INNER DYNAMICS OF
THE PEOPLE OF HİZMET

INNER DYNAMICS OF THE PEOPLE OF HİZMET

Fatih Değirmenli

New Jersey

Originally published in Turkish as *İç Derinlikleriyle Hizmet İnsanı* in 2011

27 26 25 24   2 3 4 5

Published by Tughra Books
345 Clifton Ave.,
Clifton, NJ, 07011, USA

www.tughrabooks.com

Library of Congress Cataloging-in-Publication Data Available

ISBN: 978-1-59784-293-8

Contents

1.

LOYALTY AND FIDELITY

Those who maintain a friendship with one who has fallen on hard times are true, loyal friends. Those who do not support their friends during their misfortune have nothing to do with friendship.[1]

What Do Loyalty and Fidelity Tell Us?

As one of the fundamental dynamics of the people of Hizmet,[2] loyalty refers to keeping promises, giving our willpower its due, and showing reverence and respect in order to be thankful for God's blessings and grace. The other main dynamic is fidelity which means being truthful, honest, and trustworthy when giving a promise. Fidelity also means having best wishes for his brother or sister and being the best companion for the sake of God. Moreover, it refers to friendship and loyalty in fulfilling pledges, as well as keeping promises, caring for trust, and accomplishing duties that are undertaken.

Feelings of loyalty and fidelity are significant sentiments that lead someone to become esteemed in the eyes of both God and man. It is a necessary duty for a true believer to be loyal and truthful to his noble cause and values as well as to those who provide opportunities for him to flourish with these values.

---

[1] Gülen, M. Fethullah, *Pearls of Wisdom,* New Jersey: Tughra Books, 2012, p. 81

[2] Hizmet (literally, "service") means disinterested voluntary beneficial service to humanity and thus to God Almighty. This term is preferred among the participants of the Gülen Movement to describe their attitude and work.

Loyalty and fidelity require believing that every human being has some level of goodness within them, and thus, we need to act accordingly. There are many generations who hope to find truthful people for guidance. Leaving them unanswered and lost would never be a trait of a devout person who is wholeheartedly dedicated to loyalty and fidelity.

READING TEXT

Who is a Loyal Friend?

For a person, there are three important friends. One of them is loyal, while the other two are not. These are one's belongings and wealth, his relatives and friends, and his good deeds.

When death arrives, belongings fade away. Thus, the person, who is in fact a traveler in a long journey, leaves provisions that should be prepared for the destination.

His friends come to his grave for a funeral service. After sending this heavy gift to its owner, they wave their hands in pain, and yet, they leave.

The most loyal friend is one who never leaves him alone in his prayers, which are indeed provisions for the eternal journey, as well as his sufferings and troubles for the sake of God, including even the dust that he got on his clothes when striving in God's service. Only God's grace and these aforementioned deeds go beyond the grave and walk with him on the Bridge of Sirat, and thus, greet him as eternal joy and happiness.[3]

Loyalty and Fidelity: For What, Whom and How?

Let's summarize the points that note whom/what deserves our loyalty and how we should be loyal:

    1- Being loyal to Our Lord is the ultimate goal, the sole aim, and the One whom all means are destined to arrive. This is only pos-

---

[3] Akar, Mehmet, *Mesel Ufku*, İstanbul: Timaş, 2008, p. 76

sible through becoming perfect servants, which is best described in the Qur'an and in the words of the noble Prophet.

2- Loyalty to the Messenger of God. It could be done through spreading the noble message of Islam, which was conveyed and represented by him despite innumerous troubles and sufferings he faced. Of course, in introducing Islam's message and the beloved Prophet to all humanity, we should follow the Messenger's path, and thus, convey the message in accordance with his practices.

3- Loyalty to the Qur'an. We can show our loyalty to the Qur'an by reading it a lot, practicing its teachings, regarding it as the ultimate source in both material and spiritual senses, and attempting to convey noble feelings and lofty truths that we acquire from it to all humanity.

4- Being loyal to Islam, because it is Our Lord's greatest gift to humanity and is the final and perfect religion. Loyalty to it can be accomplished by doing our best in its path, like a steed that constantly runs until it finally dies of exhaustion. Thus, we need to develop an inner sensitivity that disturbs us until this collection of Divine truths that are a recipe for humanity's material and spiritual salvation, are heard throughout the world.

5- Loyalty to all the great masters, from the times of the Companions of the Messenger to our age, in the path of Islam. We can be loyal to them by remembering them and their causes frequently, through showing respect to them, and through sharing the good values that we learned from them with the world.

6- Being loyal to our elderly who guide us in the path of serving faith and Our Lord in this contemporary age. They are the ones that show us how to understand and practice the truths of Islam under today's circumstances. Our loyalty to them means having heart-to-heart talks with them, making an effort to become what they expect to see, i.e. an ideal man of service for humanity, and finally, praying to God for them frequently.

READING TEXT

True Loyalty Is the One That Is Exercised for the Sake of God

Shams at-Tabrizi was having a conversation with his friends who were known to seek God's pleasure. He was talking about mysterious matters. After some time, he said, "If someone shows loyalty to us in the path of God only once and later shows cruel action towards us a thousand times, we appreciate his one-time loyalty and forgive his cruelty. That is because true loyalty, which is the one that is conducted for the sake of God, is invaluable. Those who know the value of true loyalty disregard cruelty."

God is the one who is the most loyal friend. One loyal action in His path overcomes thousands of disloyal acts. This is because true loyalty is for the sake of God and the sake of God is beyond everything; it is impossible to measure.

If Shams showed preference for a single loyal act over thousands of acts of cruelty, we cannot possibly imagine how God will reward loyalty expressed in His path for His sake and how He will forgive many of our sins and shortcomings as a result. As long as an individual exhibits true loyalty with perfect sincerity once in his lifetime, it is a great success: "A moment of life enlightened through this connection (to God) is preferable to a million years of life devoid of such light."[4] In other words, a single moment of light is always preferred over thousands of hours of darkness because their outcomes vary significantly.

How Did God's Messenger Demonstrate Loyalty?

God's Messenger was a loyal man. He always kept his promises and fulfilled his pledges. He never broke his agreements nor forgot those who helped himself and his Companions. He was the type of person who always sought to protect his friends and always asked them how they were doing and if they needed anything.

---

[4] Nursi, Said, *The Letters*, New Jersey: The Light, 2007, p. 310

Loyalty is best expressed by the personality of God's Messenger. He advised Muslims to be loyal friends. Let's look at several examples from his life. One of the Companions, Abdullah ibn Abdul Hamsa, narrates: "I conducted a trade with God's Messenger. I told him, 'Wait for me, I will arrive soon.' Yet, I forgot my promise to him. Three days later, when I remembered and came back to the same place, he was still there, waiting for me."[5]

As we see from this example, our Prophet was a trustworthy person in his transactions, and he was extremely loyal to his promises. He not only waited for his friend for three days, but was also deeply concerned that his friend was in trouble.

Mut'im ibn Adiyy was one of the leaders of the unbelievers from the Quraysh tribe. When the Messenger of God returned home from Taif, his enemies tried to block him from reentering Mecca. Upon learning of this development, God's Messenger requested protection from a variety of the leaders of Mecca. Yet, all of them rejected his request except Mut'im, who armed his sons and protected our Prophet's entry into the city.

Many years passed. Together with the other unbelievers, Mut'im fought against the Muslims in the Battle of Badr and was killed. Hassan, our Prophet's favorite Muslim poet, wrote a poem after the death of Mut'im, praising him for his protection of God's Messenger many years before. Our Prophet was always pleased by acts of loyalty performed towards him. To demonstrate how strong our Prophet's feelings of loyalty were, it is meaningful to note that he said the following as the Muslims were discussing what to do with the prisoners of war from the Battle of Badr: "If Mut'im ibn Adiyy were alive and if he requested the prisoners back, I would have freed them all without any compensation."[6]

Our Prophet was also loyal to his allies. For instance, the Tribe of Khuza'a that allied themselves with the Muslims in the Peace Treaty of Hudaybiya were attacked by the Tribe of Bakr, a tribe allied with the

---

[5] Ibn Sa'd, *Tabaqat*, 7/59; Shibli, *Asr Sa'adah*, 1/137

[6] *Sahih al-Bukhari*, Fardu'l Khamsa, 2906

Quraysh in the Treaty. The people of Quraysh, in fact, were behind this attack and supported it. The Khuza'a tribe leaders came to our Prophet to complain about the issue, and God's Messenger immediately issued an ultimatum and prepared an army. This event is known in history books as the cause of the conquest of Mecca. Thus, our Prophet did not leave his allies alone when they were under attack.[7]

Moreover, our Prophet was very loyal to those who helped his Companions. Once, messengers of the Abyssinian King came to God's Messenger. Our Prophet showed great hospitality towards them. Some of the Companions said to him, "O God's Messenger! Please have rest! We can host them in the best manner!"

Yet, he replied back in the negative saying, "They provided a safe haven for my Companions who migrated to their land and hosted them. Now, as reciprocity, I would like to serve them."

Our Prophet did his best hosting the tribes that visited the city of Medina. For the representatives of the tribes who came from rural areas in order to learn about Islam, God's Messenger prepared guesthouses. He hosted them in these places and offered them a warm welcome; he appointed teachers for them and assigned some of his friends to help meet their needs. When they left to go back to their tribes, he gave them gifts, new clothes and filled their bags of food (for travel). He personally wished them a safe journey with strong feelings of loyalty in hopes that they would never forget it, because these people were interested in Islam and visited him to learn more about Islam.[8]

How Can We Show Loyalty to Our Prophet?

One of the most important ways of showing loyalty to the beloved Prophet is to respect and protect his legacy, both in a material and a spiritual sense. The Companions not only did their best to uphold his sacred cause but also regarded his physical being as a holy trust, and therefore, protected it as they protect their own souls. The hairs on his head, the

---

7   Azzam, Abdurrahman, *Büyükler Büyüğü Resuli Ekrem'in Örnek Ahlakı ve Kahraman-lığı*, translated by Hayrettin Karaman, İstanbul: Yağmur, 1985, p. 37

8   Algül, Hüseyin, *Peygamberimizin Şemâili Ahlâk ve Âdâbı*, İstanbul: Işık, 2001

hairs from his beard, and his nails are just some examples of this; indeed, they protected almost everything about him very carefully. As an indication of their love for the Prophet, some of the Companions wished to have these precious legacies in their graves. Still, however, many of these sacred trusts have remained into the modern age. Similar to the Qur'an and the Sunnah, which cure our souls and minds, these trusts are a cure for our eyes!

Abdullah ibn Umar is an outstanding figure amongst those who followed the Sunnah, and remembered the noble Prophet's material and spiritual trusts with deep respect. He was a distinguished Companion who strongly pursued the pleasure of God's Messenger. Abdullah ibn Umar had an extraordinary desire to follow the Prophet's practices. He used to imitate God's Messenger in all aspects of his life, including his way of walking, eating, and drinking. At times, he used to sit under trees that the Noble Messenger rested under and even watered them to protect them from dying. After the Prophet's death, Ibn Umar broke down in tears as remembering God's Messenger. Asim ibn Muhammad reported that Abdullah ibn Umar cried whenever our Prophet's name was mentioned. Because he truly missed God's Messenger, Abdullah ibn Umar took every opportunity to show respect to the Prophet's inheritance. Living with the memories of God's Messenger, he touched the Prophet's pulpit and then brought his hands to his face and eyes. He made a special effort to pray where God's Messenger prayed.

During the conquest of Mecca, right after the noble Prophet prayed inside the Ka'ba, all of the Companions rushed to get inside; Abdullah ibn Umar asked Bilal where the Messenger of God had prayed so he could pray in the same place. Similarly, as he traveled around the city of Medina, Ibn Umar asked the people where God's Messenger had prayed in their mosques.[9]

Being loyal to God's Messenger demands that we uphold and respect his trust, and invoke peace and blessings upon him. In fact, both the Companions of the Prophet and our ancestors showed this loyalty, and thus, set a good example to guide us.

---

[9] *Al-Muwatta*, The Qur'an, 35

Loyalty and fidelity are the most important qualities of a man of service, i.e. someone who is dedicated to serve in God's cause. Fethullah Gülen Hocaefendi (pronounced as "Hodjaefendi," an honorific meaning "respected teacher") depicts such a man of service in the following poem:

A Man with a Cause

Along the winding road to the Truth
A hero, all selfishness banished,
The key to the mystery of creation in his heart,
Weaves his way through time to reach his goal.
Moving ever upwards he breathes the air of eternity
He has met with Khidr: He knows the way.
And to fellow wayfarers he gives the good news of dawn
A message of hope in a night of choking darkness.
In his hands burns a torch; he spreads light everywhere
And he brightens the Way for all who would follow.
His ascendance radiates peace and serenity
His amber fragrance permeates every atom of creation.
Wherever he treads finds life and becomes green
The hills and valleys, plains and mountains are all dressed in color
And on every breeze is borne the perfume of spring;
Blossoms appear, flowers burst into life, trees are quickened.
His mind nurtured ever by eternity,
An everlasting melody flows from his lips
All he sees is the richly colored tapestry of life to come,
The belief in which is part of his every being. [10]

READING TEXT
How to be Loyal to Our Cause?

God created mountains to provide stability on the Earth; mountains have roots under the ground that are twice as big or even more than their appearance to our eyes. Similarly, those who whole-heartedly support this noble cause should become mountain-like spiritual heroes—seeking the ways to travel with Khidr, drinking from Khidr's fountain

---

[10] Gülen, M. Fethullah, *Kırık Mızrap*, İstanbul: Nil, 2006, pp. 34–35

and trying to find everlasting life. They should become enlightened like a day at night, so deep in their inner world that they weep before God.

We need to be very cautious in our everyday life. We know that all parts of an airplane are closely checked for problems before they take off. Similarly, we need to be cautious about the well being of our inner faculties and all our inner feelings.

Here is an indicator of self-control: If a man of service keeps talking about "serving people" and "God's pleasure" amongst the people, and yet does not display similar good feelings when he is alone, then, he perhaps is showing a sign of hypocrisy.[11]

The most important duty of a true man of cause is to show loyalty to his cause. It is not up to us to evaluate those beyond our intellectual world such as Abu Bakr and Umar. And yet, consider Abu Bakr As-Siddiq. His loyalty was so great that he did not even take his daughter Aisha, who was 7 or 8 years old, with him when he migrated to Medina. Likewise, when Umar migrated to Medina, his little son, Abdullah, was not with him.

Pointing out Salman al-Farisi, God's Messenger said, "If faith were at (the place of) Ath-Thuraiya (the Pleiades, the highest star), even then some would attain it." In fact, even if the truths of the religion were hung at a star cluster, a man of cause should show his loyalty to them by bringing them down to the Earth.

Moreover, for a man of cause, there is a strong correlation between the accomplishment of his duty and his degree of belief in the cause. Nowadays, we witness the organization of soccer games for super cups such as the Presidential Cup and the Prime Minister's Cup. Those who are dedicated to the cause of Islam indeed compete for winning such a Cup. In fact, for winning such a Cup, everything can be sacrificed![12]

QUESTIONS

1. In general terms, how can God's servant be loyal to his Lord?
    a. By making this world a comfortable place to live

---

[11] Gülen, M. Fethullah, *Fasıldan Fasıla-1*, İzmir: Nil, 1997, p. 99
[12] *Ibid.*, p. 113

b. By expressing his feelings of loyalty with his tongue

c. By being a servant of God in the way that is described in the Qur'an and by God's Messenger

d. By putting intercessors between himself and his Lord

2. Which Companion said the following: "I conducted a trade with God's Messenger. I told him, 'Wait for me, I will arrive soon.' Yet, I forgot my promise to him. Three days later, when I remembered and came back to the same place, he was still there, waiting for me."

a. Abdullah ibn Abdul Hamsa

b. Abdullah ibn Umar

c. Abdullah ibn Jahsh

d. Abdullah ibn Mubarak

3. Among Umar ibn al-Khattab's sons, one was a distinguished Companion in terms of his adherence to the Sunnah and his treatment of the Prophet's material and spiritual trusts with deep respect. What is his name?

a. Abdullah

b. Asim

c. Hamza

d. Urwa

4. "……….. refers to keeping promises, giving our willpower its due, and showing reverence and respect in order to be thankful for God's blessings and grace. ……… means being truthful, honest, and trustworthy when given a promise." Which concepts should consecutively be put in the blanks?

a. Sincerity-fidelity

b. Fidelity-loyalty

c. Loyalty-fidelity

d. Fidelity-sincerity

5. How should we show our loyalty to the Qur'an?

a. Memorizing the rules of *Tajwid*, i.e. the established norms in reciting the Qur'an

b. Reciting the Qur'an after our relatives pass away

c. Placing the Qur'an in our houses where it is not seen
d. Reading the Qur'an frequently and implementing its teach-ings

2.

MODESTY AND CHASTITY

Anas ibn Malik narrated, God's Messenger said: "Impudence, rowdiness, and wildness spoil whatever they are involved in and make them ugly. By contrast, modesty, which is the feeling of shyness, embellishes whatever it is involved in and makes it beautiful."[13]

What is Modesty?

Modesty means to be shy and ashamed, as well as to protect one's chastity and honor. Modesty refers to one knowing his limits and not going too far and placing oneself in a position that protects his good relations with God first and then with people.

Modesty is such a vital quality that it makes one a true human being. Modesty is the spiritual ornament of an individual and it is the best disposition that God wants to see in His servants. In this sense, modesty also refers to one's avoidance of all bad habits that God does not want to see in people's behavior.

In the Qur'an, Our Lord declares that He forbids all sorts of immodesty and impudence.[14] Also, it is stated, "All religions have a code of ethics. The ethics of Islam is modesty."[15] God's Messenger emphasized how this characteristic is vital in a Muslim's everyday life.

The *hadith* reported below clearly underscores the importance of modesty. Abdullah ibn Umar narrated: "Our Prophet encountered a man who was advising his brother not to be too modest, and, upon

---

[13] *Sunan at-Tirmidhi*, Birr, 47

[14] Al-A'raf 7:33

[15] *Al-Muwatta*, Husn al-Huluq, 2

hearing this, he told the man, "Leave him alone, for modesty is a part of *iman* (faith)."[16]

Another *hadith* states the following: "Faith has over seventy branches; the uppermost of these branches is the declaration 'None has the right to be worshipped but God,' and the least of these branches is the removal of a harmful object from the road. Modesty is a branch of faith."[17]

The scholars of Islam commented on the *hadith* above in the following way:

> Although modesty is a characteristic that comes at birth as a God-given quality, this *hadith* presents it as a part of faith. That is because one who shows modesty stays away from sins. In this sense, modesty becomes a barrier between an individual and sins and thus performs a function of faith that prevents one from committing sinful acts. In the *hadith*, it is stated that modesty is a part of faith. We know that one's faith is reflected in the obedience of God's orders and the avoidance of what He forbids. When an individual avoids sins due to his modesty, therefore, we can see how modesty becomes a part of faith.[18]

Our Prophet stated, "Be modest towards God!"

The Companions said, "O God's Messenger! How can we be modest towards God?"

He replied, "The person who is modest towards God is the one who guards his head and its associated organs and his belly and its associate organs, and who is not spoiled by the adornment of the World and never forgets death."[19]

In this *hadith*, guarding the head means using our feelings and ideas in the path of goodness. Protecting the other organs that are associated with the head refers to keeping our eyes away from all that is forbidden, our ears away from bad words, and our mouth away from forbidden things such as lying. Guarding the belly could refer to avoiding eating what is forbidden. According to scholars of *hadith*,

---

[16] *Sahih al-Bukhari*, Book of Faith, 3, 16; *Sahih Muslim*, Iman, 12, 59
[17] *Sahih Muslim*, Iman, 58
[18] Ibn al-Asir, *An-Nihayah*, 1/470
[19] *Sunan at-Tirmidhi*, Al-Qiyamah, 23

protecting "the organ that is connected to the belly" could be done by avoiding adultery. Guarding all of these organs is necessary to be modest to God.

The one who would like to reach happiness in this world and the Hereafter should acquire propriety and modesty. That one that lacks propriety and modesty also lacks his ability to do good deeds. Modesty and faith complement each other; when one of them is absent, the other one vanishes, too.

God's Messenger states that "modesty only brings goodness,"[20] and, in another similar *hadith*, he emphasized the importance of modesty saying, "All sorts of modesty is good." [21]

Do As You Wish If You Are Not Ashamed!

Considering the meaning of being embarrassed and bashful, modesty acquires a very significant place in Islamic ethics. It is enough to ask a modest person "Aren't you embarrassed?" in order to make him avoid a bad action. Our ancestors said, "One who does not feel embarrassed before people also lacks the feeling of embarrassment before God."

The one who truly has a feeling of embarrassment is the person who avoids evil not only when there are people who could see him but also in other situations where he is alone. Those who have this feeling enjoy good mental health and a comfortable conscience.

The Companion Qurrah ibn Iyas narrates:

> We were together with God's Messenger. People talked about modesty. A questioner asked, "O God's Messenger! Is modesty from Islam?"

> Our Prophet responded saying, "Modesty is the whole of Islam. Certainly, observing modesty, avoiding *haram* (what God forbids), controlling the tongue, and being chaste are from the faith. Lessening worldly gains increases one's blessings and merit in the Hereafter. Yet

---

[20] *Sahih Muslim*, Iman, 12

[21] *Ibid*.

when they are compared, the resulting gains in the Hereafter overcome
the immediate loss in this world."[22]

One can expect to witness all sorts of evil-doing from a person who
lacks the feeling of shame. In other words, an individual who never feels
embarrassed can become involved in all types of bad actions and disre-
spect. Consider the following example:

> One day, the esteemed great Imam Abu Hanifa went to a public
> bathhouse. As the Imam was taking a shower, a man appeared with-
> out any clothes on him. As soon as the Imam saw him, he closed his
> eyes so as not to see his nakedness. The man had no feelings of
> shame. Moreover, he is so bold as to make fun of Imam.
>
> He said, "O Imam! When did they take your eyes' light?"
>
> The Imam replied to the rude man, "At the time when they removed
> your curtain of modesty."

Indeed, if someone removes their curtain of modesty, he could
show all types of actions that lack propriety and modesty. In one of his
sayings, our Prophet maintains the following: "One of the statements
that has been repeated by all Prophets since the time of Adam, peace
be upon him, is 'Do as you wish if you are not ashamed.'"[23]

The statement in the *hadith*, "Do as you wish if you are not
ashamed" should not be understood to mean that one can do whatever he wants so long as they are not ashamed by their actions. Instead,
this type of understanding misses our Prophet's main point and goes
against common sense. Rather his words should be understood in the
following way:

1. Do as you wish but also consider the consequences of your
    actions. Losing the feeling of shame does not save you from
    being accountable. None of your bad deeds will be excused
    just because you no longer feel ashamed of them.

2. Do as you wish, because what makes an individual a real
    human being is the feeling of shame. If you lose this crucial

---

[22] *Sunan al-Darimi*, Introduction, 43

[23] *Sahih al-Bukhari*, Book of the Prophets, 7/100; *Sunan ibn Majah*, Book of Asceticism,
2; Ahmad ibn Hanbal, *Al- Musnad* 4/121

feeling, there is no force that can stop you from doing evil nor shout at your conscience about your evil actions. In this case, you will be such an impudent person who accepts everything as permissible without paying attention to whether it is good or bad. In this case, you will be an animal-like person who lacks human feelings.[24]

How Many Types of Modesty Are There?

The feeling of modesty can be seen as twofold. First, there is the inborn feeling of modesty that everyone acquires (or should acquire). This feeling causes a person to feel embarrassed to reveal his private parts (the parts that are forbidden to be revealed in others' presence). In Islam, this is called *satr al-awrah* (covering the private parts). As you know, *awrah* refers to the whole body except for the hands and the face for women; it refers to the parts between the navel and the knee (including the knee joints and the navel) for men. Showing these private parts to others is a shame. This is the first feeling of modesty that appears in one's life; at the age of 4 or 5, a child starts to experience this feeling. Later, the child develops other moral values based on this feeling.

The second type of modesty refers to one's avoidance of disturbing other people (and of making them feeling ashamed) as well as conforming to the ethical conducts of modesty and moral codes. This type of modesty can be divided into three labels:

1. Modesty before God. The bare minimum indication and sign of this modesty is one's performance of the *fard* (that which God commands) and his or her avoidance of the *haram*.
2. Modesty before people. This is expressed by avoiding acts that are against good manners, and thus, not hurting other people.
3. Modesty in our inner selves. One's avoidance of sin even when he is alone is an indication of this type of modesty.

Our Prophet taught that a scarcity of modesty would eventually lead a person towards disbelief. He also explained how immodesty poses such a potential danger that could cause someone to find himself

---

[24] Akşit, Vehbi, "Utanma Duygusu ve Hayâ", *Diyanet Dergisi*, pp. 49–51

on the brink of destruction by saying, "Modesty is the structure of faith. When the structure of something is ruined, it becomes broken and scattered. The morality of Islam is modesty."[25]

Our Lord expresses the characteristics of the believers in the following verses:

> Prosperous indeed are the believers. They are in their Prayer humble and fully submissive (being overwhelmed by the awe and majesty of God). They always turn away from and avoid whatever is vain and frivolous. They are in a constant effort to give alms and purify their won selves and wealth. They strictly guard their private parts, their chastity and modesty. Save from their spouses or (as permission for men) those (bondmaids) whom their right hands possess, for with regard to them they are free from blame. But whoever seeks beyond that, such are they who exceed the bounds (set by God). They are faithful and true to their trusts (which either God, society, or an individual places in their charge), and to their pledges (between them and God or other persons or society). They are ever mindful guardians of their Prayers (including all the rites of which they are constituted). (al-Mu'minun 23:1–9)

As understood from these verses, each believer should possess the qualities of faith, *salah* (the Daily Prayers), *zakah* (prescribed purifying alms), chastity, modesty, trustworthiness, and truthfulness, because these attributes are the traits that offer happiness to believers in both this world and in the Hereafter.

READING TEXT

A Good House without a Foundation

One day, a wise person with scholarly knowledge and insight saw a handsome young man who had some problems regarding modesty. Realizing these problems, the wise man told him the following statement that is full of wisdom and lessons. He said, "It's a good house, but I wish it had a strong foundation, too!"

The fundamentals and foundations of all things are modesty and shame. Without this quality, other good things become meaningless.

---

[25] *Sunan ibn Majah*, Asceticism, 17

Just as a building that lacks a foundation cannot possibly stand, a person who lacks modesty cannot stand even if his other qualities were good. Therefore, one should first and foremost try to acquire modesty; in other words, one should lay a strong foundation.

When Becoming Alone, Is It Really the Case?

A person observes modesty when he knows that others would see him. For example, when someone is watching us, we would not do some of the same actions we would perform if we thought no one was watching. In fact, this feeling stops us from committing sins and making bad choices. Of course, this also depends on an individual's level of modesty. To express this fact, our knowledgeable elders said, "A person that commits sins in public is as bad as his level of shamelessness; likewise, he would be ashamed of committing sins according to his level of modesty."

At this point, let's ask ourselves a tough question: Is an individual ever really alone even when nobody is around him? Of course not... There is God and His angels in charge, who record all the things that are done by human beings. In other words, someone is watching over an individual constantly. Someone who has this feeling and understanding would be aware of the fact that he is never alone. Feeling embarrassment, he would sense that the very actions he would not do among other people should be avoided before the Lord who is All-Hearing, All-Seeing, and All-Knowing and His Angels right next to himself.

Because of the aforementioned reason, a believer should want to acquire modesty and should never ever lose this feeling and understanding. Indeed, this feeling of modesty is what made the Companion Uthman rise to the position of Caliph.

Uthman ibn Affan was a person who symbolized modesty and shame. In the words of Necip Fazıl:

> Abu Bakr symbolizes compassion and mercy; Umar symbolizes fervor and justice; Uthman symbolizes modesty and good manners; Ali symbolizes reason and wisdom. These four Companions encompass

the esteemed values of all humanity combined. All four of them are the four glass faces of a lantern. The light is inside this lantern. [26]

One of the most distinguishing characteristics of Uthman ibn Affan was certainly his modesty and shamefulness. When talking about this attribute of his, the mother of the believers, Aisha, narrated the following incident that gives us a lesson:

> God's Messenger was lying in the bed in my apartment with his thigh uncovered when Abu Bakr sought permission to enter. Permission was given to him and he conversed in the same state (with the Prophet's thigh uncovered). Then Umar sought permission to enter, it was given to him, and he, too, conversed with the Prophet in that state. Then Uthman sought permission to enter; God's Messenger sat up and he adjusted his clothes. Uthman then entered and conversed and, as he went out, I said, "Abu Bakr entered and you did not stir and did not observe much care (in arranging your clothes), then Umar entered and you did not stir and did not arrange your clothes, then Uthman entered and you got up and set your clothes right." Thereupon, he replied, "Should I not show modesty to the one whom even the Angels show modesty?"

With his modesty, Uthman ibn Affan became distinctive and rose to the third place among the Companions. Surely, this quality symbolized by Uthman is a very important value for eternal salvation of people in the contemporary age. A believer should avoid the behaviors and environments that could embarrass him before God in the Hereafter. Young people should especially be careful to observe chastity and to not exceed the limits of privacy. They should not let feelings that they have in their young age to lead them to do things that will embarrass them and cause them regret later.

READING TEXT

To the Youth That Exceed the Limits of Privacy

After his greetings, the young woman on the other line of the phone asked a question about exceeding the limits of privacy: "I and my

---

[26] Kısakürek, Necip Fazıl, *Batı Tefekkürü ve İslâm Tasavvufu*, İstanbul: Büyük Doğu, 1999, p. 86

friend from school would like to conduct a religious, unofficial marriage. What do you think about this type of marriage that would not be known by our families? Would you suggest it?"

Since I know what kind of grave regrets these acts of transgression (of the limits of privacy) invite, I am afraid I was a bit harsh in my answer: "I am against all sorts of suicide. Taking the risk of getting married unofficially in her youth—without the knowledge of her family and without finishing her education—could lead a young girl to commit suicide or some other dreadful acts. This kind of situation may not result in such a tragedy for the young man, but for a young, innocent lady, it might be the end result."

She insisted in asking if there was ever a solution for this issue. Therefore, I continued saying, "Yes, there is! Have an official marriage contract, which sets and ensures both sides' rights. In this way, you ensure your own safety and relieve your family from the burden. Simply, do it officially!"

"But," she said, "There is no way out for us. Our families would not approve of it. Neither of our families would approve of it nor are our ages, finances, and school conditions appropriate for this!"

"Then, under these circumstances in which your age, schooling, and finances do not allow you to get married officially, why do you dare to be married secretly and unofficially? What is the reason to accept the risk of all these negative things and make your future dark?"

Her answer was a typical response that we hear frequently. "In the beginning," she said, "we were not careful in our conduct regarding limits of privacy. We freely chatted as if we were so close. After a while, I guess, we fell in love with each other!"

Certainly, destroying the limits of privacy and not avoiding hanging out with a stranger can result in the conditions in which these two youngsters find themselves and cannot thoroughly think about their action's consequences. Now, they must accept their mistake that will make them regretful their entire life. That is because they already destroyed the limits of privacy, which were functioning as a protector and a defender against wrongdoing. They incited their youthful feelings that are hard to extinguish. Now, their fake cover to justify their behavior to themselves is ready: They are in love and assume that it is impossible to be separated.

Such a youngster who trespasses the limits of privacy is not so different than a very angry youngster who foams with rage, losing control of his anger and then coldly pulls his weapon's trigger to kill someone. Never thinking about the consequences, he pulls the trigger and hits the target, and thus, makes a mistake that leads to a lifetime of regret and crying for help. Then, it is full of screams of regrets to be heard for miles. This scream, however, is useless. It is because the bullet is already out of the barrel and hit the target. Now, there is only a corpse in the picture. Who is going to be blamed for the corpse?

"Then, is there any way out for our salvation?" asked young women insistently.

"Yes, there is!" I replied. "Caring for yourself by acting within the limits of privacy! Also, graduating from your school successfully, and then, preparing financial resources so that you can conduct an official marriage to share your happiness with your family."

I do not know what that young lady who was lost in thought did later on. Yet, I would like to turn to the youth and tell them the following:

Dear Young People!

Guard yourselves to be safe in your school age. Our beloved Prophet apprised us of the irreparable drawbacks that dating would invite with his warning, "A man is never alone with a woman except that *Satan* is the *third*."[27] If you do not care and do not avoid dating, the flow of feelings will dangerously electrify you and lead you to make wrong steps that would make you regretful for a lifetime.

Thus, to avoid taking a wrong path that would lead to an abyss, protect yourself within the limits of privacy. First and foremost, take aim at graduating from your schools and sharing your happiness with your family members. At this point, our duty is to make you think about this important topic, and your duty is protect yourselves from dating in which Satan is the third. Do not forget that country fruits

---

[27] *Sahih al-Buhari*, Nikah, 111–112

might be bitter to the taste, and yet, healthy. At the end, you will be the one who is successful![28]

What Does Chastity Mean?

Chastity refers to the avoidance of ugly words and actions and behaving within the boundaries of modesty and shame, while being strongly committed to truthfulness, honesty, and moral values. As originated in Arabic, the word *iffet* was transferred to the Turkish language by having similar meaning to words that express someone's esteemed characteristics of honor, dignity, and morality. Especially in old writings and poems, the word "*afif*" (who observes *iffet*) was often used for referring to those people who have honor and integrity, who avoid *haram* and seeking unlawful material gains, and who are especially alert in conducting his sensitive relations within the moral boundaries.

Moral philosophers of Islam pointed out three basic emotions that are granted to all individuals. First, the force of intellect, which refers to the ability of understanding the truth to some extent and of distinguishing what is useful or harmful. Second, the force of anger, which refers to power that breeds feelings of grudge, rage, fury, and boldness. Finally, the force of desire, which refers to the feeling that nurtures desires related to the appetite and bodily pleasures.

The extreme form of desiring potential is called dissipation, which is one's lack of the feeling of shame, and thus, becoming so immoral that he could easily commit all sorts of sins/crimes. At the other extreme, someone's indifference towards even *halal* (permissible by God) blessings is called frigidity. The moderate and upright approach regarding the aptitude of desiring potential is chastity, which refers to one's wish for permissible pleasures and tastes within legitimate limits, and at the same time, his deliberate rejection of illegitimate desires and wishes. Thus, in general, chastity means one's controlling his bodily desires by the power of his will, and his aversion toward adultery and debauchery.

---

[28] Şahin, Ahmed, "Mahremiyet sınırını aşan gençlere," *Zaman*, 2 June 2010

The Noble Qur'an highlights that true believers are the ones who have chastity and modesty and who protect their private parts[29] and tells the good news that they will be granted God's mercy, among other bounties, in the Hereafter because of their chaste lifestyle.[30] Due to the importance of the topic, the Qur'an mentions men and women one by one and commands all believers to be chaste and to avoid gazing at *haram*, which is considered as the first step towards promiscuity.[31] Moreover, it encourages good-hearted believers to be modest and pure by praising the monuments of chastity such as Prophet Joseph and Mary, the mother of Jesus, peace be upon them.

Upon calls by the vizier's wife (for committing sin), Prophet Joseph, peace be upon him, said, *"My Lord! Prison is dearer to me than what they bid me to"* (Yusuf 12:33). He accepted imprisonment for years in order to avoid taking a step toward immodesty; in this way, he set a wonderful example of modesty for all believers of all times until the end of the world.

Notwithstanding these general meanings of chastity in our minds, we can approach this concept in a broader and more comprehensive manner. As Bediüzzaman Said Nursi said, "The boundaries of *halal* are quite wide and they would satisfy our desires. Thus, there is no reason to involve in *haram*." From this perspective, chastity refers to one's observance of not trespassing the legitimate boundaries through avoiding looking at or touching, or stepping towards the forbidden. Therefore, a chaste person should learn to be satisfied by the permissible enjoyments of his organs such as the eyes, ears, hands, and feet, and he should never commit *haram*. Also, we should avoid harming our honor and reputation.[32]

READING TEXT

Guard Your Chastity!

- Chastity is such blessed dough that is comprised of honor, fidelity, and loyalty; when it is used as material for plastering,

---

[29] Al-Mu'minun 23:5–7

[30] As-Sajdah 33:35

[31] An-Nur 24:30–31

[32] Gülen, M. Fethullah, *İkindi Yağmurları*, İstanbul: Nil, 2011, pp. 335; 337

it is quite rare, if not impossible, to see such a building shaken or demolished.

- Chastity is a hero's most lofty characteristic and most important quality. By the same token, the worst misery and the worst condition of a hero is his excessive free and easy conducts regarding chastity.

- The most honorable and valuable side of a woman is her purity regarding her chastity and chastity. Those who are not sensitive in preserving their own honor and their families' chastity could certainly not be keen on protecting national dignity and national honor.

- Chastity is so sacred that all nations would make a pledge upon this quality and it is one of the most brilliant among virtuous elements. It is full of falsehood and fabrication to hear claims of honor and virtue from those who lack this quality.

- Chastity is a unique diamond and it should be preserved in the most protective cases. In this way, its value would be doubled.

- It is impossible to trust any matter to those people who are not sensitive in protecting others' chastity and honor as their own.

- Bats do not like the light. Likewise, infidels do not like systems of faith, ignorant people do not like scientific knowledge, immorality do not like morality, and the unchaste do not like chastity.[33]

Most of the Time I Cannot Keep My Chastity and Control My Own Self!

Surely, it is hard to reach that level, especially at the time when unchastity is wide spread and the veil of shame is unveiled. It is quite possible to hear the following words from our youth: "I do not have willpower. That is my problem. Most of the time, I cannot keep my chastity and control my own self. Simply, I plunge into sins. I promised myself not to do it again but, unfortunately, I could not keep my word."

---

[33] Gülen, M. Fethullah, *Ölçü veya Yoldaki Işıklar*, İstanbul: Nil, 2011, pp. 95–96

The Sublime Creator gave to his servants, like a drop in the ocean, some of His Attributes and Names. For example, He is the sole Forgiver and we, also, have an attribute of being forgivers to some extent. Likewise, with our human free will, which is a tiny part of the Divine Will, we can enlighten or darken our lives, and choose to be fortunate or not.

Just think about a palace, which is the most magnificent masterpiece of the world. Everything can be found in that palace. And every single pattern of it is in its more beautiful, decorated, precious, modern, and practical state. Electrical and lighting units are incandescent. Imagine that you have a remote control in your hands. And whatever you wish to—just press its "ok" button and it will appear before you. The same case is for electricity, too… if you press "on," then it will be enlightened right away, and by pressing the "off" button, you will darken the entire place.

Behold, you have a remote control of the palace that is as big as this world; and namely that remote control is your willpower. If you say "no" to it, then you will deny such a bounty and accuse the host of the palace. However, if you say that you are using the existing remote control of yours, then it will be a shame on you (and on your magnificent palace).

A mentor of the palace, who said: "Do not let a second look follow the first. The first look is allowed for you but not the second," now is saying to you: "If you use this remote control in an appropriate way, then you will feel comfortable in this palace as well as you will earn many other enormous palaces as gifts of the host." He, the mentor, supported his words with the operation manual of the palace or, let it say, with the sentences of a handbook.

Moreover, in that handbook and in other auxiliary books, it is written that the host of the palace is much closer to you than your jugular vein is, and that despite His immenseness, He is able to have a place in your hearts. Besides, if you do not misuse the remote control, then you will look around with His eyes.

Therefore, instead of saying, "I will not be able to do this or that," or even, "I have a weak mind," we should say: "I have willpower. I just haven't read the existing book till now well and did not obey the mentor of the palace well. From now on, I will use this remote control in an appropriate way for earning thousands of other glamorous palaces. That is why; I will appraise this enormous palace as a remote control of my carnal self." Insomuch, it's our eyes, which we wink with hundreds of times during a day even without realizing that, however now, at least for a few times, we should close our eyes considering that.

Our Prophet Was Very Meticulous concerning the Chastity of His Companions!

Messenger of God, peace and blessings be upon him, was very meticulous in matters of protecting his community against attacks of extraneous sins to come. At the time, when everyone got locked onto chastity, he turned back after standing at the Arafat (the hill where Muslim pilgrims stay for some time on the eve of the Religious Festival of Sacrifice). On the way, he was turning head of Fadl, son of Abbas, to the right and left; in doing so, he helped Fadl's sight not fall on any of women that were around.

It happened at the pilgrimage season of the Age of Happiness. A person, who rode at the back of the mount, was the Messenger of God, and a person, whose face was turned to the right and left, was Fadl, in chastity of whose no one had any doubt. When such a thing was almost impossible, our Prophet turned Fadl's face in order not a single delusion approach him and not a vagrant arrow strike his heart. Such an attitude of our beloved Prophet shows us his meticulousness concerning chastity and, in doing so, he constituted an example to his community.

There is an expression of Bediüzzaman, the Sage of the Age, who paid attention to that danger:

> The All-Originating One has equipped your nature with such faculties that some of them would not be satisfied even if they could swallow the world. Some others cannot tolerate even a microscopic particle. Like the eye that is unable to bear the weight of a single hair while the head carries a heavy stone, these faculties cannot endure the weight of even a hair, that is, an insignificant state that arises from heedlessness and misguidance. They are sometimes even extinguished and die.

So be alert and careful, always act with caution and in fear of sinking. Do not drown in a morsel, a word, a grain, a glance, a beckoning, a kiss! Do not cause your faculties that are so extensive that they can contain the whole world to drown in such a thing. For there are some small things which can in one respect, swallow many large things. See how the sky and its stars are contained in a piece of glass, and most of the pages of your life, history, and actions are inserted in your memory, which is as small as a mustard seed. Thus, there are minute things which in one respect contain and swallow larger ones.[34]

Just as looking at the corpse of a beautiful woman who deserves compassion with lust and desire destroys morality, looking lustfully at pictures of living women, which are like little corpses, troubles and diverts, shakes and destroys elevated human feelings.[35]

From that expression, it is clear that such a matter, which harms the chastity, as looking at forbidden by religion things destroy effectual power of faith, put barriers between an individual and full benefits of Islam, and cannot effectuate functions of some subtle faculties of a person. Bediüzzaman Said Nursi, invited us to be cautious all the time by saying, "Step your every step very carefully; otherwise there is always danger of slipping!"

READING TEXT
Three Heroes of Chastity

There were gallants, who were saved from the great disaster, when they were at the threshold of a sin and edge of an abyss. When it is told about seven groups of people that will be protected from horrific dangers of the Judgment Day and take refuge in the shade of the God Almighty, such heroes of chastity are indicated, too. For, that chivalrous soul, who in the matter of protecting his chastity and honor was exceptionally meticulous and determined to the utmost concerning the carnal desires, could refuse an invitation of a beautiful and rich lady by saying, "I fear from God," and overcame an obstacle with his willpower, which outwardly seemed impossible.

---

[34] Nursi, Said, *The Gleams*, New Jersey: Tughra Books, 2008, p. 188
[35] Nursi, Said, *The Words*, New Jersey: The Light, 2005, p. 429

During the Caliphate of Umar ibn al-Khattab, a young man was one of the representatives of the horizon of infallibility. Suddenly, when he was trapped in a slight inclination of a sin, he remembered the holy verse, which means: *"Those who keep from disobedience to God in reverence for Him and piety: when a suggestion from Satan touches them they are alert and remember God, and then they have clear discernment"* (al-A'raf 7:201). He remembered that verse, got embarrassed before the Almighty God, and turned back from the threshold of a sin. However, his conscience could not ascribe such a small inclination, his heart could not bear excitement caused by the fear of God and the body of that young man slumped down right there. A memory of that youngster, who can be called a "martyr of chastity" or "martyr of innocence," reached our days as a good remembrance.

In a noble *hadith,* (which is called the *Hadith* of the Cave) mentioned about a hero of chastity. Three men took refuge in a cave in order to rest there over night. When a large boulder rolled down and closed entrance of the cave, they could not get out of it. Therefore, they started to tell in turns about their righteous deeds, which, as they considered, were acceptable in the sight of the Creator. They used them as means for their prayers. They asked God to remove the stone from their way. After each one said their prayer, the stone moved a bit and finally rolled down. The three men were saved.

One of them pleaded, making an intercessor, his generous treatment to his parents. The last one asked help from the Divine Compassion for the sake of giving all his dues to his employee, wages of whom he did not give at first because he accumulated interest on money of that worker. As for the second one, he said: "O my Lord! I had a cousin, whom I loved more than anyone. I wanted to enjoy with her to the fullest, but she used to ignore me. However, once at the year of famine I got her. I gave her one hundred and twenty dinars with the condition of her spending the time with me. Incumbently, she accepted it. But when I was about to attain my wish, she said to me, "Fear God and do not harm my chastity!" Thereupon, I did not do anything to her and let her go, though I loved her most of all. I did not ask that my money be returned to me either. O my Lord, if you consider that I did such an act for gaining your content, then save us from this hardship!" He believed that protecting his chastity was acceptable before God and offered that deed of his to the Almighty.

The Heroism, found in the above-mentioned chaste personalities, will not be easily achieved. They are extremely exceptional victories of human willpower. Under similar conditions, not everyone can attain such self-control. Many are unable to remain standing and slip on such a slippery surface. Therefore, similar situations must be prevented before reaching that critical point. Best of all, it is required not to enter such dangerous zones, approach edges of abyss at all, and never ever walk at coasts of sin.[36]

What Should We Do to Remain Chaste and Control Our Carnal Selves?

If we observe history of humankind, we will come to know that whenever people went astray from shame and propriety, and chose the path of unchastity, they confronted many disasters and hardships, which brought them to their end. The one, who strays from shame—strays from his own essence. In considerable number of noble verses of the Holy Qur'an, it is mentioned about collapses of shameless civilizations. Nations of Ad, Thamud and Lut were buried in the depth of history: *"We certainly tested those who preceded them. (This is Our unchanging way) so that God will certainly mark out those who prove true (in their profession of faith), and He will certainly mark out those who prove false."* (al-Ankabut, 29:3). We can be modest and chaste only by not obeying desires of our carnal selves, namely which is our moral duty.

What should we do to protect our chastity and be a person of modesty? Very important criteria concerning this topic are put forward by Fethullah Gülen in his sermons as well as in his books. Here are some significant points:

---

[36] M. Fethullah Gülen, *İkindi Yağmurları*, pp. 341–342

1. BOREDOM MUST NOT BE REASON
FOR BEING UNCHASTE

Generally, boredom is caused by dissatisfaction of the heart, not establishing a relationship with God Almighty and His Messenger, not being attached to religious practices, and not being engaged in servitude. It means that such people have paved paths for Satan. The state of a person struck by Satan, who again walks at the places where mines of Satan are sown is alike to the state of a thirsty person, who drunk sea water and despite that, again runs to it.

It is necessary to be away from the places, where sins flow like floods unless it is matter of service of the Qur'an and faith.

Let's give its dues to roads that we pass. Respected Companions of the Messenger many times used to go out just to tell about the truth and justice. Abu Bakr, Umar ibn al-Khattab, and Abu Dharr, may God be pleased with them, used to do the same thing. Those, who go out with that purpose give its dues to roads that they pass and, in doing so, protect themselves from sins.

Our noble Prophet, peace and blessings be upon him, used to forbid his Companions to sit at roadsides. When they said, "O Messenger of God, there is good and proper use in our gathering outside," he answered: "If so then pay its dues to outside, in other words, purify each and every stone and thorn, greet everyone, and preach to others by enjoining good and forbidding evil."[37] Hence, we should have such a sincere intention.

We should be alert outside. A person must be as cautious against sins as he could have been at a minefield or the place where enemies are. Otherwise, if he goes out accompanied with his feelings and emotions, without being ready for that and spiritually unarmed, if he remains unprotected, without a spiritual shield against venomous arrows of Satan, then his soul will be spoiled and open to sins and all kinds of other evil. And if that recurs one more time in particular, then he will have no more of those spiritual feelings, his soul will not be restrained from sins and evil. As a

---

[37] *Sahih al-Bukhari*, Mazalim, 22

result, outside he will be left in an unrestricted state concerning forbidden things, which is desired by Satan all the time.

Before going out, we must attain spiritual alertness. Before going out, we must read a religious book or watch something spiritual, which will rejoice our hearts, increase our excitement, water our eyes, and mobilize our feelings. Namely with that spiritual alertness, we must go out in order for us to have a defensive mechanism against sins.

2. WE MUST GIVE UP ADDICTION TO OUR CARNAL SELVES

Habits and desires of a carnal self are like a deadly poison and a load, which pulls a person to vile. The soul grows and improves inversely proportional to the carnal self. In other words, as carnal self gets nourished, the soul becomes contracted, tightened, and heavy. Eventually, there appear some kind of clumsiness of heart, senses, and spiritual feelings.

In *hadith*s, the Messenger of God said that Satan goes about within the veins of people. He advised us to squeeze places, where Satan goes about,[38] by not fulfilling desires of our carnal selves. It is quite normal for those, who eat whatever comes to their minds, feed themselves with different kinds of dishes and appetizers, to be deprived of shame and chastity.

For this reason, it is very important to diminish nourishment canals of our carnal selves by giving our willpower its dues. Carnal soul will serve as a permanent entrance for Satan. Nothing good will come from our carnal selves as well as from the Satan. Carnal self is our great opponent that leads us to evil, and enemy, because of which we should perform the major *jihad* (striving in God's cause and for humanity's good). Thereby, knowing that and getting rid of Satan are first steps of getting closer to God Almighty.

Thus, we must say "Stop!" to our carnal selves and accomplish the required zeal and endeavor to discipline it.

---

[38] *Sahih al-Bukhari*, Ahkam, 21

3. WE MUST READ BOOKS AND
CONTEMPLATE ABUNDANTLY

Everyone should follow the wide path, shown to us by Messengers of the Almighty God by deepening our contemplations and considerations, gathering, just like bees, beams of wisdom from the book of the Universe, which are spread before us. By means of that path our souls will be vital; each step of ours will give us a source of power and in doing so, such people will walk securely on the way of becoming a monument of chastity.

While the Holy Qur'an and Sunnah revive our conscience and heal all our spiritual wounds, guiding treatises such as the *Risale-i Nur* Collection, which have been renewed according to treatment methods of the current time, and immortal truths described in them, are good medicines in curing our spiritual diseases in the shortest time and, like an ointment, must always be in our reach. Priority must be given to reading persistently without being bored and fed up as it is the recommended measure within the principles (of chastity). It is very important to revive our lives by reading very detailed life stories of righteous people, which shed light on the noble life of the Messenger of God, respected Companions and their successors, for integrity and vivacity of our hearts and perceptions. A person, who can compare his own self and his life with those major paragons, with contemplations will bring himself to an account by saying: "They were like that, then why are we not like them?" In doing so, he will have such a power that will protect him from all evils.

4. WE MUST CONTROL OUR IMAGINING

Imagining is an activity of mind, which does not have any logic or limit of power and does not have any record of time or place. Sometimes, by visualizing things and events under influence of our sense organs, it can put forward some motives that are appropriate to nature of those things. Each and every scene and exposure that Satan puts in our dreams will become a movie taken with the camera of our dreams, which will lead to the Zaqqum tree (Zaqqum is an extremely bitter and thorny tree that grows at the bottom of Hellfire and of which the people of Hell will eat) of polytheism, and finally to unchastity. And especially, if it is in the hands of our carnal selves, then it will easily to be turned to actual circumstances. In that case, we must consider such thoughts as venomous, and try not to be caught by them, and if we have been caught by, then try to evade them.

We will have the images of the atmosphere we are in. When we are watching something that is desired by our carnal selves, will we ever be able to dream about the circles around the Holy Ka'ba? If so, then those who want to have the sacred meanings must frequently be at places, where spirituality is found, and with people, who are spiritual.

5. DEATH MUST BE REMEMBERED OFTEN

God's Messenger, peace and blessings be upon him, wants us to remember death frequently, which displeases all the carnal pleasures.[39] If people grasp the reality of death, if they engrave it in their senses, feelings, and mind, and dominate this reality over their imagining and thinking by convincing themselves about the existence of the life after death, then their prospects about this world and the other will alter completely.

Remembering death is like a vaccine, which removes the harm of the viruses of sin presented by Satan, and which blocks his whisperings.

"Anyway I will die and be brought to an account. If so, then there is no point in dolorous pleasures of this world, committing sins and being shameless! Why should I choose the forbidden path while I can choose the legally acceptable one? And why should I become unchaste?" The idea of death in the above mentioned way is a strong dissuasive on one hand and a rejoicing efficacy on the other hand.

The idea of death, from its deterrent and incentive ways makes us bend double with a sense of personal responsibility and give account of our deeds to God on one hand, and on the other hand, it makes our hearts beat within congruity of hope and fear, which inspires us, as well as leaves positive effects on our souls and attitudes.

---

[39] *Sunan at-Tirmidhi*, Qiyama, 26

6. WE SHOULD NOT REMAIN LONELY.
WE MUST MAKE FRIENDS WITH GOOD PEOPLE!

A person, who does not intermingle with the community, is like a leaf and a feather under the feet of others. If you blow at it from one side, it will move to the other side. Even the Companions of the Messenger of God felt a necessity of being in a community and constituting a unity. That is why, the only refuge is a virtuous community as it will protect us against innumerous traps of Satan, our spiritual enemy, carnal selves, and storms of sins. Calling people to that kind of reflection is among the most vital matters of today.

God created humans as social beings. A lonely person can be weak against the winds of heedlessness. He may become a target of Satan's venomous arrows.

A person, who lives alone, eventually, may fall into a trap of Satan, be a victim of him, and fall under red clutches of him. Each and every evil thought, loneliness and boredom, which Satan puts in our minds and delusions, is like a seed that will grow and blossom on its ground. A lonely person, whose mind, heart, and soul are full of seeds of evil and sins, will sooner or later taste the poisonous fruits of an evil and wicked tree unless he begs the forgiveness of the All-Merciful God.

A person must avoid loneliness as much as he would avoid a venomous animal. For, loneliness will open doors for evil thoughts, which will later wrap around the entire soul. The same kind of danger may be there for two people, too. Though possibility of conspiring of two people upon bad and evil is low, but it is still there. As for three people, it is hardly possible for all of them to come to an agreement in matters concerning sins and evil deeds.

7. THERE SHOULD BE SPARED A DAY IN
A WEEK FOR SPIRITUAL NOURISHMENT

There is a saying which goes, "Do practice your gained knowledge." Most probably you have already heard of it. This statement is said about those people who put their knowledge into practice. Listening to advices of those people nourishes our willpower, softens our hearts, keeps us safe against Satan's whisperings and the pressure of sins.

A human being has not only a body and mind but also a spirit, a heart, and a conscience. In that respect, it is very important for him to get deep into his inner world, flourish his spiritual world, and improve his contemplation practice.

Each person has a passion to satisfy his spiritual thirst. The Messenger of God tells that "Religion is *nasiha* (corrective advice, good counsel and sincere conduct)."[40] Therefore, listening to those, who enlighten the minds, soften the hearts, and incite people for the eternal life is as important and necessary as air and food.

This is why a person should never say: "I know it. Why should I listen to it again?" As we always repeat taking meals, let alone with being fed up with, we even need them continuously; in the same way, we need sermons and spiritual talks at least once a week. For, they are considered to be nourishment of hearts and souls, and play a major role in protecting against Satan and sins.

8. YOU SHOULD NOT LOAF AROUND, BUT HAVE A DUTY

An idle person is open to shamelessness and unchastity. In doing so, he will give a good chance for Satan. Consequently, a person should not loaf around and must seek for occupations that always give him a spiritual energy and rejoicing.

Most of all Satan deals with lazy people, who sluggishly sit in their places. He will impose himself on those who do not do anything, kill their time, wander around, and talk rubbish things. Such people are easy preys of Satan.

Satan makes use of our sluggishness and laziness by emitting improper thoughts and delusions to our hearts, engaging our imagination with his own visions, forcing us to think about sins and commit them. Then we should pursue good and useful activities so that Satan cannot find a chance to deceive us.

---

[40] *Sahih Muslim*, Iman, 95

9. WE SHOULD KEEP AWAY FROM PLACES THAT AROUSE OUR CORPORAL DESIRES

In order to be modest, we must avoid places and activities which provoke indecency, and be away from incentive delusions, views, and conversations.

We can give more examples that come across us in our daily lives. Our Lord gave us a willpower, which we should use only in uprightness of righteous deeds and be out and away from ambiences that call us to commit sins.

10. WE SHOULD SUPPLICATE ABUNDANTLY

Supplication is a worship and essence of servitude. God Almighty encourages us to make supplications by saying: *"Pray to Me, (and) I will answer you."* (al-Mumin, 40:60). He also enunciated importance of supplicating by stating: *"Say: "My Lord would not care for you were it not for your prayer"* (al-Furqan, 25:77).

The most powerful means of protection is supplication. In a Divine *hadith*, it is said that if we remember God, then God will remember us and, just like in the case of Prophet Ibrahim, in the toughest of times, when all the grounds and reasons come to an end, He will stretch the hand of help and turn the fire to a cool and safe place for you.[41]

Let's finish this section with a poem of Fethullah Gülen:

Young Man

> Young man, Give some thought to the terrible maladies,
> now a century old, that afflict this society
> on every side. There is no remedy known
> for such fainting hearts and feverish minds:
> crowds in the street shouting for no reason;
> people, become like fish in the aquarium,
> Blundering anywhere in aimless confusion-
> how should, how could, they perceive?
> How in such chaos could community survive-

---

[41] Compiled from Gülen, M. Fethullah, *İnancın Gölgesinde-2*, İstanbul: Nil, 2011, pp. 145–191

Its people blind, deaf, emotionally numbed,
Their streets running filth sewage canals,
their young licensed to indulge every wantonness;
chastity publicly disgraced, decency a tattered veil,
dishonesty the norm, and deception swaggering like a king
A maggot has burrowed into the fiber of community:
the spirit of society has scattered therefore, the people suffered
You, young man, are
the one whose courage can end this wretchedness,
the one for long years expected in visions and dreams...
See, where dawn is breaking's stretch to your full height
now that a light is everywhere overwhelming darkness....
Do not pause with the water hose in your hand. But rush
to attack the flames in every place-for that is your duty.
let the darkness vanish, that the clear road may appear:
step forward and stand true to the cause of holy Trust.
You, young man, are
the hero, the one for centuries awaited. Come now.
Come now-for with us is left no power to resist.[42]

QUESTIONS

1. In the noble *hadith* of "One of the first words heard by people from all the Messengers since the time of first Prophethood is ...." Fill in the gap with one of the following expressions:
   a. If you have no shame, do whatever you want to
   b. Believe in God and be saved
   c. Propriety and only
   d. Be modest and protect your chastity
2. Which Companion was the one, "whom even the Angels show modesty," in the words of Our Prophet?
   a. Abu Bakr
   b. Umar ibn al-Khattab
   c. Uthman ibn Affan
   d. Ali ibn Abu Talib

---

[42] Gülen, M. Fethullah, *Kırık Mızrap*, İstanbul: Nil, 2006, pp. 23–24

3. How do you call a state of keeping away from ill-favored words and actions, being within the circle of modesty, and living with moral values, truthfulness, and integrity?

   a. Mindfulness
   b. Consciousness
   c. Fidelity
   d. Chastity

4. The statement, "The boundaries of *halal* (permissible conducts) are quite wide and they would satisfy our desires. Thus, there is no reason to involve in *haram* (forbidden conducts by God)" belongs to whom?

   a. M. Fethullah Gülen
   b. Bediüzzaman Said Nursi
   c. Imam al-Ghazali
   d. Rumi

5. What is the name of the Companion of the Messenger, whose head was turned by the Prophet to the right and left in order him not to look at forbidden things?

   a. Anas ibn Malik
   b. Zayd
   c. Fadl
   d. Muadh ibn Jabal

6. Which one of the following is not a discipline of remaining chaste and controlling one's carnal self?

   a. A person must be a prosecutor regarding his own self and an advocate regarding others
   b. One should abandon his sensuality
   c. One should read books and contemplate abundantly
   d. We should not remain lonely. We must make friends with good people

3.

SUBMISSION

What Is Submission?

O you who believe! Obey God and obey the Messenger, and those from among you who are invested with authority; and if you are to dispute among yourselves about anything, refer it to God and the Messenger, if indeed you believe in God and the Last Day. This is the best (for you), and fairest in the end." (an-Nisa 4:59)

According to the dictionary, "submission" ("*itaat*") is a word, which has the following meanings—to surrender, to comply with the command, fulfillment of the command, and act according to a given command. The word "*taat*" is derived from the same root, which means to fulfill someone's command and to do what was said to. An antonym of the word "submission" is "disobedience."

The word "submission" is mentioned many times in the Holy Qur'an with a meaning of obeying with a sincere submission and compliance to God's and His Messenger's commands.[43]

A believer must be definitely contented with righteousness of Prophethood and Sunnah. He should not have any doubt or trouble concerning his submission. For a human being, who has to live in a society, there is necessity of fidelity and submission in order for him to avoid turmoil and disrupting. Otherwise, there would be chaos in a society.

---

[43] Al Imran 3:83; an-Nisa 4:59, 65; ar-Ra'd 13:15; Fussilat 41:11

How Does God Explain to Us What Submission Is?

In the Holy Qur'an, the word "submission" is mentioned one hundred and twenty nine times. This fact exemplifies to us the significance of submission. In verses of the Holy Qur'an, the word "submission" is used with its original meaning, i.e. "to obey someone, to comply with a command and to accept it." Observing those verses, we will come to know that we were told about two kinds of submission:

1. Submission to God

2. Submission to someone else other than God

Submission to God consists of submitting to God, His commands and Messengers.

> O you who believe! Obey God and obey the Messenger, and those from among you who are invested with authority; and if you are to dispute among yourselves about anything, refer it to God and the Messenger, if indeed you believe in God and the Last Day. This is the best (for you), and fairest in the end. (an-Nisa 4:59)

Here, submission to administrators meant in the above verse is a reflection of submission to God and His Messengers. Submission to God is like submission to the Prophets.[44] For, submission to a Messenger means at the same time submission to the One, who sent the Messenger. Hence, God Almighty decreed:

> He who obeys the Messenger (thereby) obeys God, and he who turns away from him (and his way), (do not be grieved, O Messenger, for) We have not sent you as a keeper and watcher over them (to prevent their misdeeds and be accountable for them). (an-Nisa 4:80)

In fact, the following verse clearly states that Prophets were supposed to be submitted:

> (Everyone should know well that) We have never sent a Messenger but that he should be obeyed by God's leave. If, when they wronged themselves (by committing a sin), they but came to you and

---

[44] Al-Baqarah 2:32, 132; an-Nisa, 4:13, 69; al-Ma'idah 5:92; al-Anfal 8:1, 20, 46; at-Tawbah 9:71; an-Nur 24:52, 54; al-Ahzab 33:71; Muhammad 47:33; at-Taghabun 64:12; Nuh 71:3

implored God to forgive them—with the Messenger praying to God for their forgiveness—they would find that God is One Who returns the repentance of His servants with liberal forgiveness and additional reward, and All-Compassionate. (an-Nisa 4:64)

As for submission to others rather than God Almighty, then it is, including all kinds of submission, the submission which is not referring to God, and that is forbidden. The Holy Qur'an states that the entire physical world, with its absolute knowledge and power, submits to the Creator.[45] From the point of view of humanity, it is, along with its being an inevitable behavior pattern of people, who were created as conscious beings, they are left free to choose their object of submission. In this world, only humans have permissiveness of submitting to someone (to some object) or not. As a matter of fact, when verses, concerning submission, were studied precisely, it became evident that people submitted to other individuals and groups of people of different positions. We can put them in the following order:

Disbelievers and hypocrites: "*And pay no heed to (the offers of) the unbelievers and the hypocrites, and do not mind the sufferings they cause you, and put your trust in God. God suffices as the One to rely on and to Whom affairs should be referred*" (al-Ahzab 33:48).

Those, whose hearts were detained from believing in God because of their revolts and obstinacy, followed their corporal desires and exceeded their limits: "*...And pay no heed to (the desires of) him whose heart We have made unmindful of Our remembrance, who follows his lusts and fancies, and whose affair exceeds all bounds (of right and decency)*" (al-Kahf 18:28).

Ill-mannered and sinful people: "*Pay no heed to any contemptible oath-maker (who swears much with no consideration of truth, and no will to act on his word); a defamer, circulating slander (in all directions), who hinders the doing of good; a transgressor of all bounds (of sense or decency); one addicted to sinning, cruel and ignoble; and in addition to all that, morally corrupt*" (al-Qalam 68:10–13).

---

[45] Fussilat 41:11; ar-Rahman 55:6

Those who went beyond the limits: *"And do not follow the commands of those who are wasteful (of God-given faculties) and commit excesses,"* (ash-Shu'ara 26:151).

Groups of people, who divert their employees from the path of God:

> Surely God has cursed (eternally excluded from His Mercy) the unbelievers, and has prepared for them the Blaze, to abide therein forever. They will find neither guardian nor helper. On the Day when their faces are turned over and over in the Fire, they will exclaim, "Oh, woe to us! Would that we had obeyed God and obeyed the Messenger!" and they will say: "Our Lord! Surely we obeyed our chiefs and our great ones, and they caused us to follow a misleading path. Our Lord! Cause them to suffer the punishment doubled, and curse them with a mighty curse (so that they are utterly excluded, absolutely and eternally, from Your Mercy)!" (al-Ahzab 33:64–68)

Their submission is considered an issue of belief and appraises states of those, who did not care warnings about, as the ones, who went astray from the path of God.[46]

In other verses, where the word *"ittiba"* (obedience, following) is mentioned, indirectly we can conceive submission.[47] In fact, believers obeyed and submitted to the Messenger of God as a manifestation of their love to God Almighty and a condition of earning His consent and love. And ultimately, great rewards were promised to them.[48]

READING TEXT

All Creatures Do Submit to the Host of the Palace of Universe

Cars that are parked in a military post are in submission and indicate presence of a ruler. Reservoirs, weapons, and military training centers are also in submission. They also do indicate the same ruler. Along with

---

[46] Al Imran 3:99–104; al-An'am 6:116-117, 121; Alper, Ömer Mahir, "İtâat", *DİA*, 23/444–445

[47] An-Nisa 4:125; al-An'am 6:106, 153, 155; al-A'raf 7:3, 157; Yunus 10:109; an-Nahl 16:50; ash-Shuara 26:151–152 ; Luqman 31:21; al-Ahzab 33:2; Ya-Sin 36:11; az-Zumar 39:55

[48] Al-Baqarah 2:132; an-Nisa 4:13, 69

submission of those non-living things, soldiers and commanders are also submitted to the ruler. Therefore, there is only one ruler who governs them all.

Just like in the example above, everything in the Universe starting from sun, moon, stars and the seas, mountains, and stones as well as all the plants, animals, and humans, are in submission. So, this holistic submission indicates to the All-Majestic Ruler.

For example, as soon as trees got a command of staying at the same place, they would never move from there. They withstand winds and resist against floods. Namely that pays their heed to submission. There is an example of a camel, too, who kneels down for loads to be loaded on his back, i.e, he kneels for a thing, which is not in his favor. However, in doing so, he complies with a law of submission and, hence, worships.

As for planets, then, contrary to trees, they received a command of movement. That is why, exactly do they comply with that a command and even for a single moment they do not stop at any place to rest.

People, as well, do submit to many commands sensitively for continuation of their worldly lives. For instance, they breathe the air, see with their eyes, listen with their ears, and speak with their tongues.

All these kinds of submissions show and indicate presence of the All-Majestic Maker, Ruler of the Universe, even to blind eyes.[49]

Iblis Became a Satan Because of His Disobedience

God created Prophet Adam, peace be upon him, breathed into him out of His Spirit, and ordered the angels to prostrate before His vicegerent, a human.[50] The command of prostration was an inscription of a person's being vicegerent on the Earth. Actually, it was only God Almighty, who was prostrated before. For, there is no one to be prostrated but He. Adam was here only a direction of prostration. However, his being selected as a direction of prostrations was based on his being selected as an vicegerent of God. As for angels, they welcomed that

---

[49] Kırkıncı, Mehmet, *Nükteler*, İstanbul: Zafer, 2004, p. 50
[50] Al-Hijr 15:28–29

Divine preference with respect and prostrated before Adam. In doing so, they showed their submission to God.

All the angels had immediately prostrated except one. It was the one, who was defeated by his pride and conceit and could not fathom that secret of real greatness is hidden in prostration. Iblis turned away from prostrating and, because of that, went out of the circle of submission. The Holy Qur'an explains in different verses about the fact of Iblis' refusal with all its justifications:

> And (remember) when We said to the angels: "Prostrate before Adam!" They all prostrated, but Iblis did not; he refused, and grew arrogant, and displayed himself as an unbeliever. (al-Baqarah 2:34)

Satan, who was a worshiper and an ascetic devotee for thousands of years, lighted on a clay matter of Adam, that is why, he could not see the profundity of his nature. His pride and conceit hindered him from seeing that. He disobeyed that command because he could not fathom a subtlety of submitting to command and, though he realized the meaning of a real service, he could not accept it with all his heart, could not overawe it to his heart and, especially, to his mind. And namely, because of his that disobedience God Almighty sent him away from His abode of mercy forever and negated all his pious deeds.

The Holy Qur'an Explains Us Submission Based on Example of Talut

One of the examples of submission that is given in the Holy Qur'an is the example of Talut and his army. Who was Talut? To know that about, we need to look at the history of Sons of Israel.

In the history of the Sons of Israel, after Prophet Yusha, peace be upon him, there started a period of rulers, which lasted for about five hundred years. The last ruler of that period was Samuel. According to the statement of the Old Testament, the Prophet mentioned in the Holy Qur'an with no given name was Prophet Samuel, peace be upon him. It took place one thousand years before Christ. Prophet Samuel was not only a ruler of his nation, but was also a Prophet. During those times, there was a nation of Amalika which was located in the territory between Egypt and Palestine. Their ruler's name was Jalut. Along with his army, Jalut attacked the Sons of Israel, sent them away from their country, and separated them from their families. After such a humiliation, the Sons of Israel appealed to their Prophet with a request of designating to them a commander, who could be at the same time a ruler of theirs, too.

The Prophet was well cognizant with a character of his nation. He knew well that whenever his nation confronted a difficulty, they may disobey him and be untrustworthy. For, such an appeal required an obligation of war. In case he gave such a command and his nation turned to be treacherous again, then they would have an extremely intense dilemma. That is why he openly expressed his feelings by saying: "What if you turn away from fighting after receiving a command for war?"

The Sons of Israel assured their Prophet of not letting him down and said that they did not have any other choice besides fighting. For, they were made to leave their country and, moreover, most of them lost their children and wives. Such a humiliation should be responded with a war. However, cowardice and untrustworthiness was practices by many of them. Namely that is why; Prophet Samuel felt the need for warning his nation.

Because of Divine revelation, Prophet Samuel designated Talut as a commander. However, the Sons of Israel had some objections concerning that choice of their Prophet. Nevertheless, from the very beginning they promised to obey, but their promise was not registered with all its necessary terms. Their Prophet was supposed to choose a commander but despite that, now, they were not glad with it. In fact, such a preference was a consequence of the revelation.[51] As a result, they accepted Talut as a commander but unwillingly.

Therefore, Talut organized an army and went into action. However, it was not yet obvious that all participants of the army were completely sincere and committed ones. This nation was humiliated for years. And now, they were defeated, too. Their actions were very important, especially at the time when they confront the side, which overcame

---

[51] Al-Baqarah 2:247

them. For, battle must be undertaken with that army, which is ready and brave. It is almost impossible for armies, soldiers of which are coward, untrustworthy, immoral and have a very weak feeling of submission, to resists at difficult moments.

On the other side, coward and untrustworthy people were prone to influence badly to others and wreak havoc. That is why it was very important for such an army to hold a test of sincerity, submission and support.

After having walked for a while, soldiers got really thirsty. And right at that time, Talut said to them that God Almighty will test them with a river. Whoever drank from the river was not from him, and vice versa. He also added that they had permission to drink just a handful of it. When they reached the extraordinary river, only a few of them had drunk of it to repletion. In doing so, they disobeyed Talut. They could not pass their first trial. Whereas, it was their test and they failed it.

Such a state is explained in the Holy Qur'an with following expression:

> And when Saul (Talut) set out with the army and said (to them): "God will put you to a test by (means of) a river: Whoever then drinks of it is not of my company, and whoever does not taste it, he is of my company; but forgiven will he be who takes thereof in the hollow of his hand." But they drank thereof, all save a few of them; and when he crossed it, he and those who believed with him (those who, with weak faith, took of the river in the hollow of their hands) said: "Today we have no power against Goliath and his forces." But those who had certainty of their meeting with God and felt as if always standing in His Presence said: "Many a small company has overcome a numerous company by God's leave. " God is with the patient and persevering." (al-Baqarah 2:249)

In the narrations, it is said that the number of soldiers, who passed the trial of the river, was equivalent to the number of soldiers of Badr. Bara ibn Azib, one of the noble Companions, narrated:

> We used always to say that number of us, the Companions of the Messenger, who participated in the Battle of Badr, was equivalent to number of those soldiers of Talut, who passed the river together with

Talut and fought against Jalut, i.e. for about three hundred and ten people. Only believers passed the river together with Talut.[52]

Eventually, this small sized army fought against the big sized one that frightened hearts, defeated them, and completely overcame them. It was a result of their submission.

READING TEXT

There Is Nothing More Important Than
a Command of the Ruler!

Once, when Sultan Mahmut, ruler of Ghazna, went to Council, he saw that all the authorities of the country were gathered there. He intended to test his governors and viziers. He took a precious stone and held it out to his vizier.

"What kind of stone is this? Do you know its value?"

"It is a very precious stone and its price is a hundred sacks of gold loaded on donkeys", replied vizier.

"Then break this gem!" asked the ruler.

"Your highness, I cannot do that. I wish only your well-being. If I do that, then it will not be good of me."

The ruler appreciated such a behavior of his vizier and granted him many rewards.

After having talked for a while, when everyone forgot the previous suggestion of his, he handed the gem to the maker of curtains and said: "If someone wants to buy it, how much will he have to give for this?"

"A half of your domain," replied the maker of curtains.

"If so, then just break it apart, smash it."

"O ruler of all rulers, for it will be a great shame to break it, as this precious gem will suit you, the only and one of a kind ruler. I cannot do it, as it will be enmity to you and your treasury."

The ruler liked the words of a curtain maker, too, and granted him also with many gifts.

---

[52] Ahmad ibn Hanbal, *Al-Musnad*, 4/290

After a while, he gave the gem to someone else. The latter also gave him a similar reply and received valuable gifts from the ruler.

The ruler, who had tested many people of his, at the end, called a righteous servant of his, named Eyaz, and asked him the price of the gem. Later, he ordered him to break it. Without any hesitation, Eyaz simply shattered it to pieces. Other viziers were sorry for his deed and said:

"O you, Eyaz, how could you do it? Does anyone have heart to do that? You betrayed your ruler and his treasury."

Eyaz replied: "There could be nothing precious, than fulfillment of a command of the ruler, and especially for the one, who has a real affection for him."[53]

What Our Messenger Decreed about Submission?

Observing noble *hadith*s, we can say that our Messenger, too, paid great attention to submission. In one of his *hadith*s, the Messenger of God expressed it in the following way: "Whoever submits to me submits to God. And whoever disobeys me, then, for sure, he disobeys God. Whoever revolts against their commander revolts against me."[54]

"All members of my community will enter Paradise despite those who refuse it." "Who will refuse entering Paradise?" asked a Companion. "Those, who submit to me, will enter Paradise and those who disobeyed me will be considered as those, who avoided entering into Paradise (and enter Hell)."[55]

In other *hadith* our Prophet stated: "Hear and obey (your leaders), even if an Ethiopian slave whose head is like a raisin, is made your chief (who rules you with God's Book)."[56]

---

[53] Zeren, Mehmet, *Mesnevî'de Geçen Bütün Hikâyeler*, İstanbul: Nar, 2008, p. 239

[54] *Sahih al-Bukhari*, Ahkam, 1, 9/77; *Sahih Muslim*, Imarah, 32–33; *Sunan an-Nasa'i*, Bay'at, 27, 7/138; *Sunan ibn Majah*, Jihad, 39

[55] *Sahih al-Bukhari*, I'tisam, 12

[56] *Sahih al-Bukhari*, Ahkam, 4

Similar to these, there are many other *hadith*s in the Books of Tradition. Merely, we want to tell about Usama ibn Zayd so that you understand the above mentioned *hadith* well.

Usama ibn Zayd was a son of black slave named Zayd ibn Harisa. The Messenger of God designated him as a commander of an army, which was supposed to expedite to Damascus. In the army there were many of Companions who were more prominent and elder by age than Usama.[57] At that time, Usama was only eighteen.

Some people found commandership of too young Usama very odd, while there were such leading Companions as Abu Bakr, Umar ibn al-Khattab, and Abu Ubayda ibn Jarrah. That is why they started to talk scandals about. And most probably hypocrites had their hand in that scandal. When the state reached our noble Messenger, he said: "You do object commandership of Usama. In the past you did the same for commandership of his father, Zayd ibn Harisa, too. By God, he was the most appropriate for a position of a commander and the most beloved person by me. And now, his son, Usama ibn Zayd, also is as suitable for that as his father was. At the same time, after his father, Usama is one of the most beloved persons by me. I do recommend him to you, as he is one of the righteous among you."[58]

Really, commandership of young Usama was found strange. Simply our beloved Prophet wanted a feeling of submission to emerge in the hearts of his Companions and the whole community. One more thing to point out is that, when the Messenger of God evaluated people, he did it not according to their ages, but according to their capabilities. That is why he designated Usama as a commander of army without even considering his age and social status about. He opposed to all the criticism and laid an example of evaluating an appropriate person at an appropriate place and for an appropriate duty.

Many other leading Companions, with Umar ibn al-Khattab in the instance, sincerely respected such a preference of the noble Prophet and submitted to Usama. Even once, when Umar ibn al-Khattab

---

[57] Ibn Hisham, *As-Sirah*, 3/436
[58] *Sahih Muslim*, Fadailu's-Sahaba, 63–64; *Sahih al-Bukhari*, Al-Maghazi, 87

saw Usama, he greeted him with following words: "Peace be upon you, O Chief of Believers!" Hearing that, Usama replied: "May God bestow you His forgiveness, O Chief of Believers! Are you saying those words to me?" "I will always refer to you like that, because at the time when the Messenger passed away, you were my Chief," added Umar ibn al-Khattab.[59]

Usama was a son of a poor slave. By submitting people to an indigent youngster, God's Messenger gathered everyone's attention on what submission was.

How Should We Perceive Submission to Our Leaders?

In the noble verse[60] mentioned above, the All-Just God commanded us to submit to our leaders. How should we perceive the expression of "*ulu al-amr?*" What should be our degree of submission to them?

According to Fethullah Gülen "*ulu al-amr,*" means, "being subjected to all leaders and mentors that supervise various numbers of people and lead the path shown by God and enlightened with a torch of the Messenger of God, who are resolute and decisive of staying on that way."

The verse tells us about three kinds of submission. They are submissions to God Almighty, His Messenger, and to our leaders. The noble Prophet earned greatness of his personality by being chosen as a God's Messenger. Indeed, he is a human being; however he is the means of our purpose of reaching God. As for us, we just follow that inducement. This way is not only enlightened here, in our world, but will be so in eternity, too. Our Messenger commanded, decided, and wanted submission from us on behalf of God; in the same way, those invested with authority, must follow the path of the Messenger of God, must listen and submit to him. Our great leaders as Abu Bakr as-Siddiq, the Truthful One, Umar al-Faruq, the one who distinguishes between right and wrong, Uthman ibn Affan, the owner of two pure lights, Ali ibn Abu Talib, the attacking lion and the King of Chivalry,

---

[59] Kattani, *Taratib*, 1/136
[60] An-Nisa 4:59

may God be please with them, did not oppose our Messenger even for a single moment.

Submission is a very wide circle. Our Prophet, in one of his *hadith*s said: "If you stay somewhere in a company of three people, then may one be a chief of you."[61] So, one of the three must be a chief and others must submit to him. If they set on a journey, then every necessity of their journey must be asked from their chief. Hence, the circle of submission starts from there.

Believers, the sympathizers of the sacred course, should never act on their own, especially, in matters concerning Islam. They'll have meetings, discussions, and consultations. And if it is necessary, the case will be brought before an ultimate authority, after which everything will be determined according to his decree and everyone would have to submit to his decision. In fact, believers, who abide to those invested with authority and submit to him, will be considered as though they submitted to God Almighty.

Submission is a peculiar state and a quality of being a community. From the very moment, when people started acting as a community in big or small circles, all the time, submission came into question. A believer must know what the submission is and must always submit. Our Messenger paid heed for it and did everything possible needed for its improvement.[62]

READING TEXT

Religion Can Be Represented Only by Those Who Fathomed Consciousness of Submission

In order, the Divine Truth settle in the hearts of people, every believer must consider himself responsible to the utmost. For, such a thing was decreed for many times in verses and *hadith*s. The horizon, shown by our Prophet, was to convey the true religion to all humankind.

Conveying beauties of religion to people is not only a work of a single person but the entire community. If so, then there should be

---

[61] *Sunan Abu Dawud*, Jihad, 22

[62] Gülen, M. Fethullah, *Asrın Getirdiği Tereddütler- 4*, İstanbul: Nil: 2011, p. 168

some characteristics of that sacred community, the most important among which is submission.

If one's duty is to tell about God, and the one who takes the duty and who gives it, both do for the sake of God's content, then, definitely, they should submit willingly and fulfill their responsibilities. The most delightful examples of that sacred duty for all Muslims were set by the Companions of the Messenger. We will try to give a brief explanation on Companions' submission to the Prophet and their reasons.

1. Despite our Prophet's not being different from them as a human, and because of his being a Messenger of God by duty and giving duties for the sake of God, all the Companions did their work with yearning.

Because our Messenger and all Caliphs that came after him, asked nothing concerning desires of their carnal selves, people knew well that they did everything for the sake of God and receive rewards that for in the Hereafter; and this is why, they did their duties with enthusiasm.

2. There is no country without a ruler, no nation without a governor, and no army without a commander. When following certain aims, where actions should be taken as a community, there definitely must be one, who distributes duties. Sometimes, it could be a Messenger or his successors that give duties on behalf of the Messenger. No matter what it takes, but a community, adherers of which acted on their own, submitted not to anyone and were disobedient, would never earn success. There are many armies that were defeated by rebellious soldiers. That is why for earning success on behalf of truth, everyone should fulfill their given duties.

And now, let's conceive consciousness of submission of people of horizon by reviewing the following examples:

Mus'ab ibn Umayr, was a son of one of the richest people of Mecca. He recognized the Messenger of God when he was only fourteen. When the Messenger of God sent him, the first teacher of Islam, to Medina, he said only "Go!" That teenager crossed a distance between Mecca and Medina (about 300 miles) all alone, by foot, and went to a place, where there was no one to protect him, just by the word of Messenger "Go!"

Khalid ibn Walid, who ruined the Empire of Sassanids in one motion and brought Byzantine to a motionless halt, was dismissed by Umar ibn al-Khattab, especially at the time, when he earned victory, and joined the army under commandership of Abu Ubayda. He abandoned his carnal self, egoism, fame and reputation, and accepted Messenger's Caliph's command in submission.

The religion of God that was spread worldwide from Mecca could be represented only by those, who fathomed the meaning of consciousness of submission.

In our days, too, it was just said "Go!" to those who are fond of Divine Truth. With that command they crossed distances from Siberia to China and from Australia to Thailand. Yes, if you want to tell about God Almighty and His Messenger, then "Go!"

Because of that consciousness of submission they left their countries, families, friends and just went. That who submits to God will submit to His Messenger. Those, who submit to God's Messenger, will submit to his representatives that talk on behalf of him. And as for God, then He will qualify those people with qualifications of the Companions of God's Messenger.

What Would Happen If One Does Not Submit to a Command?

If one does not submit, then he will have frustrations only. There is an example of that: During the Battle of Uhud, cavalries of the army attacked trice, and each time were tasseled back by assault of archers'. Truly, horses could not even move because of the rain of arrows. And now, wise purpose of warning of our Messenger "Come what may but never leave the hill!" that was told sensitively and insistently to fifty archeries, was even clearer. However, running of defeated hypocrites was a cause of emerging differences of thoughts at the hill of archeries. Seeing retreat, a part of archeries said the following to their fellows: "Go ahead... and take the booties! If God gave us victory, then why do you waste your time here? Fortunately, we overcame the enemy. If so, then just come behind hypocrites and gather the war-gains together with your friends."

These words expressed the first breaking point of the Battle of Uhud. They looked like they've forgotten consequences of not committing to the command of the Messenger. Apparently, they interpreted that as to be there present till the end of the battle. However, the Messenger of God told them persistently to remain there till he gave instructions to move and yet at the beginning of the plan, he drew their attentions on that point. Frankly, it made a breach in the plan and such people like Abdullah ibn Jubayr and others startled hearing such words and responded to them: "How could you forget so fast the words of the Messenger of God: 'Protect us from dangers that may come from our behind. Though you see us being killed, never ever leave your posts and come to help us! Though you see that we are gathering war-gains, still you do not come to us to take part in it. You just protect us from coming dangers!'"

According to them, the words of their fellowmen were not clear as well as those of the Messenger. Moreover, they had their own substantiations: "The Messenger of God did not mean that." Instead, they put forward their points of view. Such a condition made them go behind the retreated army to pick up the war-gains. It was to such an extent that only a few of Companions remained with Abdullah ibn Jubayr.

On the other side, a two hundred cavalries' army, lead by Khalid ibn Walid, who had not yet converted to Islam, was awaiting such a chance. They realized that fact and started to get ready to attack by deactivating those few archers. Ikrima ibn Abu Jahl also supported Khalid ibn Walid.

A seemingly small possibility was about to change everything. Obviously, God Almighty gave lesson to coming generations on behalf of those archeries. Thus, commands, given by authorities, must be fulfilled without interpreting and explaining them away and submit to them completely.

READING TEXT

Those Who Submit Will Always Gain

When walking at night time with his army, Dhu al-Qarnayn, peace be upon him, commanded them: "Gather everything and whatever you stumble over."

As soon as soldiers heard about that, a command one group among them said: "We have walked pretty much and become exhausted. Why should we carry things that we stumble over at such a late time in vain? It is better that we do not gather anything." They said like that, and really did not pick up anything.

The second group of soldiers said: "Since our commander ordered us, then let's gather only a little bit in order to not oppose him. For, we need to submit to the army commander." They said it and gathered only a few things.

As for the third group, they said: "Nothing will be said by our commander in vain. For sure, he might know something we do not. There must be some wisdom behind that." They said it and filled all their vessels up to the brims.

In the morning, they noticed that at night, they had walked on a gold mine, and things that they stumbled over were gold. Simply in the dark, they could not understand it. When they realized that, the first group, who did not take any of them, said: "If only we had taken them! If only we submitted to our commander and gathered them! At least we ought to take just one piece of it." They regretted very much.

As for the second group, who took a small amount of gold, said: "If only we could have gathered a bit more than this! If only we stuffed all our pockets and covers with them." In doing so, they reprimanded themselves.

And soldiers of the third group said: "If only we threw all our unnecessary stuff and gathered even more. If only we could fill everything and gather even more!" Despite their gathering much gold, they were sad, too!

QUESTIONS

1. What is the name of a commander that was designated by Prophet Samuel, who was inspired by a Divine revelation?

   a. Jalut

   b. Talut

   c. Dhu al-Qarnayn

   d. Prophet Dawid

2. What was the name of a young Companion of the Messenger, whom he designated as a commander of the army and wanted to send to Damascus?

   a. Zayd

   b. Harisa

   c. Abu Ubayda

   d. Usama

3. What does "*ulu al-amr*" mean?

   a. Those invested with authority

   b. Four great Prophets mentioned in the Holy Qur'an

   c. Great Angels

   d. Our Prophet

4. What was the name of a commander of fifty archers, who were ordered by the Messenger of God as "Come what may but never leave the hill!"?

   a. Abdullah ibn Masud

   b. Abdullah ibn Ubada

   c. Abdullah ibn Jubayr

   d. Abdullah ibn Zubayr

5. What was the name of a commander who said to his army at a night time: "Gather everything whatever you stumble over"?

   a. Zayd ibn Harisa

   b. Prophet Dawid

   c. Talut

   d. Dhu al-Qarnayn

4.

SUFFERING, ANGUISH, PATIENCE, PERSEVERANCE AND INCONSTANCY

(Given the history of humankind in this world,) do you think that you will enter Paradise while there has not yet come upon you the like of what came upon those who passed away before you? They were visited by such adversities and hardships, and were so shaken as by earthquake that the Messenger and those who believed in his company nearly cried out: "When comes God's help?" Beware! The help of God is surely near! (al-Baqarah 2:214)

What are Suffering and Anguish?

In the words of Fethullah Gülen, suffering and anguish are very important means to reach the exalted goals and obtain high results. A traveler to the truth is cleansed by suffering, becomes purified by it and attains his essence with it. Neither maturation nor union with one's spirit can be spoken of where there is no suffering.

All great causes and altruistic purposes unfurl in the shadow of deprivation, suffering and anguish.[63] No great truth and high ideal were attained without facing difficulty and enduring some deprivation.

A Cause Requires Suffering and Anguish

Service to Islam and success on this path always occurred with the same method, and so many kinds of suffering and anguish were endured. Examples related to the life of suffering and anguish that accompanies

---

[63] Gülen, M. Fethullah, *Prizma-3*, İstanbul: Nil, 2008, p. 31

walking on God's path are also seen in the lives of the first people who lived centuries ago and their Prophets.

For example, if the words spoken to Prophet Noah by his tribe, as explained in the Qur'an, were spoken to any of us on the street and if we were insulted in this manner, we would be bent over by pain in our consciences. One of the five greatest Prophets, this Messenger went from door to door everyday and touching their doorknobs said, "Say that there is no deity but God and be saved"; the people, on the other hand, sometimes tied a rope to his foot and dragged him, sometimes ganged up on and beat him, sometimes threw dirt on him and sometimes made the most merciless insults.

When Prophet Abraham's life is examined, it can be seen what great difficulties he endured. He faced the heaviest suffering and anguish like being thrown into the fire, taking his wife far away and leaving her, and attempting to sacrifice his son.

One of Prophet Jesus' disciples betrayed him. In fact, his tribe treacherously surrounded his house and raced with one another to crucify their own Prophet.

In short, all the Prophets endured suffering. The path is the path they trod on. Consequently, Yunus Emre (d. 1321 CE) said:

This road is long; its stages are many

There are no passes, only deep water.

When we look from this respect, those who walk on God's path should be prepared for every kind of difficulty and hardship, suffering and anguish. Those who believe should accept from the beginning that there can be calamities on their heads in the path of explaining God and the truth to needy hearts, and they should know well and accept that it will be necessary for them to endure these.

What Is Patience?

Patience is a person's being able to tolerate every kind of trouble and difficulty, and being able to endure unpleasant situations without being bothered. It is a person who encounters calamity or catastrophe being able to await the outcome without complaint and being able to overcome obstacles appearing before them in order to reach a result.

Man was sent to this world for trial. Due to trial a person's capabilities develop and, consequently, he will become worthy of God's pleasure and seeing His sacred and infinite beauty. As a necessity of trial on this path, surpassing trouble and difficulty can only be done with patience. Patience is a virtuous attribute that will take a believer to the horizon of being together with God and that will enable him to attain God's good tidings. The existence of a believer's faithfulness to God is tied to patience. Faithfulness cannot be spoken of where there is no patience.

God informed us that He definitely would test believing servants in order to make apparent those who are patient and those who are not. He gave good tidings to the patient ones, informed us that His acceptance and pleasure were together with those who have patience, and He expressed that He would give unlimited reward to the patient ones.[64]

Being patient is accepting with pleasure God's absolutely wise and merciful dispositions in the universe which is His own property. Impatience is rejection and rebellion. It is necessary to show patience with the difficulties that God has sent as a trial.

Patience requires resignation to God, resolution, sound will power and sharp determination. Patience lies in the foundation of every kind of material and spiritual success. For this reason, patience is the key to every kind of salvation.

How Many Kinds of Patience Are There?

Bediüzzaman Said Nursi separates patience into three kinds:

1. Patience against sins: A believer shows patience against the provocative attraction of every kind of sin and tries not to commit sin.

---

[64] Muhammad 47:31; al-Baqarah 2:153, 155, 249

2. Patience against calamities: This kind of patience is that made before every kind of material and spiritual calamity and disaster he meets in worldly life.

3. Patience in worship: Worship puts an apparent weight on a person like praying five times every day, making ablution, and fasting. A believer should also show patience towards these and earn Paradise.[65]

Fethullah Gülen adds another kind of patience to these three categories: Patience against the attractive beauties of this world. This is a very important matter particularly in regard to today's Muslims. Their life standards have risen greatly, and houses, cars, summer houses, winter retreats, etc. have unfortunately distanced some people from feelings and thoughts regarding the other life. This is pointed out in this verse, *"Made innately appealing to men are passionate love for women, children, (hoarded) treasures of gold and silver, branded horses, cattle, and plantations. Such are enjoyments of the present, worldly life; yet with God is the best of the goals to pursue"* (Al Imran 3:14). The expression "innately appealing" emphasizes that it is not possible for people not to be dazzled before these beautiful things. Overcoming this can be done with very strong faith and patience which keeps faith constantly in action.

Patience against the exasperations of the time… patience in the form of indifference to spiritual distinctions… In fact, the patience to force oneself to remain in this world of suffering even if the doors to Paradise have been opened wide for the sake of service on God's path is another kind of patience.[66]

What Is "Active Patience"?

There is a concept in our literature called "active patience." It is beneficial to dwell on this briefly.

Let's think of a hen lying on her eggs. Seeing the hen in this state, we say, "This animal is lying indolently on its eggs." However, for three weeks it has endured great pain and suffering. The hen is careful to

---

[65] Nursi, Said, *The Letters*, New Jersey: The Light, 2007, p. 300

[66] Gülen, M. Fethullah, *Fasıldan Fasıla-3*, İstanbul: Nil, 2011, pp. 122–123

keep the eggs at a certain temperature; while she turns them, the hen shows maximum effort not to harm or break them. Thus, with this extremely sensitive, careful and active stand, this hen is displaying an example of active patience.

Let me give another example: In order to make dinner, a mother prepares vegetables, meat, oil, onions, spices… whatever there is, puts it on the stove and begins to wait for the food to cook. Active patience is continuing her wish after the food was put on the stove by praying for her goal to be obtained while she is waiting.

In a different example, two people talk, agree and get married. The period of waiting for a baby is the active patience period. The couple cannot do very much, but they pray for the baby to be sound and healthy.

In summary, a person's serving cooked food, beginning the meal with the *basmala*, nursing the newborn baby, taking care of it… these all require preparation. At this point the individual is responsible for continuing his or her task with determination and patience, and by embracing prayer and putting on a garment of piety, to stand firmly in place. Perhaps some events will take place, storms will rage and waves will rise. However, a believer will stand firmly in place like the pole star and actively wait for the storm to pass.

READING TEXT
Jewels of Measurement Regarding Patience

- Like an herb that eases pain, patience both burns one's body and treats the sickness.
- Every difficulty is pregnant with easiness, but it is necessary to be patient during the pregnancy period.
- Even if patience and success appear to be different, they are twins.
- Seas are formed from drops, but no one has the power to determine the time when a drop will become a part of the sea.
- Mistakes are the things found most in a mixture of one who hurries.

- The path of peaks begins in the valleys… of course, for those who are patient…
- If there is anything whose beginning is poison, but whose result is sugar-sweet syrup, it is patience.
- The name of positive attitude before events is patience; for this reason, saints considered asking for patience before its season to be ill-advised.[67]

Patience Is Mandatory for Success

A man with a cause should not be daunted by difficulties arising on his path. He should see these difficulties as a necessity of the task and he should see the struggle with difficulties as an opportunity to develop his capabilities. The person who wants to attain success should dedicate himself to the task and become passionate, even obsessed with his objective. Let's not forget that it is not the power of the drop that bores into the rock; it is constancy.

Struggling against difficulties requires enduring some hardships. One who does not envisage difficulties and suffering cannot be successful. A person who wants to be successful should take lessons from good examples that will lead him to success.

While Ibn Sina was a student he was not very good at mathematics. One day he left school for this reason. He set off for his homeland. After walking a lot, he became thirsty and went to the mouth of a well. He lowered the bucket into the well and as he was pulling the bucket out with a rope, he saw that the rope had worn away the marble. Saying, "If a rope can wear away marble, can't I do mathematics," he turned back. He worked hard, was patient before difficulties and, as a result, he became a world-renowned scholar and man of ideas.

Abul-Hajjaj al-Uqsuri said, "A cat guided me." He explained as follows to those who thought he was making fun of them: "It was a cold winter night. I had not yet slept. I was walking around outside. I suddenly saw that a cat wanted to get on the lantern pole. The pole was slippery. The cat climbed, but it could not go up and it fell down.

---

[67] Gülen, M. Fethullah, *Ölçü veya Yoldaki Işıklar*, pp. 219–220

It tried dozens of times. After returning from prayer, I saw that the cat had climbed up. Plus it was sitting next to the lantern. I learned from the cat not to be daunted by obstacles."

Difficulties push man to search, wake him up and open the door to dynamism. Overcoming obstacles gives pleasure to man. It fires him up for new purposes.

READING TEXT

An Ache in the Oyster!

In its usual state, an oyster had a plain but happy life. It was clinging to a rock in the depths of the sea, and was living its life there. It found food in the salty seawater, and its hard shell was able to protect it from enemies. Most of its time was spent watching fish that passed in front of it gliding from right to left.

Suddenly one day an ache began inside the oyster. The inner pain it felt took away its calm life and left difficult and painful days in its place. The oyster did not take long to learn the reason for the pain: sand. A tiny grain of sand had entered the oyster and was now making it writhe with pain.

One day the oyster began to think to itself about what it could do about the grain of sand. It knew there was no use or benefit in asking questions like, "Why did this trouble come to me? How did this happen?" The best thing would be to try and live together with this guest.

After this decision, the oyster's pain did not end, but it subsided. The difficulty that would have increased many-fold if the oyster had complained remained at a tolerable level. Days, months and years passed. It is interesting, the oyster's aches and pains had almost gone and in their place was an oyster that everyone enjoyed visiting.

For the grain of sand that had caused the oyster's life to pass in pain for a long time had turned into a pearl by means of patience. The other sea creatures living where the oyster was frequently visited it and from time to time watched the magnificent pearl that appeared when the oyster opened its shell.

And they could not decide about something. They wondered if that wonderful pearl was beautifying the oyster or was the oyster which stood like a symbol of patience and serenity showing the pearl to be so beautiful.

What do you think?

There Is No Unjust Treatment or Suffering I Have Not Seen!

A hero with a cause continues on his path without bowing down or being daunted before events. This attitude shows his respect, loyalty and fidelity to his cause. When it was asked to the scholar Sayyid Qutb before he was executed that he apologize to Egyptian President Nasser and that if he did, he would be pardoned, Sayyid Qutb said: "If this decision for execution is just, then I accept it. If it is false, I will not bend down to apologize to falsehood." Saying this, he showed that he was a man with a cause.

Great men of religion served their causes under great calamity and difficulties. Due to his views, Ahmad ibn Hanbal was sentenced to 28 years in prison. He said, "I ask for salvation from God for those who have whipped me on God's path." He wrote the magnificent work *Al-Musnad* while he was imprisoned.

Hanafi scholar Imam as-Sarakhsi was imprisoned in a blind well. He taught students who came to the mouth of the well from the bottom of the well. He wrote the 30-volume work entitled *Kitab al-Mabsut* inside the well.

With his unshakable spiritual state and legendary life, Bediüzzaman gave the best example to the question, "How should a man of cause be?" See how he described the suffering and pain he experienced:

"They haven't left any pains that I didn't suffer from and any tortures that I didn't agonize. I was treated in martial courts as if I was a mass murderer. I was sent into exile from one region to another like a vagrant. I was prohibited from communication for months in countryside prisons. I was poisoned so many times and was exposed to many sorts of insults..."

My nature cannot bear humiliation and insult. Islamic courage and reason forbid me from being in this state. When faced with such an incident, I will not belittle myself no matter with whom I may be dealing, be it even the cruelest, most barbaric enemy commander. I will strike him in the face with his cruelty and barbarity. He may throw me in a dungeon or even lead me to the executioner's block. It is of no importance. Indeed, that is what happened. I have seen all of these things. If the heart, the conscience, of that barbaric commander had been able to resist such cruelty a few minutes more, Said would today have been hanged and joined the assembly of the innocent.

All my life has passed with such trouble and difficulty, disaster and catastrophe. I have sacrificed my soul, my world, on the path of belief, happiness, and soundness of the society. So let it be. I do not even curse them, because thanks to this, the *Risale-i Nur* has at least reached a few hundred thousand people, or a few million. I do not know the number, but that is what they say. The Afyon prosecutor said five hundred thousand. Maybe it has been a means of saving more people's belief.

By dying I would have saved only myself, but by remaining alive and bearing difficulty and troubles I have helped to save so much belief. A thousand thanks to God…"[68]

As expressed in a *hadith*, "A believer is like a green crop. The wind constantly shakes it. (It shakes the believer with calamity and difficulties). The state of a hypocrite is like a tree. It never shakes until it is cut."[69]

Faith and patience lighten calamity and difficulties. Those who believe in God and surrender to Him see difficulties as a necessity of His path.

At a jail they beat a student of the *Risale-i Nur* until he fainted. When he came to he prayed, "My Lord, they do not know. Forgive them." Just as the Messenger of God said regarding those who gave him trouble and sadness: "My Lord, they do not know; give them salvation!"

---

[68] Nursi, Said, *Tarihçe-i Hayat*, İstanbul: Şahdamar, 2010, p. 616
[69] *Sahih Muslim*, Sifatu'l-Munafiqin, 69

When those who are saddened by calamity and difficulties they face in this world see the fruit they are given in Paradise in return for their sadness, they will say, "We wish out sorrow and trouble had been more."

READING TEXT

Troubled Ones!

The points of action for those who dedicate their lives to a cause are their ideals. They program their lives according to their ideals, discipline their feelings and thoughts along the lines of their ideals, and harness their desires and wishes within this framework. The life they lead is not their life; it is the life demanded by their ideals. In our language we call them idealists, in more serious terms "a man with a cause," and in a more sincere expression "troubled ones."

It can be seen that masses of people follow causes. However, among those masses few people can be shown who have placed their lives on an "idealistic axis." Perhaps, as they are called in the dictionary, the best word to describe the crowds is "sympathizers."

The difference between a man with a cause and a sympathizer is that a man of cause does his "daily and worldly" tasks in his "free time," and a sympathizer considers a cause as a way to "evaluate free time and as a hobby." The reason for existence, Prophet Muhammad, peace and blessings be upon him, said, "If they give me the sun in my right hand and the moon in my left hand, still I will not forego this cause." His statement is the shiniest example from the perspective that the "heartfelt cause" is greater than the world and everything in it.

While a person of stature, who had studied and been inspired by "the greatest man of troubles," said in his dying breath, "No cause as great as this cause of faith will come again to this earth and no honor equal to the honor of those dying for this cause will come into existence," he became a spokesman for the final horizon of sacrifice of a spirit with troubles.

With the statement, "If I see that my nation's faith is secure, I am willing to burn in the flames of Hell, because while my body is burning, my heart will be a rose garden," the last "troubled one" in the same chain of ideals that has extended to our century expresses what kind of spiritual state a "troubled one" should possess.

One fortunate one in a group of friends emphasized that an idealist can only be a "man living his cause" with his statement, "My ears are full but my eyes have just come out of famine." These words shout the reality of this task to those who claim to be men of cause. Otherwise, it is very difficult to reach a goal, attain a purpose or hit one's target as a sympathizer. For "Those who do not live what they believe begin to believe as they live."[70]

Patience and Perseverance Are the Solution to Being Successful in the Test

A believer is constantly being tested throughout his life. The formula for being successful in the test is comprised of patience and perseverance: *"O you who believe! Be patient (persevere through what befalls you in the world, in God's cause); encourage each other to patience, vying in it with one another and outdoing all others in it; and observe your duties to God in solidarity, and keep from disobedience to God in due reverence for Him and piety, so that you may prosper (in both worlds)!"* (Al Imran 3:200).

A purpose for which no difficulty is experienced or no calamity or trouble are endured cannot be a cause. What raises purpose to the level of cause is the difficulty and suffering. A cause cannot reach success without pain. A believer faces unexpected difficulties with patience. He does not panic. He is a person for hard times. He knows facing trouble is his destiny. As Yunus expressed, one advances from one stage to the next:

> This road is full of traps: It's too long, with huge laps;
> Blocks on it leave no gaps; it leads to deep waters.

A man of cause is tied to his cause with passion. He shows his loyalty by enduring the torment of his beloved. He accepts everything coming from God and says,

---

[70] Tokul, Ali, *Sızıntı*, November 1988, p. 118

> If harshness comes from the Majesty of God
> Or generosity from His Grace,
> Both are delights to the soul.
> Both His blessings and His wrath are pleasing.

Our noble Prophet said in a *hadith*:

"There are some kiosks in Paradise that are not hung from above or supported from below."

"O Messenger of God, how do their owners enter them?" one of the Companions asked.

He replied: "They enter and leave their kiosks like birds."

"O Messenger of God, to whom do they belong?" asked a Companion.

He said: "They are for those who were subjected to illness, pain and calamity and showed patience in face of them."[71]

Imam Azam Abu Hanifa was offered the position of judge. When he did not accept it, they tortured him. His mother said, "O my son! Knowledge has brought you nothing but difficulty and trouble." The imam replied, "Don't feel bad, mother, they want to give me this world, but I want the next world. Rather than being subject to God's wrath in the next life, I will endure torture in this world." And he endured worldly difficulties for happiness in the next world.

READING TEXT

Which Lessons Were Given at the Café Talks?

A person possesses compassion and patience to the degree of his faith. People's coming to faith is more valuable than everything over which the sun rises and sets. Friends of God who grasp this secret are subjected to serious trials on this path. Let's present an example from the present:

"After Fethullah Gülen began preaching, first the mosque and then the courtyard filled up; later on the congregation began spilling over into the streets. However, he did not appear to be pleased with this. His mind was focused on the youth: "Where are the youth," he would ask. "Since they do not come to the mosque, we should go to

---

[71] İmam Gazali, *Ölüm ve Ötesi*, İstanbul: Sağlam, 1999, p. 189

them," he said. When he decided to begin café talks, we all objected. However, he was very determined. The first café talk was to be held at the Station Café in Mersinli, İzmir.

There were pictures of Mao and Lenin in the café. Everyone was playing backgammon and card games. Some asked, "Where did he come from?" Later on verbal provocation like, "Look at this backward man; shut him up," and other insults began. In fact, they even threw bottles in front of him. We were beside ourselves. He also heard, but he continued his talk as if he had not heard. It was as if he were in another dimension.

The talk lasted a full three and one-half hours. One hour passed without taking notice of insults. Later questions began to come. Slowly the talk began to get the attention of the people at the café. Materialists began to ask questions one after another like, "Was matter or spirit created first?" He took every question into serious consideration, gave answers satisfying to the heart and convincing to the mind and waited for new questions. Most of the audience remained standing up.

It was the year 1968. There were 28 café talks. Several years passed. One day those sitting in the mosque courtyard decided to introduce themselves as was custom. Everyone said either before or after their name, "From this or that café talk." [72]

In these paragraphs taken from the article entitled "Café Talks," which pass on to history important values in the name of sociology and human psychology, this event shows how faith and patience are inseparable parts of a whole in Fethullah Gülen's attitude. We will be tried and we will show patience in the degree of our faith.

Two Conditions for Success: Perseverance and Remembering God

Our Lord says in one verse, "*O you who believe! When you meet a host in battle, stand firm, and remember and mention God much, that you may triumph*" (al-Anfal 8:45). We see in this verse that "perseverance" and "remembering God" are used together.

---

[72] Gürsoy, İdris, *Unutulmasın Diye*, İstanbul: Işık, 2008, pp. 145–147

Perseverance does not mean patience. Even though we use them together as equal words, it is a fact that perseverance carries a different meaning from patience. Patience is used for continuing a task without interruption until the end. For example, it has been used for enduring and remaining enlivened before worship, sins and calamities.

The word perseverance means determination, remaining firm in your word, thinking soundly and then not reneging on a matter that has been decided. Perseverance is an important principle and a powerful source of virtue. A person of perseverance and fortitude thinks very carefully before he acts, weighs carefully the pros and cons of the matter, makes an appropriate decision and does not go back on it or act with inconstancy. Considered to be an important sign of will, perseverance is a vital human virtue and neither joy nor sadness nor self-interest nor fear of defeat can turn such a person back on his decision.

In the rest of the verse it is said, "Remember God often." *Dhikr* means a person's remembering God. In a moment when a life and death struggle is being made and in the most difficult moment, God gives success sooner or later to a person whose heart is filled with God. However, a person's being able to say "God" and think of God in such critical moments and difficult times is tied somewhat to his remembering God in other more comfortable times. At any rate, a person will naturally call to God in times of difficulty. For this reason, the essentially important thing is not saying "God" in times of trouble, but to make this a dimension of our nature and to always be in an atmosphere of remembering God.

And the verse's summary is in the form, "It is hoped that you will reach success." This means the condition for success on the plane of causes is making perseverance and *dhikr* a dimension of our nature.

READING TEXT

There Is Perseverance; There Is Absolutely No Inconstancy!

- However important it is to find the truth and dedicate oneself to it, it is that much important after finding it to be loyal and show perseverance on that path; this is a matter that needs to be carefully taken into consideration. Someone whose spirit has been enlightened with the truth will not easily change his path and direction! Coming to those who constantly change their altar, they are some unfortunate people who have not found the truth or those who have not grasped the significance of it.

- The fortunate ones are those who are on the shore of the ocean of truth with an insatiable desire and who melt the waves coming from the ocean in their hearts and are well-known for asking, "Is there more?" These have finished their search, found their altar and have settled in the spirit. Coming to those who are constantly rolling back and forth, either they are some unmannered ones who do not know the method of searching or those without the ability to judge who mix up searching and finding. Only those who seek will find; those who find remain in their place; those bewildered ones who only think they have found the truth simply turn around on the same spot throughout their lives.

- Every fugitive who has escaped from the front has sentenced himself first in his own conscience, then in history and then before coming generations; consequently, they can be considered to have been dealt a blow contrary to their purpose. In every exalted cause standing firm and protecting the front is a sign of courage. Servants of the ego which swims according to the wind—even if they do not understand or do not want to understand this—after a real human being understands the truth once then self-interest will not chain his feet, fear will not stand in his way; and lust will not block him. He will overcome all of these as if he is flying.

- Just as those who constantly change their ideas and place in a group dedicated to service shake the feelings of others' trust and confidence in them, they have always shattered the hope of other friends in the cause. Just as one person's sliding and getting out of line in a group that is walking in unison with love and enthusiasm destroys the rhythm of the group's movement and causes confusion, someone breaking away from an idealistic team bound to one another gives shock, despondency and malediction to friends and joy to enemies.

- Those who frequently break their pledge and fall into indecision will at some time lose the trust of others and slowly fall under the influence of others. Losing their whole character in time, these paralyzed spirits become a harmful factor to both themselves and to the group they are in.[73]

What Do Today's Youth Need to Be Patient with Most?

If a believer who has shouldered the honor of serving Islam lives the virtues of faith and becomes a good role model, he is like a person from the Age of Happiness. Since we understand an event as a sign from its meaning, any act made by such a believer is equal to ten acts in God's eyes. In comparison to the Companions living 10/10, if a youth today lives 1/10 of Islam straight upright like the letter *alif* in view of many factors that trigger his feelings of lust and animal desires, I hope that God will accept him as living Islam 10/10.

There are many duties befalling Muslim youth in this century. It should not be forgotten that one of the three types of patience is enduring against a person's rebellion and sin and being patient before them. Patience that is more relevant to today's believers is persevering in being a Muslim against the sins coming at us wave upon wave.

Today there are many factors that entice our youth to fornication, drag them towards stealing and even push them to indolence. If in spite of this our youth are patient and live Islam as it should be lived, they will receive the reward incumbent upon this patience in the highest degree.

The youth of this century should live the principles of Islam and try and remain as remote as possible from sins and sinful environments. God willing, such youth will eventually take their place next to the Companions.

---

[73] Gülen, M. Fethullah, *Ölçü veya Yoldaki Işıklar*, İstanbul: Nil, 2011, p. 223–226

READING TEXT

Sensitive and Stolid Souls

Tears are the drops that fall from the eyes of a believer when sublime feelings such as fear, hope, respect and love fully wrap around his soul. The one who washes his face with these tears is called a hero of heart. As of the ones who are not deeply moved, and whose eyelashes are not moistened, could be called mere misfortunate people.

Nowadays, there are crucial inconsistencies between our religion that we believers have been practicing in a rather flawed fashion, and the real situation of us. And our general position includes lamentable pictures. Although we have been exposed to serious tests, worldly and spiritually, in all units of life, some people can still laugh at something and enjoy themselves nonsensically. In this regard, while a part of society gets so carefree, it falls to the other part to shed tears in misery. If it were my mission and if I really could, I would weep non-stop 24 hours, even like Prophet Jacob, till it blinds me, in order to soften obdurate hearts, those carefree people.

In fact, it is certain that those obdurate hearts determined with wickedness could not be softened by either tears or even the rivers of Paradise. That kind of people, as a matter of fact, are those misfortunate who are so far away from grace and compassion that they would stay fully dry even if they fell in the ocean of grief. Yes, on one side there are those who get moistened even under the open sky—I would sacrifice my life for them!—those rude and fully obdurate souls who cannot get wet even in the ocean…

Today, there is so much to shed tears for! Sometimes, I am unable to know for what I shall cry and feel sorry. For the possibility of that the egg may be broken, the chick be trampled, the winds of autumn may blow and scatter the harvest everywhere, spring be missed, and the season may pass in vain? Or should I cry for the possibility of being stabbed among people sharing my thoughts and feelings, as it happened in front of Vienna after the Girays had opened the bridge gate to the enemy and stabbed in the back of the Ottoman Army?

You, those who have forgotten to cry all through the history! Come on now, come on! Let's shed tears all together, in order to promote our enthusiasm to deal with the matters that seem to be impasse, and to give up our ages-old indifference and insensitiveness!

Along this holy path that is filled with troubles and agony, and that much to cry for, patience should be the most prominent viaticum of the believer. Referring to the troubles they had suffered for their faith, God's Messenger addressed to the Yasir Family in this way: "Keep your patience, O Yasir family! It is Paradise itself, promised to you!" That is, every single emergence passes by swallowing the thorn of "patience" like the Yasir family. You will feel it getting stuck in your gullet, in your stomach, and becoming a griping pain in your bowels; and it will follow a process by writhing in agony and suffer. A little more patience... The end of this path is Paradise. There will surely be one day in the Hereafter when those who, here, unleash magpies onto roses, surrender rose gardens to thorns, and making evil plans on breaking the seedlings, will be deeply regretful and cry. However, on that day books will have already been closed and it will be too little too late.[74]

For Whom Did Bediüzzaman Bear Suffering and Anguish?

This man of suffering and anguish who sacrificed this world and the next on the path to save the society's faith; who knew no worldly pleasure during his more than eighty years of earthly life; whose whole life passed on battlefields and in prisons; who endured every kind of punishment and was treated like a murderer in the martial law court; who was prohibited from having visitors for months on end in the country's prisons, who was poisoned many times and was subject to various insults;[75] who said, "There were times when I would have preferred death to life a thousand times over. If my religion had not prohibited me from committing suicide, perhaps today Said would have rotted

---

[74] Gülen, M. Fethullah, *Fasıldan Fasıla–5*, İstanbul: Nil, 2011, pp. 50–52
[75] Nursi, Said, *Tarihçe-i Hayat*, İstanbul: Şahdamar, 2010, p. 553

under the ground";[76] and who did not even curse those who saw him worthy of such unbearable treatment[77]—for whom did he endure this pain and punishment?

Enlightening the age with his light, shaking the century with his deep voice, conquering minds with his words, and touching hearts with his humility and modesty, amazing everyone with his abstinence and piety, astounding people of conscience with his self-sufficiency, blending Islamic works and making from them the most appropriate prescription for the illnesses of the age and presenting it to the world in his 6,000-page *Risale-i Nur Collection*, and at the same time reading the science and philosophy of the age,[78] he said, "There is a huge fire in front of me. The flames are rising to the heavens; my child is burning, my faith is burning. I am running to put out that fire and to save my faith.[79] As people saved from the fire by him, how much have we been able to help that glorious master and heroic fireman?

Have we been able to read and understand him in a way he deserves? Have we been able to share as much as was expected from us the trouble and suffering of a man who says, "The only things that give me pain are the dangers Islam faces...,"[80] first felt the blows to the Islamic world in his own heart?[81] Has the time come to question ourselves?

Gülen mentions about the man of suffering and anguish in one of his poems:

Suffering Man

He wavers like a candle, and his chest aches sorrowfully.
He walks on the mountains lightened by dawn.
Even if he's in Paradise, still there's gloom in his soul.
In his daydreams he always walks through happy ages...
His horizon is pitch-black like treeless mountains.
All the purple summits and lively islands are dark.

---

[76] *Ibid.*

[77] Nursi, Said, *Emirdağ Lahikası*, İstanbul: Şahdamar, 2010, p. 223

[78] Nursi, Said, *Tarihçe-i Hayat*, İstanbul: Şahdamar, 2010, p. 553

[79] *Ibid.*, p. 552

[80] *Ibid.*

[81] *Ibid.*, p. 54

When his chest shakes with "autumn" every morning...
And his spirit is beaten in broken mortars.
His heart is timid like the birds, his eyes are feverish.
Events make the sound of a mallet in his spirit.
He fights with time every night and day-dreams every day.
He always walks singing a song of suffering.
Time comes when he overflows with hope, a secret pleasure in him,
His head is where the transient are separated from the Eternal One.
When he shouts loudly with a voice of steel,
Shudders are aroused in hearts in rising pitches.
He aches with love in the most remote places.
He always moans and walks; the roads moan with him.
Every day he pursues a new prey, every day in a trench.
He awaits the season that will enlighten the horizons.
Sometimes loyalty gives no echo, everything is speechless...
And blood-red nails pierce his spirit.
Sometimes spring scents waft fragrantly.
You see the wind singing a lullaby with a thousand aromas.[82]

READING TEXT
The Legendary Suffering of Habbab ibn Arat

In the first years of Islam, Muslims were generally poor, destitute and impoverished people. The Meccan polytheists made unimaginable torture to these Muslims. When the oppression became unbearable, Muslims went to the Messenger of God and asked that he pray for them to be saved from it. Advising them that they show patience, our noble Prophet indicated that believers from previous times had also been persecuted.

One of those subject to the oppression and torture from the Meccan polytheists was Habbab ibn Arat. Habbab was a member of the Tamin tribe. He was one of the first Muslims. It is reported that he was the sixteenth to enter Islam.

Habbab was the slave of a woman named Ummu Anmar, a polytheist. This woman went mad when she learned that Habbab had become Muslim. How could her slave become Muslim without her permission! She immediately ordered her slave to turn back from this

---

[82] Gülen, M. Fethullah, *Kırk Mızrap*, İstanbul: Nil, 2006, pp. 179–180

religion; when he did not, she began to torture him with unbearable treatment. So much so that she would heat iron in a fire; when it became red hot, she would sear Habbab's back and head with it. Habbab would endure this. However, this torture did not cease.

One day Habbab complained about this situation to God's Messenger. Prophet Muhammad, peace and blessings be upon him, prayed: "My God! Help Habbab!" Before long the woman torturing Habbab began to have a problem with her head. She was wrenching with heavy pain. And she began to howl like a dog. She tried everything to treat the pain. She was advised to sear her head with a hot iron, otherwise, she would not be able to escape the pain. Look at God's wisdom! This time it was Habbab's turn. He took the hot iron and seared Ummu Anmar's head as she ordered. [83]

While torture was continuing relentlessly, one day some Companions went to our noble Prophet and complained about the torture they were facing from the polytheists. They asked, "Will you ask for God's help and grace for us?"

The Messenger of God replied: "There were people from communities before you who were buried to their waists in sand. After that a saw would be brought and they would be cut in two. Or their flesh would be separated from the bone with iron rakes. However, still they did not turn back from their religion. I swear that God will complete this religion. In fact, a day will come when a horseback rider will be able to take his herd safely from Damascus to Hadhramaut without any fear except for fear of God and worry that wolves will attack the herd. But you are impatient in regard to this matter." [84]

QUESTIONS

1. Which one of the following is not a kind of patience?
    a. Patience against sins
    b. Patience against difficulties

---

[83] Ibn al-Asir, *Usudu'l-Ghaba*, 2/102; Ibn Sa'd, *Tabaqat*, 3/164

[84] *Sahih al-Bukhari*, Manakib, 25

    c. Patience against the apparent heaviness of worship

    d. Patience against noise

2. Which great scholar said, "If a rope can wear away marble, can't I learn mathematics?"

    a. Ibn Sina

    b. Harizmi

    c. Ali Kuşçu

    d. Piri Reis

3. Which of the following was tried by either foregoing his faith or being thrown into ditches of fire?

    a. Ashab as-Suffa

    b. Ashab ar-Ray

    c. Ashab al-Uhdud

    d. Ashab al-Kahf

4. Which of the following great scholars said, "There is no punishment I did not suffer"?

    a. Bediüzzaman Said Nursi

    b. Abdulhakim Arvasi

    c. Elmalılı Hamdi Yazır

    d. Atıf Hodja from İskilip

5. Which of the following was designated in this section as a condition on the plane of causes for having success in a task?

    a. Patience and discipline

    b. Perseverance and remembrance of God

    c. Difficulty and pain

    d. Struggle and effort

5.

DHIKR, RECITATION, *JAWSHAN*

O you who believe! Remember and mention God much, and glorify
Him (in that He is absolutely above all defects and having partners) in
the morning and in the evening (day and night)! (al-Ahzab 33:41-42)

What Does *Dhikr* Mean?

In respect to its definition, *dhikr* means to remember God, to
recite certain prayers in a specified number and particular form,
and for a person to see messages from God in almost everything
when the world is looked at from a contemplative perspective. In this
respect it is a form of worship that takes people closer to God in the
most rapid way.

Undoubtedly, *dhikr* is one of the most important concepts in the
Qur'an regarding remembering God. The Qur'an's expressing that a
believing servant is making *dhikr* in his every attitude and movement
explains beautifully the dimensions of both *dhikr* and servanthood:

> They remember and mention God (with their tongues and hearts),
> standing and sitting and lying down on their sides (whether during
> the Prayer or not), and reflect on the creation of the heavens and
> the earth... (Al Imran 3:191)

Dhikr is life itself; it is remembering God even in moments of our
physical needs like eating, drinking and sleeping.

How Is *Dhikr* Explained in the Holy Qur'an?

When we look at the Holy Qur'an, we see that the word *dhikr* and its
derivatives are found in 292 places, and the word *dhikr* itself is used in
76 different places. This shows us the importance of *dhikr*.

In the Qur'an the word *dhikr* was used in many different meanings such as to say, to mention, to talk, to remember, to remind, to commemorate, to remember and do what is necessary, to appreciate, to remember while contemplating, to reward, to praise, to show gratitude, to pronounce the *takbir*, to say the *talbiya*, prayer and pleading, words, utterances, stories, news, Book, revelation of the Book, the Qur'an, holy books other than the Qur'an, Prophet, glory, honor, honorable matters, advice and matters leading to thinking, thought, warning and advice, proof, admonition and exhortation.[85]

It can be understood clearly from these definitions that *dhikr* does not just mean to say "God!" or to repeat a word or expression that reminds us of Him.

First of all, remembering God and His Beautiful Names, mentioning them, thanking Him and showing gratitude, reciting His Names, proclaiming His greatness with *takbir*, reading the Word of God, praying... All of these belong to the section of *dhikr* related to language.

Secondly, thinking of the proofs of God's existence and His Attributes and Names, God's judgments, commands and prohibitions, proposals, promises, the duties of a servant towards God and the wisdom and proofs of these, all subjective and objective created things and the mysteries of their creation, and seeing the Divine wisdom present in every atom of creation... This is *dhikr* of the heart and mind.

The body's being busy and full of duties and staying far away from things prohibited to it is the third kind of *dhikr* and it is physical *dhikr*.

The essence of *dhikr* is remembering with the heart and not being heedless before God. This has three main kinds:

1. To think of proofs of God's existence and, discarding doubts, to contemplate God's Names and Attributes.

2. To think of the rules God has laid down, the duties of a servant, the responsibilities He informed us of, rules related to them, commands and prohibitions, God's promise and warning and proof of these.

---

[85] Çanga, Mahmut, *Kur'ân-ı Kerim Lügâtı*, İstanbul: Timaş, 2010, p. 193–195

3. Observing material and spiritual creatures and thinking about the mysteries of their creation and seeing the atom as a mirror of the sacred world. This mirror reflects lights of the beauty and greatness of that realm to the eyes of those who look as they should. Even a momentary feeling of the pleasure of witnessing this or a glimmer lasting just for a blink of an eye is worth worlds. There is no end or peak of this *dhikr* station.[86]

What Does God's Messenger Say in Relation to *Dhikr*?

When we look at *hadith*s, we see that our beloved Prophet emphasized *dhikr* a great deal. There is a lot of information related to this in *hadith* books. I would like to choose a few examples and share them with you: Abu Hurayra relates: "God's Messenger was travelling along the path leading to Mecca that he happened to pass by a mountain called Jumdan. He said: 'Proceed on, it is Jumdan; the ascetics have gone ahead.' They (the Companions) said: 'O the Messenger of God, who are the ascetics?' He said: 'They are those males and females who remember God much.'"

According to another narrative, he said, "There are those who live on an axis of *dhikr* to the degree of love and passion; the *dhikr* they make will lighten their loads and on the Day of Judgment they will be relieved of their burdens and will come comfortably into the presence of God." [87]

Another Companion, Muaz ibn Anas, said: "A man asked the Messenger of God, 'Which of the warrior's reward is greatest?' God's Messenger replied, 'The one who remembers God most.' Then the man asked, 'Which of the pious servant's reward is the greatest?' God's Messenger answered, 'The one who remembers God most.' The man asked the same question in regard to those who pray, those who give *zakah* and those who go on pilgrimage, and God's Messenger said each time, 'The one who remembers God most.' When Abu Bakr then asked

---

[86] Yazır, Elmalılı Hamdi, *Hak Dini Kur'ân Dili-1*, İstanbul: Hisar, 2011, pp. 445–447

[87] *Sahih Muslim*, 4/2062

Umar, 'O Aba Hafs! Didn't those who remember God leave any reward for us,' God's Messenger replied, 'Yes.'"[88]

This *hadith* is one of the most important *hadith*s explaining the significance of *dhikr*. Our noble Prophet's cousin Abdullah ibn Abbas said: "One day while the Messenger of God passed by Abdullah ibn Rawaha who was giving some advice to his friends, he said to them, 'You are a community that God has commanded me to have patience together with.' He continued his words: 'Listen well! However many people are sitting here, there are that many angels sitting with you. When you recite God's Names, they recite also; when you praise God, they praise Him too; when you revere God, they do so also saying God is great.'

Later on they go to God's presence. Although God knows much better than the angels what His servants have done, the angels say, 'Our Lord! Your servants recited Your Names and so did we. They said God is great and so did we. They praised You and we praised You, too.'

Our Lord says, 'O my angels! I take you as witnesses and I have forgiven them.' The angels say, 'But among them were such and such sinners.' God replies, 'They are such a congregation that anyone who sits with them cannot be a miserable person.'"[89]

Dhikr Is the Surest Path of Taking a Person to God

Our Lord evaluates every kind of mental activity you can imagine under the umbrella of *dhikr*. For example, if someone is talking about God and those listening remember Him due to his words, this means that *dhikr* is being made in this gathering. In other words, just as recitation of God's Names individually or several together is *dhikr*, every kind of talk that brings God to mind is also *dhikr*.

Daily acts like the *tasbih* made after the Prayer, the reading of prayer books and *Jawshanu'l-Kabir* (The Great Shield), and daily repetitions of litanies are included in *dhikr*.

> Recitation, irrespective of its style, is the safest and soundest way leading to God. Without recitation, it is difficult to reach God.

---

[88] Haythami, *Majmau'z-Zawaid*, 10/71

[89] Ibn Hibban, *As-Sahih*, 3/139

When the traveler remembers Him in his or her conscience and puts this remembrance into words with his or her tongue and other faculties, an inexhaustible source of support and (spiritual) provision is tapped.[90]

Along with our material life, there is also a spiritual life and our hearts are in the center of it. There is an aspect open to good and evil in our hearts. Together with being able to soar to God when we use our heart on the path it was created for, we can fall to a level that would embarrass the devil when we misuse it. Just as faith is found in the heart, *kufr* and dissension also develop in the heart; together with sincerity being a work of the heart, self-pride, hypocrisy and conceitedness also can find their place in the heart. We are asked to protect our hearts from the poisonous arrows of Satan; we need to keep it closed to everything except God. Just at this point *dhikr* takes on great importance. A believer who uses his tongue and heart together to draw closer to God as a "spiral leading to the nearness to God" will be like the one who has taken a magical elevator. He will ascend to the Most Exalted, he will flap his wings in the emerald hills of the heart and he will rise.

READING TEXT

Medicine Has Been Found for the Illness of Sin

Abu Yazid (Bayazid) al-Bistami (d. 804–874) was passing in front of an insane asylum one day. He saw that a servant of the asylum was hitting something with a pestle and he asked: "What are you doing?"

Servant replied: "This is an insane asylum. I am making medicine for the crazy."

"Can you recommend a medicine for my illness?" Al-Bistami asked.

"What is your illness?"

"My illness is the illness of sin. I commit a lot of sins."

"I know nothing about the illness of sin. I am making medicine for the crazy..."

---

[90] Gülen, M. Fethullah, *Emerald Hills of the Heart-1*, New Jersey: Tughra, 2011, p. 133

A crazy person (!) who heard the conversation from behind bars said to Bayazid al-Bistami: "Come here grandfather, come here! I will tell you the cure for your illness."

Drawing near to the madman, Bayazid al-Bistami said: "Tell me, what is the cure for my trouble?"

The madman (!) recommended this medicine: "Mix a repentance root with a leaf of penitence. Ground it in the mortar of the heart with the pestle of *tawhid*, pass it through a sieve of mercy, knead it with tears and bake it in the oven of love. Eat a large amount morning and evening. Then you will see that nothing remains of your illness."

Learning this good medicine, Al-Bistami said: "This is really strange! So they brought you here as a madman."

Then he left.

This medicine is still worthy of recommendation to those with the illness of sin. In other words, the formula still works.

Does *Dhikr* Have a Specified Time?

Another important matter related to *dhikr* is its not being tied to a particular time or approach. *Dhikr* has no specified time. It has the right of free circulation in almost every segment of time and it is not limited by any kind of state. The Qur'an says regarding this truth, *"They remember and mention God (with their tongues and hearts), standing and sitting and lying down on their sides (whether during the Prayer or not), and reflect on the creation of the heavens and the earth"* (Al-Imran 3:191).

Mentioning God by different Names and Attributes was done first of all by our noble Prophet. Actually the Messenger of God never passed a moment without Him. Even when his eyes slept, his heart did not; he did not live even one moment separate from God. Together with this, he adorned his daily life with different *dhikr*s, and fulfilled the requirement of being a perfect human being. Although he was the human being most remote from sins, he made repentance more than one hundred times a day and turned to God with requests for forgiveness. He made various recommendations of *dhikr* to his friends, and doing what he said first, he taught all of mankind about the servant-God relationship.

There is no specified time or place for *dhikr*. A person should not hesitate from taking every opportunity to remember God in words and in his inner world. Fethullah Gülen gave this warning in a talk:

> On the subject of keeping the area of *dhikr* broad, it is possible for you to constantly remember God by including it in your daily work like while walking on the street, walking on a treadmill and driving a car. For example, if every day you ride in a car one hour and walk for 30 minutes, you can read perhaps half or all of your daily Qur'an portion in that half hour or forty minutes. Turn on the tape recorder; either listen to the Qur'an or a hymn and you can find a way from it to draw closer to God. You can give your heart a work-out, make your spirit talk and, breaking the nose of your ego, tell Satan off.

> If you have someone travelling with you, you can chat with him a while, but a little later it will be possible for you to begin reading something and become a good example. It is not right to tie such behavior to observations about road safety, because there is egoism in such a thought. It is Sunnah to say the following while riding and remember God with praise and glorification: *"All-Glorified is He Who has subjugated this to our use. We were never capable (of accomplishing this by ourselves). And surely, to our Lord we are indeed bound to return"* (az-Zukhruf 43:13–14).

> While riding horses and camels, our ancestors would recite this verse and would be filled with a feeling of gratitude. Then, if possible, this prayer should be repeated while riding a taxi, bus, train or plane, for these are each a blessing from God. It is necessary to say, "We praise and revere You for You allowed us to ride this car, train or plane." Thus, while being subject to God's blessings and benefitting from them, you can turn it into full *dhikr* by reading something and mentioning God's Names and Attributes.[91]

Which *Dhikr*s Did God's Messenger Recommend?

There are many *dhikr*s that our noble Prophet recommended to his *ummah*. Let me try and mention some of them:

---

[91] Gülen, M. Fethullah, *Kırk Testi-4*, İstanbul. Nil, 2011, p. 253

In a *hadith* related by Jabir, he said, "The best *dhikr* is 'La ilaha illallah.'" [92]

Another *dhikr* mentioned by our noble Prophet is "*Subhanallahi ve bihamdihi. Subhanallahil azim.*" It means: "My God who is free from all deficiencies and faults! I praise You. My God who is free from all deficiencies and faults! You are the Most Exalted." While presenting this at prayer, the Messenger of God said, "Two words; light on the tongue but heavy in the Scales, love to the Merciful: "*Subhanallahi ve bihamdihi. Subhanallahil azim.*"[93]

There are two words that are easy to say. The tongue can pronounce them easily. When merits and sins are weighed on the Judgment Day, they have a special quality that will make the scales heavy. Also they are words very much loved by the Owner of Infinite Mercy. God likes very much to be mentioned with these words. They are the words, "*Subhanallahi ve bihamdihi. Subhanallahil azim.*" It must be because their spiritual value is great that Imam Bukhari put this *hadith* at the end of his valuable book on *hadith, Sahih al-Bukhari*, for an ending with musk.

Repeating these blessed words one hundred times a day takes only 5 minutes of a person's time. However, there is no doubt that much more is gained for the spiritual life.

Still another expression in our Prophet's *dhikr* bouquet is "*La hawla wa la kuwwata illa billah'il-aliyyil azim.*" It means: "There is no power or strength other than the power and strength of the Most Exalted God."

The following are a few narratives related to our Prophet's presentation of this prayer:

One day the Messenger of God set out at the head of his army towards Khaybar for a military expedition. While passing through a valley, some of the Companions began to shout *takbir*. Our noble Prophet said, "Make *takbir* slowly, because you are neither praying to a deaf person nor the unknown. It is certain that you are praying to God who hears everything and who is very close to you. He is always with you."

---

[92] *Sunan ibn Majah*, Adab, 55

[93] *Sahih al-Bukhari*, Dawat, 65; *Sahih Muslim*, Dhikr, 31

Abdullah ibn Qays, one of our Prophet's friends, said: "I was behind our Prophet's mount and I began to say, *"La hawla wala kuwwata illa billah."* God's Messenger heard my voice and called out, "O Abdullah." I said, "Yes, O Messenger of God." "Shall I tell you about one of the treasures of Paradise?" he asked. I said, "Tell me, O Messenger of God, may my mother and father be sacrificed for you." He said, "The treasure is *"La hawla wala kuwwata illa billah."* [94]

It is very meaningful that our Prophet said "one of the treasures of Paradise" regarding this prayer. It means that Paradise has its own treasures and one of them is this *dhikr* expression. It can be understood that a person's making this *dhikr* from the treasures of Paradise makes him worthy of and entitled to Paradise. Those who can say this prayer understanding its meaning and feeling it deeply can taste what those in Paradise taste and obtain the state of those there while they are still in this world. In other words, those who say this *dhikr* frequently will possess a treasure from Paradise and they will see the benefit of this in both worlds.

READING TEXT
How Much Scripture and *Dhikr*
Should We Recite Daily?

Fethullah Gülen answers this question as follows: "Since everyone is in a position to perform the requirements, there should be remembrance and recitations. For example, I should feel that I need to read as much as 10 people recite. And I should say to myself, 'Since this many people turn to you, then more than others you should give that its due and, keeping the connection with God strong, give thanks for this blessing and, on the other hand, ask for the blessing to continue like this.' Yes, this is what I say and try and do.

In view of this, the heads of different Islamic service units like muezzins (callers to prayer), imams, preachers, muftis (local administrators of religious affairs), etc. should increase remembrance and recitations according to their positions and their Lord will definitely strengthen

---

[94] Ahmad ibn Hanbal, *Al-Musnad*, 5/156

their relations. Otherwise, they will not have given their position its due.

Please, no one should make excuses like, 'We cannot find time among our heavy workload; we return home tired late at night.' If those who hide behind such excuses would turn and look at their daily lives, they would be embarrassed to see how much valuable time they spend for nothing. I previously expressed this as follows: 'Turks are time victims. Sometimes they spend hours for a glass of tea, and sometimes they cannot find time for the most vital jobs.' We can find many examples like this when we examine our daily lives. It is not necessary to say that we spend a world of time for empty and simple things... Now we will find it difficult to compensate for generously spending our time, on the one hand, and not finding time for the most vital matters, on the other hand.

As a result, I would like to remind you one more time that everyone should put some time aside for remembrance and recitations and should not make any excuses on this subject."[95]

We Should Not Neglect Daily Recitations

When *tasbihat* is mentioned, we first think of the recitations made after the Prayers. Our beloved Prophet indicated in many *hadith*s the recitations and prayers to be made after the Prayers, and he recommended that we do them: One day our noble Prophet asked, "Shall I teach you something that when you do it, those before you will not surpass you and those who come after you will not be superior to you?"

Abu al-Darda replied: "Yes, O Messenger of God (teach us)."

He said: "Recite thirty-three *tasbih* (*subhanallah*), *tahmid* (*alhamdulillah*) and *takbir* (*Allahu akbar*) after every Prayer."[96]

This matter is expressed as follows in another *hadith*: "Whoever recites *tasbih* thirty-three times, makes *tahmid* thirty-three times and makes *takbir* thirty-three times after each Prayer and then recites, "*La ilaha illallahu wahdahu la sharika lah, lahulmulku ve lahulhamd ve huwa*

---

[95] Gülen, M. Fethullah, *Fasıldan Fasıla-3*, İstanbul: Nil, 2011, p. 49

[96] *Sunan Abu Dawud*, Imarah, 20; Ahmad ibn Hanbal, *Al-Musnad*, 5/196

ala kulli shayin qadir," will be forgiven even if his mistakes and sins are as plentiful as the froth on the sea." [97]

It can be understood how important *tasbihat* is from these *hadith*s. We can sometimes sacrifice our recitations to neglect for right or wrong reasons. We have to evaluate the thought, "At any rate, *tasbihat* is Sunnah. It's OK if I don't do it (!)" as a concession, because human nature is very amenable to this. To begin with, a person who abandons the *tasbihat* can, in time, abandon what is Sunnah. And this situation—God forbid—can take a person to completely abandoning the Prayers. A believer should look at Sunnah acts as a kind of making connection with our noble Prophet, and he should make them, beginning with the *tasbihat*, a vital part of his life.

Sometimes we can be very busy in our daily lives. Consequently, we may have to pray and return to our work without making the *tasbihat*. Even in these situations the *tasbihat* should not be abandoned; even if done standing up, the *tasbihat* should be made. If this is not possible, then *tasbihat* should be left for later and it should be completed when more convenient.

In addition to the *tasbihat* everyone knows and which is mentioned in the above *hadith*s, there is a famous "Prayer *tasbihat*" which is a little longer than the other. Comprised by bringing together wording from the Qur'an and *hadith*s by our spiritual elders, this recitation includes prayers recommended in *hadith*s, *salawat*, *Al-Asma al-Husna* and *Al-Ism al-Azam* in addition to the *tasbihat* that is known and recited at mosques. Without restricting ourselves on the topic of *tasbihat*, it will be better if we make this recitation after the Prayers.

READING TEXT

The *Tasbihat* That Saved the Butcher Tahir from Execution

A large, courageous man from the shoe-makers trade was known as "Calamity Tahir" because he extorted money from the people of Afyon

---

[97] *Sahih Muslim*, Masajid, 144

and its surroundings. When he killed a man who acted indecently towards his wife, he began to be known as "Butcher Tahir."

Sentenced to execution, Tahir was shackled from both his hands and feet; he had to wear these even when he was taken from his cell to the prison yard to get some fresh air. One day he met Master Bediüzzaman in the yard.

Discerning the Master's character from his face, Butcher Tahir, throwing his trouble into the ocean, pleaded: "Please pray for me! Save me from this situation."

The Master gave the following advice: "These shackles are not chains to your execution sentence. These are your prayer beads! Begin to pray, make your *tasbih*, I will also pray for you and, God willing, you will be saved."

Synchronizing his heart frequency with God's friend from that moment on, Tahir became physically and spiritually cleansed and began to perform his Prayers. At the end of his Prayer he counted the rings of his chains. What did he see? There were exactly thirty-three rings (like on some Prayer beads). From that moment on, that chain became his Prayer beads.

After days, weeks and months had passed, Bediüzzaman's wonder came true and, after first gaining spiritual freedom, Tahir gained physical freedom with a pardon in 1950.[98]

What Is *Jawshan*?

One of the best expressions of *dhikr* to our Lord is reading the *Jawshan*. A Persian word, *jawshan* is defined in the dictionary as "a kind of armor or shield" Actually, *Jawshan* is a book of prayer traced back to the Messenger of God by means of Musa al-Qazim, Jafar as-Sadık, Muhammad al-Bakir, Zayn al-Abidin, Hussain and Ali, may God be pleased with them, and which contains many of God's Names and Attributes.

According to a report, at a time during one of the battles that occurred during the Age of Happiness (according to one report it was

---

[98] Refik, İbrahim, *Hayatın Renkleri*, İstanbul: Albatros, 2001, p. 145

at Uhud) when the battle was intense and the Prophet's armor gave him discomfort, our noble Prophet opened his arms and prayed to God. The doors of heaven opened and Gabriel came and said, "O Muhammad! Your Lord sends you *salam* and wants you to take off your armor and read this prayer. This prayer will give you and your *ummah* more safety than armor."

Later on the *Jawshan* passed into the hands of God's friends by means of Shiite imams and since then many lovers of the Truth have read the *Jawshan* scriptures and *dhikr*. Because it came from Shiite sources, Sunni imams looked at it suspiciously and did not favor it much. The meticulousness of the *Ahl as-Sunnah* on this matter and their sensitivity towards Shiite sources prevented these blessed Names from becoming a part of Sunni sources.

The *Jawshanu'l-Kabir* is a long prayer comprised of one hundred sections composed of ten of God's Names and Attributes. At the end of each section there is a repetition of the expression, "*Subhanaka ya la ilaha illa anta'l-aman al-aman khallisna/ajirna/najjina mina'n-nar*" (All-Glorified You are! There is no deity but You! We ask for safe keeping from You; protect us from Hell!)

At the beginning of twenty-five of the one-hundred sections there is the phrase "*wa as'aluka bi-asmaik*" (and I entreat You by Your Names) and God's Names "Ya Allah, ya Rahman, ya Rahim." There are prayers in the form of different litanies that begin with the phrase "*Ya Khayra'l-Ghafirin*" usually in three paragraphs between each section that begins with the above phrase. Thus, the full prayer includes two-hundred and fifty of God's Names and seven-hundred and fifty Attributes and litanies. The main purpose of all these litanies—as can be understood from the content of the prayer and the expression at the end of each section "*Al-Aman, al-Aman. Khallisna mina'n-nar*" (Mercy! Mercy! Save us from the Fire!)—is salvation from world calamities and punishment in the next world. [99]

---

[99] Aydüz, Davud, "Cevşen Üzerine", *Yeni Ümit*, issue 51, p. 27

How Does Bediüzzaman Explain the *Jawshan*?

Bediüzzaman explains that the *Jawshan* is our beloved Prophet's prayer and that he recited it as follows: "Humanity, in exactly the same way and upon whom numerous Divine Names are manifested, has many duties and is the target of many kinds of enmity. Thus we seek refuge in God by invoking many of His Names. In fact, Prophet Muhammad, the pride of humanity and the most perfect human being, prayed to God through 1,001 of His Names in his *Al-Jawshan al-Kabir* supplication, and sought refuge in Him from Hellfire."[100]

In another place Bediüzzaman says that there is no equal to the prayers made to God in the *Jawshan*.[101] Stating that the *Jawshan* is a litany taken from the Qur'an, he says that its content is suitable to the Qur'an and that it is a sign of our Prophet's Messengership.[102]

When the *Jawshan* is read regularly, undoubtedly it provides the reader with many material-spiritual benefits. The most important example of this is Bediüzzaman's own life. He mentions the benefits he gained from reading the *Jawshan* as follows: "The *Jawshan* and Shah Naqshibandi's *Awrad al-Qudsiya* have saved me perhaps twenty times from death with their blessedness against the material and spiritual poisoning by my hypocritical enemies... My brothers, do not worry. The *Jawshan* and *Awrad al-Qudsiya* have again defeated the terrible danger of poison. The danger has passed, but the sickness continues."[103]

READING TEXT

How Does Fethullah Gülen Respond to Claims Regarding the *Jawshan*?

Question: There are varying views about the *Jawshan* among Muslims. While some hold it in high esteem, some others are as indifferent as possible, and even unaware of it. Would you please clarify this situation of the *Jawshan*?

---

100   Nursi, Said, *The Words*, New Jersey: The Light, 2005, p. 354
101   Nursi, Said, *The Rays*, New Jersey: Tughra, 2010, p. 146
102   *Ibid.*, p. 278
103   Nursi, Said, *Emirdağ Lahikası*, İstanbul: Şahdamar, 2010, p. 131

Many views and ideas have been put forward about the *Jawshan* so far. The fact that it has mostly been reported through Shiite resources has led the *Ahl-al Sunnah* to hold themselves at a distance towards the *Jawshan*. However, our consideration on the *Jawshan* bears somewhat specialty. Due to this fact, instead of transferring the views of others, we would rather like to convey our own considerations here:

1. The *Jawshan* is a prayer performed in a full sincerity. Whichever sentence or word of it you take, you will witness a prayer loaded with sincerity, drop by drop. As this is the factual situation, whomever it is referred to should not influence on this feature within the essence. Of course, we do not mean that "There is no difference between referring a word to our Prophet or someone else". What we mean is that the minimal feature of the *Jawshan* is that it is a prayer. Even if it does not bear any other feature, just this feature of the *Jawshan* is a sufficient cause to refer the *Jawshan* a particular worth and value. In fact, it has so many other specific features that we shall point out in following entries. So, a critique of the *Jawshan* that originates merely from its reporting-chain may not be considered as a right behavior.

2. The words belonging to our noble Prophet essentially bear superiority to all the words of the rest of the humanity. That the *Jawshan* owns a style adorned with Prophetic expressions from beginning to end is a reality that shall not remain veiled to those who have gained expertise on identification of the words belonging to him. Due to this fact, too, to employ the items belonging to him through prayer is both significant and more apt to be approved. But still, it is a matter of preference. Indeed, the language preferred in the prayers outside the Daily Prayers does not bear an influence of the essence of the prayer, as God knows all the languages and attaches importance of the sincerity and willingness of the prayer. In fact, is not the diversity of languages and colors one of the verses marking His might?

3. As mentioned above, the Sunni resources do not give a place to the *Jawshan*. We may only see a few articles from the *Jawshan* only in Hakim an-Nishaburi's *Al-Mustadrak*. Along the works except it, I have not witnessed that the clauses and expressions belonging to the *Jawshan* are reported, even a few of them. However, this situation is nothing but the manifestation of the common attitude totally based upon the reporting-chain. And this does not bear a weight impacting on the worth of the *Jawshan* in a negative way. Indeed, there are many *hadith*s reported by Bukhari and Muslim which appear in Al-Kulayni's *Al-Kafi*, with little nuances, sometimes even in the same form. However, the scholars from the *Ahl-al Sunnah* have not reported even a single narration from Kulayni. In fact, *hadith*s appearing in that book are impossible to refute—in terms of both reporting-chain and wording—as they are included in the books of Bukhari and Muslim, as well. The *hadith*s in *Al-Kafi*, however, have mostly been reported by Shiite imams, which has let the people from the *Ahl-al Sunnah* react in a skeptical concern to those *hadith*s, at the very beginning. The same has happened to the *Jawshan*. If the *Jawshan* had not been reported through Shiite imams, I suppose, it would be warmly received by all the people of the *Ahl-al Sunnah* and put on a pedestal. However, as the *Jawshan* has undergone such a misfortune regarding to the reporting-chain, so many people have been deprived of its bright, bountiful and blessed climate. For the time being, we are not of the strength to prevent such a misfortune. Though not impossible, it is very difficult to remove such an opinion accumulated through ages.

4. Sometimes, the traditional *hadith* criteria may not be the mere criteria for firmness. It has not been of rarity that People of God (*Ahlullah*) have taken some *hadith*s from our beloved Prophet, directly, in a specific dimension of time and place. Imam Rabbani states in a translated text: "I started to avoid reciting Muawwizatayn (the last two *surah*s in the Qur'an, al-Falaq and an-Nas) in obligatory prays just after meeting the

report from Ibn Masud narrating that those *surah*s did not belong to the Qur'an. As soon as I got a warning from the Messenger of God that they were indeed from the Qur'an, I proceeded to recite them as before in the Prayers, as well." The fact that some people consider what we recite as Qunut prayers as *surah*s from the Qur'an may be considered as another evidence for the issue we have been contriving to point out above. Still, another example from Imam Rabbani: "I used to imitate Imam Shafi about particular issues. However, I was insinuated that Imam Abu Hanifa represents the profession of Prophethood. And, I got subjected to Abu Hanifa after all..." Of course, this position, too, requires a particular set of criteria. Otherwise, everybody may declare that he has taken something in this specific way of spiritual discovery, and the agenda shall be filled up with those kinds of fictitious spiritual discoveries. However, to count some great figures in this category shall be a huge mistake, on the other side. They have absolutely taken in that way whatever they claim to have taken in a specific spiritual discovery; and it is no doubt right whatever they say. However, it is impossible to analyze these statements regarding to particular *hadith* criteria. Because of this, *hadith* scholars have not accredited those kinds of expressions. But, this does not mean that those expressions are not right.

All what we say is also valid for the *Jawshan* in the same way. Because of this, we definitely say that the *Jawshan* reached to our noble Prophet through revelation or inspiration, regarding to its meaning. Afterwards, a saintly person took the *Jawshan* from our Prophet through spiritual discovery, and it has reached up to our time in this way. In addition, a learned man like Imam al-Ghazali, a great saint like Gumushhanawi, and a master like Bediüzzaman have accepted the *Jawshan* and recited it regularly along their prayers. Imam Rabbani even penned a commentary about it. Even if there existed no more evidence of the power and holiness in the source of the *Jawshan*, only the acceptance of those great people whose names we mention here, and that hundreds of thousands of people refer a particular value and are attached to it by heart, are evidences that are strong enough to make us at least speak in caution. Talking against the *Jawshan* merely due to a gap in its chain of reporting shall be unfairness, in the most modest term.[104]

A Book of *Dhikr* Prepared for Today's Person: *Al-Qulub ad-Daria*

After explaining the importance of *dhikr*, *tasbihat* and *Jawshan* this much, now I would like to mention a *dhikr* book for today's person that gathers together the best *dhikr* from our noble Prophet's time to present: *Al-Qulub ad-Daria*.

This book was compiled by Fethullah Gülen from several works, especially from the three volumes of *"Majmuat al-Ahzab,"* an approved prayer collection made by Ahmad Ziyauddin Gumushhanawi, a Naqsh-bandi-Khalidi sheik.

Majmuat al-Ahzab is an approximately 2,000-page book of *dhikr*. Gumushhanawi carefully prepared this work with painstaking attention together with his students. The author and name of each entry and when and how it is to be read are included in the directory.

Bediüzzaman's reading the sections of the *Majmuat al-Ahzab* without interruption and making them litanies undoubtedly makes this collection of prayers even more important for travelers on the enlightened path of Islam.

The prayer book *Al-Qulub ad-Daria* (meaning "imploring hearts" reminds us of the expression in the Qur'an *"... the helpless one in distress when he prays to Him"* (an-Naml 27:62) is a work that was neglected and forgotten by us, and it has been prepared to please new generations in particular and enable them to benefit from this work. Close to 600 pages long, this worthy work includes various prayers of many of God's friends. In addition, at the end of the work there is a comprehensive part for the invocation of peace and blessings upon our beloved Prophet, written personally by Fethullah Gülen.

---

104   Gülen, M. Fethullah, *Prizma-1*, İstanbul: Nil, 2011, 123–126

Remember God So He Will Remember You!

The virtue of constantly remembering God and holding Him in our memory is a matter known by every Muslim. More *dhikr* means more closeness to God. Our noble Prophet, the perfect human being closest to God, remembered Him in almost every moment of his life. He remembered God at the beginning and end of eating; while resting and awakening; while entering and leaving the toilet; while entering and leaving his home and the mosque and at many other times. He gave a good example to Muslims on behalf of the servant and God relationship.

We believe with all our heart that a Muslim should put aside time for his Lord—in addition to times of the Prayers—and at that time he should recite the Beautiful Names of Almighty God.

You will remember the Lord of the Realms in a way that becomes Him. And He will remember and honor you in a way becoming His sacredness.

You will remember Him with *tasbihat*, collections of prayers and *Jawshan*. And He will pour necessary blessings upon you. Thus, you will be subject to the verse, *"So always remember and make mention of Me (when service to Me is due), that I may remember and make mention of you"* (al-Baqarah 2:152).

Do not abandon Him in tongue and heart when you are comfortable. He will send you breezes of mercy before events that will chase away your comfort.

You will not forget Him and put Him off during your worldly affairs, and He will see and watch out for you in both this world and the next. He will disperse your troubles.

As a person of love, you will be determined to live and remember Him rightfully. Rewarding your effort and determination, He will make you feel His closeness in your heart.

While passing your lives in accordance with the other commands and prohibitions of Muslimness, you will also turn towards God with this extra servanthood, and He will make you happy in this world and the next. Your extras will be met with "more." Blessings you could not dream of will nourish you.

And, thus, God will realize your desire or, in other words, your purpose of creation, and you will gain very important strides on your path to become a "perfect human being." He will resurrect you in the next world with the Prophets, friends of God, martyrs and pious ones. Showing you His holy beauty, He will honor you with favors that surpass your capacity.

Those who have attained high stations on the plane of Truth to date were able to reach these levels by remembering God and by living on His path. Great men like Abdu'l-Qadir al-Jilani, Shah Naqshband, Muhyid-Din ibn al-Arabi, al-Ghazali, Rufai, Ahmad Badawi, Hasan Shazali, and Imam Rabbani, all stars in the heavens of mankind, attained very high levels and stations by remembering God and giving this remembrance its due.

QUESTIONS

1- In the statement of our noble Prophet, "Proceed on, it is Jumdan; the ascetics have gone ahead," who were the ascetics?

   a. Those who make a lot of *dhikr*

   b. Those who fast

   c. Those who pray correctly

   d. Those who make ablution

2- Saying, "Shall I teach you something that when you do it, those before you will not surpass you and those who come after you will not be superior to you," which Companion did the Messenger of God ask?

   a. Uthman

   b. Abu Ubayda

   c. Abu al-Darda

   d. Fatima

3- Which is the best expression of *dhikr*?

   a. *Astaghfirullah*.

   b. *Allahu Akbar*.

c. *Alhamdulillah.*

d. *La ilaha illallah.*

4- Which is the prayer our noble Prophet referred to as follows: "Light on the tongue, heavy in the Scales, love to Mercy"?

    a. *Subhanallahi wa bihamdihi. Subhanallahil azim.*

    b. *La ilaha illallah, Muhammadur-Rasulullah.*

    c. *Subhanallah, alhamdulillah.*

    d. *Allahu akbar kabira, subhanallahi kathira.*

5- Which of the *dhikr* expressions was described by our noble Prophet as "a treasure from the treasures of Paradise"?

    a. *La hawla wala kuwwata illa billah.*

    b. *Astaghfirullah al-Azim.*

    c. *La ilaha illallah, Muhammadur-Rasulullah.*

    d. *Subhanallah, Alhamdulillah, Allahu Akbar.*

6- Which of the following books is a summary of *Majmuatu'l-Ahzab*, which was prepared by Naqshbandi-Khalidi sheik, Ahmad Ziyauddin Gumushhanawi?

    a. *Supplication*

    b. *The Garden of Remembrance*

    c. *Al-Qulub ad-Daria*

    d. *Effective Prayers*

6.

SINCERITY

If we consider a deed to be a body, sincerity is its soul. If a deed represents one wing of a pair of wings, sincerity is the other. A body without soul is of no worth, and nothing can fly with only one wing.[105]

What is *Ikhlas*?

L iterally it means "to clean and purify something from things that have been mixed into it and lowered its value." As a term it means "Purifying one's worship and good deeds from hypocrisy and self benefit and doing them simply for the sake of God."

A broader description of *ikhlas*: cleaning the heart from polytheism and hypocrisy, superstition, evil emotions, self benefit, and in general, the desire to boast and show-off. It means approaching every good deed with an equally good intention and, in every case, only pursuing the favor of God.[106]

A believer who wishes to gain *ikhlas* stays far away from any acts of hypocrisy or showing off and only has servitude to God. He performs all his acts only to gain His favor. The Almighty God mentions these slaves of His in the Qur'an: "*...to us are accounted our deeds, and to you, your deeds. It is we who are sincere to Him (in believing in Him and worshipping Him exclusively)*" (al-Baqarah 2:139). These sincere servants display their worship they do for God; even if their carnal souls might

---

[105] Gülen, M. Fethullah, *Emerald Hills of the Heart-1*, New Jersey: Tughra, 2011, pp. 63–64

[106] Ragib al-Isfahani, *Mufradat*, p. 155; Al-Ghazali, *Ihya*, 4/379–380

dislike it, they continue on with this behavior and never fall behind in praising God.[107]

The opposite of *ikhlas* is *riya* (hypocrisy, showing off). *Riya* means adding pompous display into deeds that should be done for the sake of God; it means doing the deeds so others could see. Our Prophet cautions us of this, "Verily, God does not accept those deeds that are not done solely for Him and His favor."[108]

A believer that turns towards God with *ikhlas* will also perform his worship because God has commanded it. A requirement of being a servant, the believer will sincerely worship God. A sincere servant will perform his duty and won't delve into God's will. This is made clear in the verse, *"Turn toward Him your faces (i.e. your whole being) whenever you rise to perform the Prayer, and call upon Him, sincere in your faith in Him and practicing the Religion for His sake"* (al-A'raf 7:29).

Ikhas is the Cure to *Riya*

The definition of *riya* was already mentioned. Now we wish to approach it in more detail. *Riya* means not being straightforward, not acting as one believes, being double-faced, and performing worship and good deeds for the purpose of showing off and having others notice oneself. *Riya* is the reason behind a person being slapped across his face by his good deeds and Prayers and means associating partners with God. It is a very dangerous behavior that leads people into the greatest punishment.

Almost everyone is generally attracted to having a place in other peoples' hearts, being popular and the center of attention by way of showing off, and having a high standing in society.

Riya comes from very bad morals and is a person's weakest spot. Essentially, *riya* means making a place for oneself in others' hearts, and in this way expecting respect and to be looked up at highly by them. For God, those people with *riya* are unattractive and condemned. For

---

[107]   Al-A'raf 7:29; Yunus 10:22; Luqman 31:32; an-Nisa 4:46; az-Zumar 39:2; al-Mu'min 40:14

[108]   *Sunan an-Nasa'i*, Jihad, 24

these kinds of people God decrees, *"And woe to those worshippers (denying the Judgment); those who are unmindful in their Prayers; those who want to be seen and noted (for their acts of worship)"* (al-Ma'un 107: 4–6).

A believer will never fall into an act of *riya*. God characterizes *riya* as a characteristic of a hypocrite and decrees: *"The hypocrites would trick God, whereas it is God who "tricks" them (by causing them to fall into their own traps). When they rise to do the Prayer, they rise lazily, and to be seen by people (to show them that they are Muslims); and they do not remember God (within or outside the Prayer), save a little"* (an-Nisa 4: 142).

Muslims must never fall into *riya* in any of their acts. Because *riya* wipes all the good deeds and Prayers performed. This is because the performed Prayers and good deeds were done to show off to the people, instead of being done for the sake of God and to win His favor. The Almighty God describes these types of deeds in the Holy Quran:

> O you who believe! Render not vain your almsgiving by putting (the receiver) under an obligation and taunting—like him who spends his wealth to show off to people and be praised by them, and believes not in God and the Last Day. The parable of his spending is that of a rock on which there is soil; a heavy rain falls upon it, and leaves it barren. They have no power (control) over what they have earned. God guides not such disbelieving people (to attain their goals). (al-Baqarah 2:264)

The Messenger of God compared having *riya* to a small *shirk* (associating partners with God) and stated: "God decreed, 'I am the Most Self-Sufficient and All-Glorified from those who associate others with Me. For those who associate another with Me in their deeds and prayers (having *riya*), I will leave them alone with that which they associate as a partner to Me (leaving them without good deeds)."[109]

Ikhas is the cure to *riya*. As long as a believer has *ikhlas*, he will have kept himself away from the cliff of *riya*. A friend of God, Abu Lays as-Samarqandi explains: "Those who perform their worship for reasons other than the sake of God are similar to the man that fills up his purse with pebbles and enters the market. When the people see his

---

109   *Sahih Muslim*, Zuhd, 46

full purse, they exclaim. 'What a rich man!' There will be no other benefit for him than this. If he wishes to purchase something from the market, no one will give him anything for his pebbles."

The person who performs an act without *ikhlas* will just have gained a burden on his back, which will also have been pointless and ineffective *riya* in the view of the people; and in the Hereafter, he will have gained punishment.

A story that is usually explained about this topic: A Bedouin performed his *salah* in the mosque so quickly that the Caliph Umar was forced to warn him after witnessing it.

"O God's servant, what kind of *salah* is this? Like a chicken that feeds. It's best for you to pray again!"

The man prays again, without rushing, and in compliance with the rules of *salah*.

Having been watching, the Caliph asks him after the *salah*:

"Tell me now, which *salah* was better?"

The man replied: "My first *salah* was better?"

"Why?"

"Because," he said. "In the first one I had only prayed for the sake of God; in this second one in your view, I prayed for your sake!"

People must have the sake of God as their main objective behind their deeds and should never even bring into mind people watching and admiring them, while also paying attention to the *fard* (obligatory), *wajib* (necessary), and the sunnah. With this, the rule that there is no *riya* in performing *fard* is certain. Wherever you are, pray your *salah* and don't even bring to mind the fear of *riya*. In this period of time where people have fallen into considerable heedlessness, prayers should be performed everywhere without hesitation. This will also cause those who see them pray to analyze their own consciences. In this way, a believer will think of his Lord and those who see will listen to the voices of their consciences.[110]

---

110   Şahin, Ahmed, *Olaylar Konuşuyor*, İstanbul: Cihan, 2001, p. 78

READING TEXT

We Have Been Waiting For You
For Years, Young Man!

A teacher friend of ours explains: In the hopes of doing something beneficial over the summer and teaching our children something about religion, we got approval from the district governor and opened a Qur'an reading class in the basement of the Hayriye Mosque at the heart of Yalova, Turkey. With four or five imams we worked in the class. There was more interest in it than we expected. Over four hundred students from high school and middle school had signed up. In those long summer days, the classes started in the morning at eight and lasted till six or seven in the evening. I felt that my friends were infinitely pleased with the work that was being done. There was no request for money and God's word and religion was being taught solely for His sake.

As the days passed by in happiness, a young man entered the room we gave the classes in, came by my side, and asked for my name. He introduced himself as an imam from İzmit and told us that he wanted to help us teach the Qur'an.

He also mentioned the name of a friend of mine in İzmit. I was overjoyed with the young man's sincere offer. I was overjoyed, but where was this young man going to live? Where was he going to sleep? What was he going to eat and drink? Maybe we could have handled his food and drink but a room to sleep in was going to be a problem. When I told the young man what was going through my head, his answer was quick and without doubt: "I will turn the benches used to teach the Qur'an upside down and sleep where the students sit down. I will ask for no food or drink from you. Give me one piece of bread everyday and that will be enough. I won't ask for tomatoes or peppers. As long as I teach God's word to a few students here, that will be my food."

O brother, where were you raised? Where did you come from? Who gave you this soul? May what you eat, drink, and wear be made *halal* and nice for you. We have been waiting for you for years, welcome...

Ikhlas Is the Soul and Life of Our Deeds

The righteousness of a deed depends on its life. A deed's soul and life is *ikhlas*. *Ikhlas* is the name and title of performing deeds for the sake of God. *Ikhlas* is closing the heart against all expectations. Not being able to push aside any expectation other than pleasing God means tainting your deeds. Because of this secret power in *ikhlas*, our noble Prophet tells us. "Have *ikhlas* in your spiritual life, little work (with sincerity) is enough."[111] Our beloved Prophet also warns us to act upon the path of *ikhlas*. "Always have *ikhlas* in your deeds, for God only accepts those deeds that are pure."[112]

An example of a tainted deed: Let's say we listened to a lecture together with our friends. The topics that were discussed softened our hearts, wetted our eyes, and a few teardrops slid down our cheeks. If there was an opportunity to be able to hide those teardrops and we didn't, and if we opened a door so that our friend's could see us in this state, this act would've tainted our good deed. It means that we would've pushed that deed outside of an act done with *ikhlas*.

Everything should be for the Most Exalted God, and every aspect of us should not explain us, but Him.

Ikhlas also has degrees in itself. Everyone can reach a level of *ikhlas* according to his own servitude. The friend's of the Truth have separated this into three categories:

The first level is the *ikhlas* of the people that lived at the time of the Prophets and the people that succeeded the time of the Prophets. These people lived under the shade of the Prophets and were near to them. The members of these groups had no expectations, either for this world or for the Hereafter. Their eyes were only focused on the favor of God; it is virtually impossible to reach their height.

In the second category come the other friend's of the Truth. The representatives of this group have no expectation at all for this world. However, for these people the mind boggling beauty of Paradise, and

---

111   Munawi, *Faydu'l-Qadir*, 1/216
112   *Ibid.*, p. 217

the horrifying terror of Hell incites in them an expectation of being forgiven on the Day of Judgment, and the desire for eternal happiness takes hold of their hearts.

The third and last group is those that have the desire for Paradise and the thought of being away from Hell, along with expectations of the worldly life according to their own levels, such as feeling spiritual joy while praying and being satisfied with worship; like that intrinsic pleasure that comes when one provides service for someone or does good while on the path of the Truth. On the other hand, people with expectations of being rich or famous cannot even find a spot for themselves in the shade of these people.

Thoughts and expectations such as gaining pleasure from the worldly aspect of worship, feeling happy in struggling, or being known publicly as someone who tries to bring people onto the path of the Truth... having an easy death and afterlife or being an intercessor for the people you know... are signs that we haven't been able to escape from the attraction of our desires yet.

READING TEXT

Who Won the Fight between the Lumberjack and Satan?

There once was a man who made his living through woodcutting. He would fulfill his servitude to God and wouldn't meddle in anyone's business. There was another village near the village he lived in. In this other village the people would worship a tree on a mountain. They thought that the tree was divine and would expect it to help them. The lumberjack one day thought: "Let me cut down this tree they worship as God and make it into wood." He decided to cut down the tree for the sake of God and thought that he would also be able to sell the wood in the market and make his bread money while also saving a group of people from rebelling against God.

While he was walking towards the mountain an odd faced and dirty man came up to him and asked him where he was going. The lumberjack replied: "I'm going to cut down the tree that the people worship as God and rebel against Him with."

The man said: "I'm Satan. I don't give you permission to cut down that tree." When the pious lumberjack heard this he became very angry and, with the intention of killing him, attacked Satan and brought him onto his back. He then sat on Satan and stuck his dagger to his throat. Satan said to the pious man: "O pious man, you can't kill me. God has given me permission till the Day of Judgment. However, come, don't cut down that tree; let us make an agreement. I'll give you a gold coin everyday if you forget about cutting down the tree. And why do you care that other people are worshipping a tree and committing a sin, take your gold coin and look after your own work."

The man let go of Satan. Satan told the man to go to sleep at night and look under his pillow in the morning. They agreed and left. The man had abandoned his decision to cut the tree and turned back to his house. When he went to sleep that night and looked under his pillow the next morning he saw a gold coin. He was pleased. Then came the second day. But this time Satan hadn't put a gold coin there. The man got angry and left off to the mountain with his axe to cut down the tree. He ran into Satan on the road again. The man was very mad at Satan and when he saw him, he said. "You crook; you tricked me, didn't you."

But completely opposite to last time, Satan immediately grabbed the man and brought him down. The man was astonished. His shocked expression seemed to be asking how this had happened. Satan answered for him.

"You're amazed, aren't you? I'll tell you why you lost to me: Yesterday you were going to cut down that tree for the sake of God. That day even if all the satans in the world had come together to stop you, we still couldn't have stopped you. But now you were not going there for the sake of God, but instead because you were mad I hadn't given you a piece of gold. So, that's why you lost to me today and I won't let you cut down the tree."

READING TEXT

What Will Satan Do to Make a Young Person's Worship Insincere?

Satan is a person's most important enemy. His goal is to whisper evil suggestions to us and make our worship worthless. And one of these whisperings is the thought of "I can't do this in complete sincerity with the fear of *riya*." It would be the biggest mistake to stop performing worship with this thought. This is exactly what Satan wants.

Satan won't leave a person alone with one whisper. Whatever he can lower in your acts or your good deeds, he takes as profit for himself. For instance, let's look at the struggle between a young person and Satan: Satan will first try to keep the person far away from worship. If the person is resolute, Satan will then try to push the age he begins to pray into the future by saying, "You're still young, go travel a little and live your life, and then you'll start!" If that young person doesn't fall for that trick and turns towards praying, then Satan will whisper to him again: "Don't make your *wudu* now, the *adhan* was just called." If that young person takes his ablution, this time Satan will whisper. "You still have time; it's okay to pray later, first finish your conversation." Satan's intention is to, for example, make the person pray late and have him abandon the sunnah part of the Prayer Asr. In this way the person will be without the good deeds of having prayed sunnah. Even this is a profit for Satan.

If the young person begins his *salah*, then this time Satan begins to bother his mind with things the person had forgotten and other important and unimportant things. Satan tries to make the person inattentive in his prayer or tries to make him pray quickly as if he were a "chicken feeding", thus preventing the person from obeying the rules of *salah*.

Despite all of this, if the young person is able to pray in sincerity and devotion, Satan will try one last trick. He will make the young person look around and urge him to think. "Is there anyone else praying in complete devotion like me?" This will then make the young person enter *riya*. Thereby the act would have been for nothing, with no good deeds, and Satan would've won.

There are many more possible examples. The matter here is being able to resist Satan's whisperings, and in spite of everything, being able to remain sincere in our worships.

Strength that comes from God will never see defeat. However, if the thoughts of self-benefit or *riya* taint our intentions, we will be rewarded accordingly. You must not forget that Satan has tricks and traps for people of every level. We must learn these and take our precautions so that we don't fall into the same traps.

How Does Bediüzzaman Explain *Ikhlas*?

Here is what Bediüzzaman says about sincerity:

> O people! Do you want to make your brief and useless life long, immortal, beneficial, and fruitful? To want this is a natural requirement of being human; so then spend your life on the way of the Truly Everlasting One. For anything turned to the Everlasting One receives the manifestation of immortality. Since everyone passionately desires a long life and yearns for immortality, and since there is a means of transforming this transitory life into an everlasting life, surely anyone who still preserves their humanity will seek out that means and try to transform that possibility into a reality, acting accordingly. The means in question are as follows: do whatever you should do for God's sake, meet with others for God's sake, and work for God's sake. Act within the sphere of "for God, for God's sake, and on account of God. Then all the minutes of your life will become like years.[113]

For a believer to continue his path, whether in servitude to Him or in helping others, one must live the principles that were listed in Bediüzzaman's "The Twenty-First Gleam" (on sincerity or purity of intention).

A believer should strive for the sake of God in his actions. There shouldn't be any other aim than this. He shouldn't criticize his brothers and sisters that walk on this same path with him, and he shouldn't

---

[113]   Nursi, Said, *The Gleams*, New Jersey: Tughra, 2008, p. 27

see himself over them. Due to the secret of brotherhood, he should be shoulder-to-shoulder with them. Three ones written side by side make a hundred and eleven. Three people who believe in the same cause and seek the favor of God have the strength of a hundred and eleven people. Strength is in *ikhlas*. This is the secret behind how an army of three thousand Muslims in Mu'tah scattered away an army of ninety thousand, and how Tariq ibn Ziyad faced an army of ninety-five thousand with five thousand people in Andalusia. History has many events that prove that small groups that shared similar beliefs and ideals were able to ruin crowded armies that were not united. As a matter of fact, this verse from the Qur'an talks about this topic: "*Many a small company has overcome a numerous company by God's leave*" (al-Baqarah 2:249).

Bediüzzaman explains this: "...each individual in a true, sincere union can also see with the eyes of his other brothers and sisters, and hear with their ears. It is as if each member of a group of ten people in true solidarity and unity has the power of seeing with twenty eyes, thinking with ten minds, hearing with twenty ears, and working with twenty hands."[114]

Providing service to others in Islam must be done with sincerity. Like the Companions of the Prophet, one must be at the forefront in providing service but at the back when looking for a reward. Also one should see every success as a gift from God and shouldn't ascribe anything to oneself. Even making it a goal to be noticed in others' eyes while doing good will take people to committing secret *shirk*.

What Principles are Explained in the Treatise of Sincerity?

Bediüzzaman has recommended "The Twentieth Gleam" and "The Twenty-First Gleam" that focus on *ikhlas* "to be read at least once every fifteen days".

In the beginning of "The Twenty-First Gleam," Bediüzzaman put forth four basic tenets and principles of *ikhlas* in order to internalize it into our lives. Let's examine these one by one:

---

[114]   *Ibid.*, p. 228

1. Not criticizing those who provide service of the Qur'an: From the *hadith* of Prophet Muhammad, peace and blessings be upon him, that says "Believers are like a single body,"[115] Bediüzzaman makes the comparison that those who practice their faiths through actions and those who practice it through providing service of the Qur'an are of a single system and similar to a human's body or a factory.

Just like how a person's organs don't compete against each other or how gears in a factory don't have rivalries with each other, it is not correct for people that are on the path of the Qur'an to have rivalries with each other. Otherwise, just like how a person's body would not be a body anymore and a factory would be without products and would become pointless, those who provide service of the Qur'an would be deprived of the spiritual strength that comes with doing it with *ikhlas*, and the groups would fall into pieces. Moreover, for Bediüzzaman a requirement of true *ikhlas* is being able to form brotherly love for that person who could be a rival to you, and to be able to praise him for his superiority over yourself.

Bediüzzaman would say: "Beware of opening the door to criticism between each other. There are many things to criticize outside the circle of your close ones. Just as I praise your virtues, you all must see each other as through your master's eyes. To the degree that all of you all should be the publishers of the others' merits."

2. Pursuing friendship: Having signified the importance of friendship and brotherhood when providing service of the Qur'an, Bediüzzaman states that those who are providing service of the Qur'an must praise their friend's merits and should be proud of each others' achievements. People of Sufism take *"Fana Fir-Rasul* (annihilation in the Messenger) and *Fana Fis-Sheikh* (annihilation in the guide)" as the base for their love. In the same way, Bediüzzaman believes that it would be more correct for those who provide service of the Qur'an to be attached to the principle of *"Fana Fil-Ikhwan* (annihilation in the brothers and sisters)"*. He explains the term as "Forgetting your own feelings and desires and mentally living through the thoughts of your friends' virtues."

---

115   *Sunan ibn Majah*, Zuhd, 38

3. Pursuing the pleasure of God in one's deeds: Bediüzzaman summarized this principle to his friends with these words: "Your deeds must have the pleasure of God. If God is pleased with a person because of his deeds, it doesn't matter whether or not the whole world is against him. If God accepts your deeds, rejection from the rest of society has no effect. Once God is pleased and has accepted your deeds, if He wishes and it is required, He could make society accept and be pleased with your deeds as well. For this reason, it is absolutely necessary to aim for the Almighty God's pleasure as your primary goal." Because, as *ikhlas* is the soul of one's worship and deeds, the only requirement for their acceptance is again *ikhlas*. Moreover, the verse in the Qur'an saying "have *iman* (faith, belief)" instead of "have *ikhlas* in your *iman*" refers to the fact that *iman* without *ikhlas* cannot even be considered perfect *iman*.[116]

The most feared thing in this topic is to ask for other people to be content with oneself, even if in secret, while providing a service to faith. Bediüzzaman touches on this topic in a good number of his letters and warns his students of this. In fact, he rejects many letters that shower him with praise just so it doesn't contradict the pleasure of God, or he accepts it in the name of the *Risale-i Nur* while also adding a few notes to try and fix it. A letter signed "Lütfi's friend, Zeki" and written by one of his students: "Dear Master! May your mission for service journey through the skies and may your name journey through epic stories." Under this letter Bediüzzaman placed a note: "I don't share this brother's feelings. God's pleasure is enough. If He loves, everything is love. If He does not love, even if the whole world applauded, it would be meaningless. If you desire the approval of people, and it is the cause behind a deed for the afterlife, that deed would be void. If it is preferable, its *ikhlas* is broken. If it is encouraged, its purity is removed."

4. Grasping the spiritual strength in *ikhlas*: Bediüzzaman would point to the importance of this and describe it as "know that all your strength lies in *ikhlas* and the truth." For him, having sincerity or being

---

[116] Al-Baqarah 2:13

righteous increased a person's strength. It is because of this strength, that *ikhlas* gives a person or a society, that even unjust people gain strength because of their *ikhlas* and sincerity in their injustices. Skills and means are important for success and victory. In other words, a nonbeliever with a Muslim attribute will win over a Muslim's illegitimate attribute, and in the end it will be the nonbeliever, not the Muslim, that will be successful.

Bediüzzaman gives an example of the strength found in *ikhlas* in his own mission for service and how even though there were a hundred or, in fact, a thousand more helpers in twenty years in İstanbul and Van, a hundred times this progress was made in the service of faith in Barla with seven or eight people. "... Here (in Barla) I am alone, a stranger, and under the surveillance of unjust officials whom I am persecuted by. I have no doubt that the strength which makes our seven or eight years of service here a hundred times more successful than my former twenty years of service comes from your sincerity."

According to Bediüzzaman, God ascribes a special significance to people with *ikhlas*. It can almost be said that the strength that arises from *ikhlas* is a cause for God's mercy. In this sense, he states in many places that he and his Nur students were "employed", and that those who have *ikhlas* and loyalty are employed by the way of God. A student of his, Süleyman, caught Bediüzzaman's attention when the student rejected any physical reward for the service the student provided for him. Bediüzzaman then said that because of that student's pure service done solely for the sake of God, the student had been employed by the way of God.

READING TEXT

Here Is the Shepherd's *Ikhlas*!

God protects His servants from misfortunes and calamities based on their *ikhlas*. Bediüzzaman asks Truthful Süleyman, who had been giving out tea at that moment, a question: "Süleyman, have you ever entered a jail?"

"I haven't been given that blessing, master," Truthful Süleyman replies. On top of this Bediüzzaman says, "Due to your devotion and sincerity, that duty has been removed from you."

"You should know that all your power lies in sincerity and truth," Bediüzzaman says. "The prayers of those who turn towards God with *ikhlas* will be accepted. Those who carry out their work with *ikhlas* will be successful." A story from M. Necati Sepetçioğlu's book called *Anadolu Efsaneleri* (Anatolian Legends) expresses this truth very nicely:

In a city in Anatolia when an alcoholic who had taken a philosophical attitude on life died, the imam and the city's people left him without a funeral prayer. The man's wife took her deceased husband onto her shoulders and began carrying him towards the mountains. She asked for help from a shepherd she then came upon. They bury her husband together. "Can you also make a prayer?" The woman asks the shepherd. The shepherd says he doesn't know any prayers but he raises his hands and quietly mutters one or two sentences and finishes his prayer.

The woman then returns home to her village and home. The leaders of the village, in fact the imam himself, sees the man in his dreams in a scene of Paradise. This news spread throughout the village. Everyone began searching for the reason behind this. Finally they decided to ask the woman: "Where did you bury your husband, and how? This is what we've heard!" The woman explained everything in its complete simplicity: "I didn't do anything! Whatever it is, it's from that shepherd's prayer!"

They go to the shepherd. "You apparently made a prayer after you buried the man; what did you say?" they asked. "O God! I fed the people that passed through here with my food and let them drink from my milk, thinking they were God's guests and Your guests. I am also sending a guest, host him according to Your Glory, O God!" the shepherd replied.[117]

This is the shepherd's *ikhlas*! Sincerity brings near what is far away, makes many out of little, and makes important what is unimportant.

---

117   Sepetçioğlu, M. Necati, *Anadolu Efsaneleri*, İstanbul, İrfan, 2005, p. 17

What Are the Ways to Gain and Protect *Ikhlas*?

Bediüzzaman mentions the two most effective ways of gaining and protecting *ikhlas*. One of these ways is the thought of death, which can also be called "living with the understanding that the world is temporary." The second one is to live with the feeling that we are, at every moment, in the presence of God, which can be called "conscious contemplation." Truly, a person will gain *ikhlas* according to the degree he is able to transfer over these two points and implement them in his life. In a more correct statement, the Almighty God will place this secret, between Him and His servants, into the hearts of His faithful and beloved servants.

Bediüzzaman summarizes this in a statement: "Another important means of attaining sincerity is, being based on certain verified beliefs and the lights of belief (guided reflective thought on God's works of art— the whole creation) which lead to knowledge of the Maker, to experience the omnipresence of the All-Compassionate Creator, and to not seek the acceptance or attention of any other than Him, and to understand that it is not the right conduct to look for help from others in His presence, and that in this way we can be saved from ostentation and attain sincerity."[118]

According to this statement, for self-reflection to form in a person he must first gain the feelings of contemplation and wisdom. Everyone cannot easily understand and wake up to the fact that the Almighty God, with his Knowledge and Power, is everywhere and sees everything, and that He knows everything a person utters, every behavior he displays, and every inclination of the heart he has. Before this, that person must make "*tafakkur*" (contemplation) and must wake up to the "knowledge of God".

Understanding self-reflection means living with the knowledge that we are being controlled. Every believer that wishes to gain *ikhlas* and protect it must live with the consciousness that the Almighty God sees him at every moment. This degree of understanding will affect the

---

[118] Nursi, Said, *The Gleams*, New Jersey: Tughra, 2008, p. 230

believer's behaviors, conversations, and even his heart's inclinations. A believer who has gained this thought will continue his life with this perspective: "Since God Almighty sees and hears us at every moment, and since we are actually always in His presence and He is always with us, then all of our actions, words, and thoughts must be appropriate to His pleasure. Since our Lord knows our every condition, then there should not exist any word, act, or misstep of the heart that He would dislike."

Verily, once He approves and is pleased, it doesn't matter if others approve or disapprove of us. If He approves, it doesn't matter if society rejects it. Once God is pleased and has accepted your deeds, if He wishes and it is required, He could make society accept it and be pleased with your deeds as well. There should be no pursuit to have people approve. For this reason, it is absolutely necessary to aim for His approval.

Living with the consciousness of being controlled will fill a person with these thoughts. It will purify his heart. His heart will close itself off to all other things than God. One with this type of heart will take every step with exceptional care. He will orient his life with the consciousness that one bite or one look could ruin him. Worrying about something's outcome will keep him from being heedless. Seriousness and dignity will become an inseparable part of him. He will constantly struggle against the stray thoughts and feelings that come into his heart. The Most-Merciful God will not leave this effort and struggle without reward, and will place *ikhlas* in the person's heart.

A person who is able to completely understand self-reflection will be able to clean and increase his heart himself; by constantly keeping his heart in control and under fear, he could keep himself away from all of life's impurities and stains. All of this means that the heart is cleaned of all heinous feelings and thoughts, and becomes flushed with *ikhlas* and sincerity.

A believer must always protect his *ikhlas* and must not fall prey to obstacles that might confront him. He must know that Satan wishes to keep him from this Divine duty and must continue straight on his path, pushing aside any barriers. In order to preserve our *ikhlas* we must always keep in mind that God sees us at every instant. We must not attach ourselves to temporary things and must remember that death is at the end of the road and that, with the thought of being held accountable for our actions, we need to increase our good deeds.

READING TEXT

Will God Ask Me About the Milk I Drained Down the Sink on the Day of Judgment?

This story came to mind when mentioning being accountable. One of our teacher friends explains: It was during the years I was a teacher at Yalova High School. The blessed Ramadan had come. At Yalova High School almost ninety percent of the students fasted. During the first days of Ramadan the canteens were astonished at this large percentage who fasted at a school like Yalova High School. The pastries, toasts, and drinks they had brought to sell to the students were all left in their hands. It was amazing! Also, the small minority of the students who weren't fasting showed exceptional care to be courteous to their other friends that were fasting by not eating or drinking by them.

One morning when I went to school and was walking towards my classroom, a girl at the front of the corridor came up to me: "Teacher, can I ask you something?"

"Go ahead," I said and she continued with her black bead-like eyes and face that was a mix of sadness and distress.

"Teacher, I was keeping my fast a secret from my mother and father. When I was coming to school this morning, my mom gave me a glass of milk and said, "Drink this then go to school!" I then took advantage of my mom when she wasn't paying attention and drained the milk down the sink and told my mom, "I drank it!" Teacher, I wonder, will God ask me about the milk I drained down the sink on the Day of Judgment?"

And I was shocked from excitement and didn't know what to say. I could've been the one to ask the question. I wonder, in view of this, will the Most Merciful Lord hold me accountable for that milk?

QUESTIONS

1- "A believer who wishes to gain *ikhlas* .... and only has servitude to God. He performs all his acts only to gain His favor." Which of the following fill the blank.

    a. stays away from all sins

    b. stays far away from any acts of hypocrisy or showing off

    c. stays away from all types of luxury

    d. pushes aside all types of pleasure

2- Which of the following were one of the principles explained in the treatise of sincerity?

    a. Criticizing those who are in the service of the Qur'an

    b. Protecting friendship

    c. Staying far away from hypocrisy and showing off

    d. Gaining the worldly benefits

3- Which sin has our Prophet called "secret *shirk*"?

    a. backbiting

    b. *riya*

    c. interest

    d. self-pride

4- "Speak softly so that the hearts open their doors; be warm-hearted so that others welcome your thoughts; act with *ikhlas* so that ....!" Which of the following best fits the blank?

    a. you always have an effect on others

    b. you become popular

    c. you become fit for Paradise

    d. you become a wise person

5- Where in the *Risale-i Nur* is the treatise of sincerity?

    a. The Nineteenth Gleam

    b. The Twentieth and The Twenty-First Gleam

    c. The Twenty-First Word

    d. The Twenty-Second Gleam

7.

TAWAKKUL (TRUST IN GOD)

Having been proven through a thousand experiences, when one says "These dynamics will take me to this goal", those dynamics will then become ruined. Our duty is to clench our teeth and trust in God in our work.[119]

What Is *Tawakkul*?

Tawakkul is the name for leaving everything to God after taking all the necessary steps and after putting in all the required effort. In other words, *tawakkul* on anything about religion or this world, means leaving the result to God once all the cautions have been taken and every move has been made about the matter.

"*In God let the believers put all their trust*" (Al Imran 3:122). This verse explains *tawakkul*. Our noble Prophet would recommend *tawakkul* to Muslims: "If only you had true *tawakkul* in God, He would provide sustenance for you just as He does the birds."[120]

Even though *tawakkul* is a state dependent on the heart, it doesn't contradict working and earning with your body. This is stated as performing the requirements of servitude with your body, becoming attached to God with your heart, and being content with just enough to live.

Tawakkul in God means finding God content in what He has chosen for him, through blessings and misfortunes, eases and hardships. Humans are hidden from the knowledge of something having a good

---

119   Gülen, M. Fethullah, *Ölçü veya Yoldaki Işıklar*, İstanbul: Nil, 2011, p. 137

120   *Sunan ibn Majah*, Zuhd, 14

outcome. What God has chosen for humans is superior to what humans would choose for themselves.

Tawakkul is having absolute trust in God in everything you do and submitting yourself to His preference. This is shown in being patient in the face of calamities and misfortunes.

READING TEXT
Some Remarks on *Tawakkul*

Imam Fakhr ad-Din ar-Razi says: "*Tawakkul* does not mean, as some uneducated people think, that people neglect themselves. If it was so, the command to consult with each other would've been an obstacle for *tawakkul*. *Tawakkul* means complying with the external appearances of cause and effect, but not attaching your heart to them and instead taking refuge in the Almighty God."

* * *

After having constructed the best ship and having sailed through the ocean and reached the shore, we must know this as God's gift and praise and thank Him because a ship's perfection and a captain's expertise cannot stand against those mountain-like waves and probable storms.

Making the ship perfect is an example of placing effort into causality. After having completed this commitment, *tawakkul* is leaving the outcome after having left the shore to God's grace.

* * *

A parable is usually explained: Prophet Solomon inquires as to how much an ant eats in the course of a year. "A grain of wheat," they replied. To test this, he put an ant in a box and threw in a grain of wheat.

A year later he opens the box and sees that the ant has eaten only half of the wheat. He asks the ant: "Don't you eat a whole grain of wheat a year?" The ant responds: "O Solomon! That was when my sustenance was provided by the All-Providing, the All-Munificent. But when you began to provide for my sustenance, I did not know what you would do in the future. What if you forgot me? However, my

Lord never forgets any being among His creation. That's why I acted with caution," the ant said.

Being Able to Live Peacefully Comes from *Tawakkul*

A person without *tawakkul* would be overwhelmed with the problems that face him in this world and due to the worries that envelop him, his soul's health could be ruined. Not having *tawakkul* means for a person to burden himself with unbearable weight. God does not place people under burdens they are unable to bear, but people put themselves under those burdens by not having *tawakkul*.

Bediüzzaman tells us the story of two men, one who has *tawakkul* in God and another who doesn't: One man boards a ship, known to have an expert captain, with his belongings. He trusts the captain, places his belongings on the floor, sits on them, and continues his journey in trust. Another man aboard the ship is scared that his belongings will be stolen. He can't trust the captain's fairness and ability to protect him. For safety measures, he carries his things upon his shoulders. As the journey lengthens, the weight upon his shoulders weakens him and finally he loses all his strength. Forget protecting his belongings, he couldn't even stand up anymore. Moreover, he is then punished because this act of his is interpreted as him taking the captain to have no power.

See that this is the condition of the person without *tawakkul*. The person will deplete his energy, not be able to do anything, and because he has a lack of belief in his Creator, he will also be punished.

Bediüzzaman refers to a person who says "I place my trust in God" as someone who "travels through the mountainous waves of events in the ship of life in complete safety."

The person who entrusts all his burdens to the Absolutely Powerful One's Power will be at ease. A person who places this trust will have attained happiness. Therefore, "Belief consists of affirming Divine Unity, which requires submitting to God, which requires relying upon God, which yields happiness in both worlds."[121] On the other hand,

---

121   Nursi, Said, *The Words*, New Jersey: The Light, 2005, p. 330

the person who does not have this trust can be crushed by the world's burdens.

Some people burden themselves not only with the weight of the present but also with the weight of the future. The misfortunes of the past and the possibility of living through similar events in the future drive some people into worry. When, in fact, these worries consume a person's strength. The person would've spread his strength over the present, the past, and the future and would've left himself weak in the face of life.

In fact, people require a power upon which they can lean onto. If a person uses up all his life's energy for the future from now, he will not have the energy to live for the future.

READING TEXT
Two Yolks Came Out From Each of the Two Eggs!

When there came a knock on the house's door, the old woman walked up to it with her weak legs. The visitors were her son's army friends.

After both of them kissed her hand, the taller one of the two said: "We don't have much time Ma'am. We caught a thirty minute break and wanted to have your prayer and blessing."

"Of course not!" the woman replied in great haste, "Will I ever let you leave without eating something?"

The old woman had blurted this out from the habit of saying it to her husband and son while they were still alive; however, she didn't know where it was going to lead.

The other soldier looked at his watch. "Well then, sure Ma'am," he replied. "We're full, but if you crack two eggs each, we'll eat."

In truth, the young man didn't want to impose on the woman and said this after seeing the chickens in the garden, wanting to make it as easy as possible on her. How was he to know that she has had only two eggs everyday for the last few days, and that there was nothing else in the house?

As the old woman began moving towards the kitchen, she was thinking about her son that had been made a martyr by traitors of the land while performing his military duty with these young men sitting in the next room. Like his friends, he also loved eggs cooked on a pan.

As she was trying to break the eggs with her quavering hands, she couldn't stop herself from feeling sad and was trying to find a way to keep her guests from noticing her poverty. Ok, but the kids had asked for two eggs each. What was going to happen when they saw only one egg each on their plates?

The old woman couldn't think about it any longer. And when she cracked the eggs with the trust in God that comes with helplessness, she was very happy to witness the favor of her Lord! Two yolks came out from each of the two eggs!

Understanding of *Tawakkul* Eases Worries

Sentences that start with "What if" about the future express worry. "What if I don't pass the test..., What if I become sick..., What if I'm fired..., What if I die..." The only way to escape from these "what if"s is *tawakkul*.

The future has still not taken place. The soldier that wastes all his ammunition out of fear will be hopeless when he faces the enemy. If the body didn't store energy, it would fail under hard conditions. The person who depletes his strength over worrying will also not have the Almighty God's strength behind him since he has not placed his trust in God.

In *tawakkul*, there is immediate gratefulness and acceptance for what the Almighty God has created for him. The person who has *tawakkul* brings together and does the required things, but understands that he is powerless to do anything himself. He doesn't suffer in the hands of senseless worry. He sees everything as coming from its true Owner, leaving nothing to pride himself on and finding spiritual joy and peace.

In *tawakkul* is peace and constant ease. Due to this, all men of piety, scholars of purity, and other blessed people, with our beloved Prophet at the forefront, have found ease and peace in *tawakkul* and have always recommended it.

Everyone in the world would like to lean on someone, use someone's name, seek refuge in a sultan, and carry out their business in his name and be at ease. As you can see, there is this type of ease in *tawakkul*. This truth is explained in the Qur'an: *"And put your trust in God. God suffices as One on Whom to rely (and to Whom to refer all affairs)"* (al-Ahzab 33:3). Prophet Ibrahim's last words before being thrown into the fire: "God is sufficient for me, and how great a Guardian He is." As an outcome to this *tawakkul*, that mountainous fire became a rose garden to ease his soul.

Life Can Sometimes Bring Distress

It is unhealthy to act as if negative events never took place. In reality, something has happened. It is not correct to completely stifle those feelings of sadness, anger, resentment, and sorrow that arise in the face of negative events. The important thing is to be able to live these feelings in moderation and under control. The emotions that we have were given to us by our Creator so that we could experience them. It is also important to experience these emotions for a person's health, as long as they are in moderation and kept under control. Sadness and resentment should urge people to become better. If we are rejected, let us be sad, but this should lash out to our eagerness to ever being rejected again.

Sometimes events can seem to be the end of the world for a person. If he is able to pull out and escape from that event, he will understand that it's not the end of the world. As a matter of fact, after some time this event could even seem to be funny.

It must be known that this world is not eternal and that a person's life, based on this, will not be without problems. Problems shouldn't be underestimated but they shouldn't be given more significance than necessary. Life is variable and is not constant. A person will not only live through a certain dimension of life. That is, a person's life will not always be happy or always sad. Sadness and happiness are for people.

Knowing that the sky will not always be starry and clear, a person should not be sad in rainy weather. We must be thankful and have *tawakkul* for every situation the All-Compassionate Creator creates for us. The ability to be grateful and turn a negative emotion into a positive one is in the hands of the person. And this is based on the person being able to control his emotions.

READING TEXT

The Sufferings in Life Are like Salt, Not Too Little, Not Too Much!

An old journeyman becomes fed up with how his apprentice complains about everything. One day he sends his apprentice out to get salt. Once the apprentice, who is unhappy with everything in his life, returns, the old journeyman tells him to put a handful of salt in a cup of water and drink it.

The apprentice does as the old man tells him, but the second he takes a gulp, he begins spitting it out. "How did it taste?" the old man asked. "Bitter," he replied in anger. Thereupon, the journeyman grabs his apprentice by the arms and takes him outside. Silently, he takes him to the nearby lake and this time tells his apprentice to throw a handful of salt into the lake and take a drink.

Once the apprentice did this, the master asks him again. "How did it taste?" "Relieving," the young apprentice answered. "Did you taste the salt?" the old man asked. "No," said the apprentice.

Then the old man comes up next to his apprentice, who was kneeling by the lake, and says:

"The sufferings in life are like salt, not too little, not too much. The amount of suffering is always the same. However, the bitterness of that suffering depends on what it's placed in. When you are suffering, the only thing you have to do is to broaden your feelings in what is giving you that pain. Therefore, stop being a cup, and start trying to become a lake."

The person that illuminates his heart with the light of God and His mercy, and enlarges it with *tawakkul* and compassion, becomes like a lake compared to a cup of water. So, in the same way, to reach spiritual joy, one must become a lake.

Does *Tawakkul* Call For Laziness?

God has established conditions and causes for everything that is wanted in this world and the Hereafter. This is one of God's laws. So, *tawakkul* is leaving the outcome to God after having appropriately addressed the causes; it is trusting in Him and accepting everything that comes from Him with content and satisfaction. Whereas, leaving causes and reason on one side and saying, "Anyway, whatever is destined to be, will be" and waiting is not *tawakkul*, it's laziness.

In fact, in the Qur'an, God decrees: *"... once you are resolved, put your trust in God"* (Al Imran 3:159). Not working and having submission to God was not commanded. Being able to resolve work requires reliance. The person who does not trust in God will either rely on himself or on the causes. With the understanding that he and the causes involved are impotent, a person can only attain true ease of heart by trusting God, the One who creates all the reasons and relates cause and effect. For this reason, belief in the Oneness, submission to the Oneness, trust in submission, and absolute reliance upon God renders happiness in both this world and the next.

Islam's view of *tawakkul* has been misunderstood by some people. This incorrect understanding resulted in many people falling into laziness and blaming God; since many people then couldn't trust in God, their dreams would be broken and they would fall into hopelessness, which does not adhere to belief. Both conditions result from an incorrect understanding of *tawakkul*.

Tawakkul is never about abandoning work and compliance to reason by saying, "What God decrees will happen" and moving off to the side. Without effort there can be no *tawakkul*. In this world everyone will be awarded for their effort. The Qur'an relates this important truth: *"And that human has only that for which he labors"* (an-Najm 53:39). Our noble Prophet, peace and blessings be upon him, said to a Bedouin who had left his camel without tying it, to "tie your camel then place your trust in God."[122]

---

122   *Sunan at-Tirmidhi*, Sifatu'l-Qiyamah, 60

Once Umar ibn al-Khattab asks a group of people walking around pointlessly, "Where are you from, who are you?" "We are the ones who have submitted. We are the ones who have *tawakkul*," they replied. Thereupon, the Caliph says, "No, you are not the ones who have submitted to God, you are the ones who eat. You are liars, the one who submits to God, first seeds the field then has *tawakkul*."

This true incident expresses very nicely what should be understood in *tawakkul*. *Tawakkul* is a result of the believer's belief in Divine destiny. The person who has *tawakkul* has absolutely submitted himself to God and is content with His destiny. Just as believing in destiny doesn't require one to leave aside everything and sit down in laziness, *tawakkul* does not require laziness and indolence.

READING TEXT

Add Some Tar to Your Prayers, Tar!

An old woman's lone camel had caught mange and was sick. If it died, everything would be ruined; she would be without a means to carry her things when she went to her garden. She thought about this for many days, but no solution came to mind. She continuously prayed and asked God to save her camel.

One day when she saw her camel, which she earned her living from, not eating or drinking, and as thin as a skeleton, her sorrow increased and she began crying. She had her hands out, praying, while also continuously crying.

It was at this moment that our noble Prophet and his Companions were passing through there. When he saw the old woman crying, he asked her, "O God's servant, why are you crying?"

She replied, "Why else, for my camel. My camel is everything for me. What will happen to me if it dies? I have been praying to my Lord for many days, asking for its sickness to go away, but they aren't being accepted."

With a smile the Messenger of God replied, "If you want them to be accepted, add some tar to your prayers, tar!"

The woman began thinking. What did it mean to add tar to your prayer? Finally, she felt like she understood. This time the woman found some tar from her neighbors and applied it to her mangy camel first. After this, she opened her hands and began to pray.

The tar completely killed all the germs on the skin of the camel and saved it from the sickness.

From this it was understood that opening up your hands to make prayer and embracing *tawakkul* are not enough to cure an illness. Alongside this, it is also critical to not neglect the needed medicine. Our noble Prophet wished to say this to the old woman, who understood the problem and did what was recommended, thus saving her camel.

Have *Tawakkul*, Be At Ease!

Tawakkul is not leaving our duties to God and abandoning causality. For instance, it isn't *tawakkul* for a person that wants to reach his goal to say "I leave my work to God" and expect success without putting in the required effort. On the contrary, to be able to reach that goal, one must work regularly, with discipline, and systematically, doing the most he can in the way of causes. Then he will expect the outcome from God and will be content with whatever it is.

An important aspect of this is to not attach the outcome to the causes. Let's clarify this through an example: Let's say someone ill seeks treatment at the best hospital, gets examined by the best doctors in the field, and uses all the given medicines on time without exception. In the end, this person finally becomes healthy again. If this person ascribes his recovery to the hospital, doctors, or medicines, it will contradict *tawakkul*; in reality, health (everything) comes from God. The One Who creates everything, the One Who heals illnesses is God. This verse reveals this truth: "*Nothing will befall us except what God has ordained for us. He is our master, and in God let all the faithful put their trust*" (at-Tawbah 9:51).

To bestow us with fruits, Our Lord has made the tree; for the tree to grow He has made the soil, the seed, the water, and the sun as simple means or causes. Since this world is a place of trial, God has bounded the gifts and blessings we receive to some causes. In fact, our All-Powerful Lord has no need for causes. However, fulfilling the causes and taking the needed measures are required as respect to the laws God has decreed.

A true believer with *tawakkul* to God works as systematically and methodically as possible in his every work; he shows the greatest diligence in fulfilling the causes, but never attaches himself to any of them. He solely relies on God, trusting Him.

He knows that God created the causes and the outcomes and wholeheartedly believes this. If he comes face to face with a calamity or trouble, he becomes patient and says, "My Most Merciful Lord knows of my condition, there must also be good in this." If he attains success or a blessing, he becomes grateful and says, "This is a favor solely from my Lord."

A person who has *tawakkul* with this understanding would not even lose hope in the face of the most terrible calamities. Even if he were to shake a bit, he would never fall. Even in front of the greatest achievements, he would refrain from becoming spoiled and being full of pride; to the contrary, he would be doubly bent down in thankfulness. And in this way, he would've found true peace.

READING TEXT

The Important Thing Is How Big the Basketball Player Inside of You Is!

The middle school student came home with a pout on his face, threw his backpack onto the floor, ran up to his room, threw himself onto his bed and began crying. He hadn't been able to achieve his greatest dream. He had done everything he could to join the school's basketball team, but he had failed.

His mom quietly came into the room and asked him what had happened, her voice full of compassion.

"I didn't make the team!" said the little boy. "They told me 'You're still young!'"

The mom sat by her son's side and wrapped her arm around him. She said: "Son, the important thing is not that you are too small to make the team, but instead how big the basketball player inside of you is."

After the mom said this and left the room, the boy sat upright on his bed. He felt stronger than he ever was. Maybe he was small, but the basketball player inside of him was very big!

The next morning he went to practice early. Every day, every week, every month... his mom's words kept repeating in his mind. As the days passed, the basketball player inside of him and his determination grew.

The next year the team had tryouts again. This time, the big basketball player inside of him showed enough of itself. He astonished the coach and made the team. He always protected his spot in the upcoming years. He continuously became better and improved.

Before long, he began receiving offers from outside. He first played in the amateur teams. Then he gradually began scaling the success ladder.

And then the whole world was introduced to basketball's most successful player, Michael Jordan. Someone who once upon a time wasn't even able to join his school's team...

Don't Think Negatively... Work, Strive, You'll Succeed!

The thought of not being able to bear the negative events in the future is a negative thought in itself. The Almighty God knows the strength of the beings He creates and has already decreed that they wouldn't be weighed down with a weight they couldn't withstand. The problem lies in the person's thoughts. Someone who says "I can't carry this" to a one kilogram weight, won't be able to carry it. He has already made up his mind that he won't be able to carry it. A person's thought of not being able to withstand his misfortunes means that he will be deeply shaken by those misfortunes.

The days ahead of us have not yet come. Today's worries won't be able to save anyone from the troubles of the future. *Tawakkul*, however, will increase the strength to withstand.

Spiritual joy in a person keeps one from becoming obsessed with dwelling on the chances of facing misfortunes. These obsessions could wrap a person's life in a web of fear. Such a person would be unable to walk on the road or get in a car. Even if every precaution were to be taken, there will still be a chance for a car to crash, a plane to fall, and a ship to sink. But these are events that are outside the control of a person's willpower.

If a person becomes obsessed with things outside of his control and doesn't have *tawakkul*, he could make his life unbearable. The person, who has a phobia over dying in an unlikely event, always has a chance to die in an unlikely event.

"God Almighty placed fear in our nature so that we might preserve our life, not ruin it. He did not give us fear to make life an unbearable burden full of pain and torment. If there is a risk of 1:2 or 1:3 or 1:4, or at most 1:5 or 6, it may be permissible and tolerable to fear and avoid the risk. But to fear a chance of 1:20, 1:30, or 1:40 is groundless suspicion, a sort of paranoia that changes life into a torment."[123]

Fears won't change the destiny a person lives through. Don't be overly attached to ease, or it will also bring along with it the worry of that ease going away over time. This negative thought is already enough to ruin a person's ease.

Consequently, a person should bear the obstacles he faces in his life with patience, remain firm in front of them, strive to resolve them, and embrace the causes till the end, leaving the outcome to his Lord. Also, we must not forget that sometimes things that look bad have many hidden truths in them for us.

READING TEXT
How Did the Armless Judo Player Become the Champion?

The nine year old Japanese boy's greatest dream was to become an amazing judo master. Having always lived with this dream, the boy then lost his left arm in a traffic accident. The family was broken with

---

123   Nursi, Said, *The Letters*, New Jersey: The Light, 2007, p. 402

sorrow, and the boy's dreams had gone down the drain. Still, the family hired one of the best judo teachers for the boy to learn from. But the family had no hope.

The teacher kept teaching the boy the same move. Even though the boy got tired of practicing the same move, he began to execute it even faster than his teacher. One day he says to his teacher,

"Teacher, enough, I want to learn other moves."

Nevertheless, the teacher doesn't turn back from his plan and still makes the boy repeat the same move. Then, one day when the boy is able to execute the move lightning quick, the teacher says, "It's time for you to join a tournament" and signs up the boy.

The boy beats all of his opponents using the same move. In the final match he is faced against a giant-like man. He also uses the same move on him and wins. "Teacher, how did I become the champion? I can't believe this," he says to his teacher.

The teacher replies, "Look son, to stop this move I taught you, your opponent has to hold your left arm."

QUESTIONS

1- Which of the following are false about *tawakkul*?

   a. Islam's understanding of *tawakkul* has placed Muslims behind.

   b. Even though *tawakkul* is a state dependent on the heart, it doesn't contradict working and earning with your body.

   c. *Tawakkul* is having absolute trust in God in everything you do and submitting yourself to His preference.

   d. Saying, "Whatever is destined to be, will be" and waiting is not *tawakkul*, it's laziness.

2- How did our noble Prophet, peace and blessings be upon him, correct the acts of a Bedouin who said he had *tawakkul* in God and left his camel untied.

   a. Tie it up really well. If you do this, you wouldn't need *tawakkul*.

b. Let it go. After all, you will live through whatever is in your destiny.

c. Let it go, it will find someone who needs it.

d. First tie your camel then have *tawakkul*.

3- "Belief, therefore, consists of affirming Divine Unity, which requires submitting to God, which requires................., which yields happiness in both worlds. Fill in the blank in this sentence of Bediüzzaman Said Nursi with one of the options provided below:

a. happiness

b. silence

c. relying upon God

d. laziness

4- What is the name for taking all the necessary steps and putting in all the required effort, then leaving that work to God?

a. *Tazakkur*

b. *Tadabbur*

c. *Tawakkul*

d. *Tafakkur*

5- One day Umar ibn al-Khattab asks a group of people walking around pointlessly, "Where are you from, who are you?" "We are the ones who have submitted. We are the ones who have *tawakkul*," they replied. Thereupon, the Caliph says, "No, you are not the ones who have submitted to God, you are the ones who eat. You are liars, the one who submits to God, first .... then has *tawakkul*."

Fill in the blank with one of the options provided below:

a. sleeps

b. seeds the field

c. knows

d. thinks

6- "*Tawakkul* is never about abandoning work and compliance to reason by saying, "What God decrees will happen" and moving off to the side. Without effort there can be no *tawakkul*."

These statements could answer which of the following questions?

a. What are the worldly benefits of having *tawakkul*?
b. What are the benefits in the Hereafter of having *tawakkul*?
c. Is it difficult to have *tawakkul*?
d. Does *tawakkul* mean being lazy?

8.

CALAMITY, TEST, DISORDER

"We will certainly test you with something of fear and hunger, and loss of wealth and lives and fruits (earnings); but give glad tidings to the persevering and patient!" (al-Baqarah 2:155).

This World Is a Place of Trial

The words calamity, tribulation, trial, and strife remind us of the test. Henceforth, in this section, we will describe all these words under the heading of "test."

The main reason for the creation of humans is worship. It is possible to determine one's level of worship through tests. Thus, one reason for humans being in this world is tests. God tests people on various things. This is sometimes through hunger, sometimes through fear, sometimes through the lessening of wealth, such as one's life and possessions,[124] and sometimes through gifts, such as bestowing wealth and children.[125]

In short, calamities and tribulations along with good and beauty are a means of testing us. Meaning, we don't know when, where, and with what we will be tested with. This uncertainty helps keep a person conscious of the thought that he could be tested by anything at any moment.

Every person who comes, completes his life and moves on to the other world. No matter how much of a guest we are in this world, our

---

124   Al-Baqarah 2:155
125   Al-Anfal 8:28; al-Anbiya 21:35; Al Imran 3:186

Lord has sent Prophets so people don't stray onto the wrong path. Naturally, our Lord who has sent these Prophets must have some things He wants from us.

Just as we expect thanks and respect from the people we help and do good for, God, even though He has no need for it, will of course ask for thankfulness in view of the countless blessings He bestows upon us; such as feeding us honey from a poisonous bug, favoring us with indescribably delicious crops from a dry, mindless, and unconscious soil, making this world a house for us and the sun a heater for it, making the moon a lamp at night and a ceiling for the sky, establishing a university of various feelings in our minds and allowing us to utilize our senses, providing oxygen for us at every moment and changing it into carbon dioxide within us, safeguarding our body temperatures, and circulating the endless other planets that are like beads in space with His All-Powerful will.

As is seen, these thanks are called "worshipping God". Through His beloved Prophet Muhammad, peace and blessings be upon him, our Lord has shown us the essence, path, and method for worshipping Him and being thankful. However much we praise and glorify God, it's insufficient.

For this reason, we need to live in this world with the understanding that we will be held accountable in the Hereafter for every step we take and every breath we breathe, regulating ourselves so that the blessings we eat here aren't causes for regret there. The Qur'an emphasizes these two points, *"without forgetting your share (which God has appointed) in this world"* (al-Qasas 28:77), which advises people to prosper from this world, while the verse, *"Were not My Revelations recited to you, and you used to deny them?"* (al-Mu'minun 23:105), acts as a reminder that life in the Hereafter is the priority and that our first duty is to not lose our eternal bliss because of this world.

God has commanded this path upon humans and our Prophet implemented this verse as the best model to follow; the following generations then passed on these principles to the ones after them by living them in their lives.

We Must Pass the Test of This World

Every human that God sends to this world as a temporary officer realizes that he is a guest here and is transient, with the essence of this life being towards having an eternal life. As is already known, everybody wants to live forever. So, our most fundamental desire of not dying, and our prayers to stay eternal were accepted by our Lord and He has created the eternal Paradise for us.

However, God has subjected us to this test in order for us to be taught manners and shame worthy of Paradise. And the test is such a test that it isn't difficult, the question is obvious, the time is obvious, and the outcome is obvious. For instance, is it harder to make *wudu* and perform the *salah* than to memorize a history textbook and take a test on it? Is fasting for one month out of a year harder than algebra and geometry? Is it hard to not be a thief? Is cheating someone on a measurement or scale as hard as memorizing a biology textbook and taking a test on it? For humans that work and strive day and night for a sixty year long life, what valid and logical excuse could they have for not striving to pass a test much easier than these worldly tests?

Certainly, there can be no valid excuse. For this reason, you must be conscious of the fact that every moment of this worldly life is a test.

This rule of worldly tests is effective for everyone. It is a custom of God to subject humans to tests. The Qur'an gives tidings of how humans will be tested with good and bad to see their sincerity in belief. Humans will also be tested with life's temporary beauties.[126] Wealth and children are tests for humans, a means of trial.[127] Just as abundant sustenance and given blessings[128] are trials, the sorrows[129] one faces, calamities and afflictions are also tests.[130]

---

[126] Ta-Ha 20:131
[127] Al-Anfal 8:28; at-Taghabun 64:15
[128] Az-Zumar 39:49
[129] Ta-Ha 20:40
[130] At-Tawbah 9:126; al-Haj 22:11

READING TEXT
What Comes to Mind When We Say Test?

Test, is a mysterious word that reminds us of passing and failing at the same time. It hides in it both hope and fear. Pleasure and pain have mixed with each other in it. It makes a person neither laugh, nor cry. Pleasure and ease come before it, torment and suffering follow it. Aren't all these, at the same time, the same qualities of the worldly test? Aren't humans being tested in this world?

Till one hits puberty, it's before the test: The phase of preparing one's paper and pencil. After reaching puberty, humans then begin filling up their test papers with their recorded deeds and the pen will continuously move till the person dies. It is known that this test will come to an end for everyone one day, but it isn't known who and when the paper will be taken from them. When one says test, many things come to mind. Let's list a few: In a test, the important thing is not to write a lot, but instead, to write correctly. There are those who aren't able to get a "one" after filling up ten pages, and there those who are able to get a "hundred" by filling up one page. If that is so, a long life should be desired to write more good things. When taking the test, sitting up in the front, wearing the best clothes, and using the most valuable pencil won't affect the outcome a single bit. These are all permissible, but not of them are necessary. What is necessary and required is to answer the questions correctly.

During the test, it isn't obvious whether or not you are fortunate or unfortunate. It isn't correct for us to desire a person's worldly opportunities when we don't know the result of the person's life. During the test, no one interferes with the other. Everyone is free to write whatever he wishes. But there is encouragement in writing the correct answer, and a threat in writing the wrong answer. Both are for the test taker's benefit.

One of the most important qualities of this worldly test is that the test takers were already notified of the correct answers. Isn't that so? Don't we all know what to do and what to abstain from? Contrary to other tests, this test has allowed collaboration with each other, actually it is even rewarded. We can go next to a hardworking student and, by looking at his paper, write the correct answer, too. And our answer will be accepted. Verily, in righteousness, truth, and beauty, helping is allowed. Making others write the wrong answer or following the wrong answer is prohibited! Whoever shows as much effort in helping others pass as passing himself will receive a gift. However much he teaches will also be added to his own score. And for this deed, he is a given a great rank: *jihad* (striving in God's cause and for humanity's good)

It isn't acceptable to only take care of oneself, it's disdained. This process of gaining and losing is not in the least bit similar to business in this world. In this test, we are not rival firms. However much we praise our neighbors, our gain will be that much more fruitful. We will be harmed in proportion to how much we praise ourselves. In this business, the wealth of the one who gives will increase, not the one who is stingy. Doesn't explaining what we know to others also give us a better understanding of it?

In the worldly test, writing the correct answer is easy and convenient. The actual hard thing to do is to write it wrong. This is a great Divine blessing for us. If it was the other way around, then it would truly be a difficult test for us. We all know how easy like breathing saying the truth is. A person won't get tired telling the truth the whole day; however, if he was required to converse for half an hour with the condition of lying in his every sentence, he would become miserable. Drinking water doesn't make one crumple one's nose in bitter taste, but one can't even look at the face of one who drinks alcohol. Lawful earnings ease the soul, whereas forbidden earnings torment the conscience.

At first glance, it seems like everyone will pass this test. But come and see, most people still stray onto the wrong path. The reason for this must be searched for in that which shows white as black, and black as white: *nafs* (carnal soul) and Satan.

The trials and tests in this world have many types. Some are tested on their wealth; others are tested on their hate of wealth. Some on their health, others on their illnesses..... Some on being in debt, others on crediting loans..... It is because everyone is being tested that, in truth, no one is in ease. The noble saying of the Prophet is like an ocean:

"There is no ease in the world." One of its meanings could be: "There is no ease in trial; there is work and effort, worry and hope, sorrow and patience..."

Before us, the rich-poor, worker-employer, commander-officer, man-woman, and strong-weak have already entered this realm of trial, sat down in it for some time and have gotten up to leave. Now, it is time for the people of this century.[131]

If There Were No Calamities, We Wouldn't Know the Value of Positive Things

Let's imagine an earth that blocks the sunlight everywhere. In this case, there is no sun or light for us. In this atmosphere, to truly understand that there is a sun that provides light, we must enter a dark room. If we open up eye holes in that pitch-black room and look outside, we will have no doubt of the existence of light and that it comes from the sun.

This world is actually like a dark room. Opposites like good and bad, blessings and evil allow us to comprehend God's endless and matchless good. Otherwise, if this world only had good, then they wouldn't be called good. The evils and calamities that walk around us actually shape our dark room. From the experience we gain from them, we are able to appreciate the value of blessings and beneficial things.

So, in this way, the interweaving of opposites in this world gives birth to the possibility of recognizing the truths and being able to name them. Without darkness there would be no degrees of light, without cold there would be no degrees of heat, without ugliness there would be no degrees of beauty, and if there were no world and everyone was created into Paradise, then Paradise wouldn't be called Paradise and the matchless activities there would have no meaning.

Consequently, this place is relatively a prison compared to Paradise. This is because opposites exist here, and that the good things here will come to us there in their true forms and qualities; thus this world will not have the worth of a shadow's shadow.

---

131   Başar, Alaaddin, *Nur'dan Kelimeler*, İstanbul: Zafer, 2000, pp. 113–115

In the same way, this world, in comparison to Hell, will be like Paradise. Because none of the goodness here will exist there, but all the hideousness, harms, and evils here will be more horrible, scary, and agonizing there.

When we see a saint perform an extraordinary wonder, we can only think of good coming from him. If we see him in pride or in another behavior inappropriate to him and yet are still able to say "There must be a reason", then how can we not believe that the things we face from God, the One who decorates us with every kind of blessing and continuously bestows us with things we need in our lives, must be full of good and blessings? The wonder that saint showed was also indeed created by God. Our Lord will surely test us. Our sole duty is to be ready for every type of test.

READING TEXT

What Are the Types of the Most Important Tests We Might Face?

Fethullah Gülen answers this question as follows:

One of the most important elements of being tested is decreed in the Qur'an, *"We try people through one another"* (al-An'am 6:53). People are tested with each other. This is the scariest kind of test and the line between passing and losing is at its thinnest. The Respected Companions have come face to face with this kind of test repeatedly and, by God's grace, they were able to immediately pass them all.

The other types of test are things such as attachment to ease, attachment to a house, attachment to children, attachment to grandchildren...etc. For people who were at higher levels of providing service to others, this was especially, at a time, always a point of trial; now, it could be the reason that most people leave. "We worked very hard. It's now time for the young ones to work. Let us take our rest and start dealing with our families and children." This thought could be said to be the beginning of this type of test. The verse Abu Ayyub al-Ansari stated during the siege of Constantinople should always be kept in remembrance, *"(So) spend in God's cause (out of whatever you have) and do not ruin yourselves by your own hands (by refraining from spending)"* (al-Baqarah 2:195).

During the siege some soldiers would warn their friends, who were fully knowingly throwing themselves into death, by reading this verse to them, *"Do not ruin yourselves by your own hands (by refraining from spending)"* (al-Baqarah 2:195). Thereupon, Abu Ayyub al-Ansari said, "You are reading the verse correctly, but interpreting it wrong." And he continued, "We, the people of Ansar (the Helpers), said after the conquest of Mecca, 'Finally Islam has become mighty. We had shared our wealth with the Muhajirin (the Emigrants), and had neglected our gardens and fields. Now let's look after our own survival.'" Then this verse was revealed; meaning, "Forsake your property and your lives for the sake of God. By not forsaking these things, do not ruin yourselves by your own hands." As is seen by this decree in the Qur'an, these kinds of thoughts can also be a test.

Personally, I also believe that desiring death is also a test. We might or might not rejoin them, that is another topic, but it is a great thing to desire rejoining the Messenger of God, the Companions, the Successors, and the generation after the Successors. But how are we to know that this is a consequence of the hardship one faces in providing service!

In short, the people whose mission it is to provide service are bothered by a world of various tests. The important thing is for the people who follow the Divine Truth to notice and be conscious of this, displaying a behavior required of a worshipper.

Don't forget! "Duty is greater than everything; the soul is inferior to everyone."[132]

Every Test Is a Mercy

If a close one became ill and the doctors altogether said that it was possible to cure him through surgery, you will immediately begin carrying out the needed transactions without any hesitation. On the day of the surgery, you will get him nicely prepared and submit him to the doc-

---

[132]   Gülen, M. Fethullah, *Prizma-3*, İstanbul: Nil, 2008, p. 58

tors. We are talking about open surgery, but even in this case what would be our reaction to viewing the surgery live through a television placed outside?

For instance, would we say "These doctors are cutting and slicing my child, I'm going to send them to court, and after the surgery I will criticize the doctors and come down on them!"? Of course not... We would patiently wait for the outcome because we know that the doctors are not cruel and they handle treatments. Moreover, after the surgery we will thank the doctors profusely and send them flowers and gifts later on to show them our gratefulness.

Similarly, the devices that make up our spiritual side have become chronically ill with behaviors that might take us towards sins and heedlessness. We can't be as meticulous as we are with our stomachs in treating these all the time. In such cases, spiritual surgeons come into play to perform spiritual surgery on us that will help us have eternal goodness.

And this surgery's method, length, and tools are decided by God, the All-Healing (Who cures all physical and spiritual diseases). Since we didn't rebel against the doctors and instead relied on them, it is then impossible for us to not rely on God; wouldn't this mean that we must thank God and worship him proportionate to the number of good those devices, which He treated with those illnesses, calamities, and various tests, that we will continuously use in the eternal world will bring or have already brought?

Humans have not come to this world only to live nicely and follow corporeal pleasures. They have come to present their differences from animals by controlling these corporeal desires and their carnal souls. Otherwise, humans, who have been given wealth and competence many times more superior than animals, will have been absolutely deceived and will have left this world they had come to, in order to decorate their devices for the eternal world, as something less than an animal.[133]

---

[133]   Al-A'raf 7:179

Truly, humans have been given this condition and it is expected for them to display their functions and to improve their potential abilities, putting forth their eternal performance by passing through a sieve in this world that has an atmosphere in which opposites clash against each other, constantly presenting them an environment in which they either become fit for Paradise or for Hell. The choice is now in their hands.

How Can Every Calamity We Face Be Good for Us?

We must separate the events people face into those that they have no control over and those that they have control over.

If a person has no control over what befalls him, it is wholly good. For that person, God is fair and good. Since it was outside that person's will, God will always desire beauty and good for him. If so, there is no option in this that isn't good. However, the outwardly appearances might be terrible, and this is anyways a part of the worldly test. If he has some patience, he will see that it also was good.

Since God is far away from any defect, He will show to us, whether in this world or in the Hereafter, the good results behind the things that were considered evil. This verse plainly decrees this, *"It may well be that you dislike a thing but it is good for you, and it may well be that you like a thing but it is bad for you"* (al-Baqarah 2:216).

On the other hand, if the person had control over the event and it only involved himself, it could happen in two ways: Based on the person's choice, a good deed or act could've come about it. This is also created by God. In this case, this creation is something that person desires and is content with. Good has come from good. Or if an evil or sin-like act was done, it was also created by God. This time, good did not come from good. However, the one who wanted this evil to be was that person and God privileged people in this world by granting them good if they wished for it, and evil if they wished for it, presenting them with the option to bear the results. If so, since the one who follows and asks for that evil is people, the reason for evil is people, but since God is the only Creator, He created the evil result. Then, here, people must accredit themselves for the advent of evil. Thus, evil has not come from good. It was asked for evil to be created from good, and for the test, He created evil.

God does not will evil; people are responsible for that evil. If God only created the good for a person and didn't create the evil he desired, then this world would not be a test.

This world's dough has added together the harmful and the beneficial things, and has been shuffled around by the Hand of Power, with the evil thrown into the good, and the good encased by the evil. Therefore, humans are asked to search and find the perfect and the correct within these opposites and decide upon them.

From the time the believer reaches puberty and takes that first step towards Paradise, he will come face to face with many tests. Every test will take him to being fit for Paradise. In this way, tests are like a Buraq (a heavenly mount) and will fly us to Paradise. The person that views tests from this perspective will certainly not fall into hopelessness and uneasiness, he would say "This will also pass by!" and will continue on his path of worship with belief and patience.

Calamities and Tribulations Make a Person Feel Helpless

With helplessness and poverty, people will notice indescribable treasures, but understanding this concept of helplessness and poverty is not easy. The best means to invite this concept are illnesses and calamities. We take our precautions against being ill and falling into calamities. With the required care and attention we don't submit our health to anyone. However, if we fall ill or under a calamity outside of our control, we also believe that it has good and look to find and live with them.

Illnesses are the most important advisers in making us notice one of our greatest blessings, health. If people weren't touched by afflictions called illnesses, they wouldn't know their blessing of health existed. Even if they saw the illnesses on others, they wouldn't be able to regard it as genuine. Thus, generally people are afflicted with large or small illness. So that the person could wholeheartedly and sincerely attain the gratefulness required for a blessing such as health. To be able to fully be thankful for health, the mirror of illness must definitely intervene. Then, if the mirror of illness presents goodness proportionate to the goodness of health, then that illness is also a means of goodness.

A famous businessman's observation on this topic is very interesting and explains a great deal.

If we accept health as a "1" and everything else we gain later on in life as a "0", and if we placed all the zeroes next to the 1, then we would get a number in the quadrillions. The zeroes next to the 1 could represent a career, a car, a house, a factory, a summer house, another factory... These, after all, have an attraction about them that opens peoples' eyes. Health, however, isn't noticed by anyone at all. But if something happened to that health, then that 1 at the front would disappear. There may be tons of zeroes at hand but the addition and multiplication of zeroes is also a large zero. Once health leaves, even if everything were to be placed in front of a person's eyes, it wouldn't mean anything for him anymore. To his surprise, all the wealth and opportunities mean a giant nothing next to health.

Health, at the same time, is also a domino piece in one's social life. The ill man will seriously desire and expect help from others. Through the warning of illness, he will then better understand that it isn't possible to live alone in this worldly life and that every person is a crucial fundamental pillar for him. He will especially notice how valuable a treasure his close relatives are.

This interaction drives people to interlock and consult with each other. In a community in which people discover wisdom through illnesses, consultation and help between each other will be strengthened. In this way, a social intimacy and harmony will slowly but increasingly become apparent.

The ill person having understood the warning of his illness and that his body is a trust given to him by God, will know that all property only and only belongs to God. By accepting that He can use His property as He wills, the person will be content with His every decree and will understand that everything that comes from Him is good, and will gain the reflex of transferring this truth into other aspects of his life.

The person will understand the blessing of the health he had before falling ill and the other blessings he had been given, and as long as he lives in this world, he will continue his life with the view of those blessings as blessings and be doubly bent in thankfulness for their use and consumption.

READING TEXT
Why Does God Test Humans with Calamities Such as Being Disabled and Poor?

Before anything, let us clarify that we can only ask this type of question to understand the wisdom behind creation. Otherwise, this would carry the meaning of—God forbid—interrogating God and no one has the right or ability to do this. Because He is the owner of the world we live in, the air we breathe, and the water we drink along with the stars, the moon, and the sun. The things we possess or can't possess all belong to Him. The true owner has total control over His possessions.

We may understand this better with this example: A very generous man takes three men to a tower that has three balconies and three separate staircases to reach them. He advises each of them to one of the staircases and gives them a gift, not because he has a debt to them but solely because of his generosity and mercy, for each stair they climb. And when they reach the balcony, he rewards each of them with a bigger gift. However, the one who ascends to the first balcony has fewer stairs to climb than the other two and receives fewer gifts. The one who ascends to the second balcony also receives fewer gifts compared to the third person. Now, could the first person look at the second and third, and could the second person look at the third and protest to that generous man, "Why were my number of steps fewer? Why did you give me fewer gifts?" If they did, wouldn't they have done a great injustice and insolence?

So, our Lord has also created us from nothing; when we could've been rocks, dust, grass, or bugs crawling on the ground, He created us as humans. Furthermore, He also bestowed us with countless blessings. Truly, He has placed the whole universe under our command. More importantly, He has honored us by making us His servants and has declared us vicegerents on earth. After all this, if a person stood up and protested, "Why is my wealth less or why am I blind, disabled?" wouldn't it be ungrateful to our Lord? God forbid, does God owe us something so that we could protest? What's left to us is not to see what our Lord hasn't given us, but to be thankful in any case for the countless blessings He has.

There is much wisdom and hidden truths we know or don't know behind why the Almighty God has created people in different statuses. I will try to explain a few that we know:

First: God has countless Names and these Names require variety in creation. For instance, the All-Providing requires the needy, and the All-Healing requires the ill so that these Names may manifest themselves. Again, God is the All-Answering for those in trouble, the All-Constricting for those who have dived into heedlessness, and the All-Expanding for those who are drowning in worry. In this way our Lord introduces His countless Names to us; after all, this is the purpose for our creation.

Second: Everything is known by its opposite. Just like how without darkness light wouldn't be known, without illnesses health, without hunger being full, without poverty being wealthy, and without worry being at ease wouldn't have had value. Without the disabled and handicapped the strong wouldn't have noticed the blessings they had, and those who are missing a body part or have a disabled one wouldn't have totally understood the value of their other body parts. Besides, conditions of illness, disability, and calamities are exceptions. Illnesses and calamities encompass a very small period of time in a person's lifetime. Also, disabled people form a very small portion of the world's population. Moreover, most of the illnesses and disabilities result from human abuse and misappropriation.

Third: This world is a place of trial and testing. God sometimes tests people with poverty, sometimes with wealth, sometimes with illnesses, and sometimes with health. Goodness, power, wealth, disability, and strength are all means of being tested. God Almighty decrees this truth in the Qur'an: *"We will certainly test you with something of fear and hunger, and loss of wealth and lives and fruits (earnings); but give glad tidings to the persevering and patient"* (al-Baqarah 2:155).

The verses immediately following this one talk about the characteristics of the patient one and how they will be given a great reward by their Lord. God will never place a burden on someone that wouldn't be able to withstand it and will not hold someone accountable for something he didn't own.

Fourth: God is the All-Just and has infinite mercy. God never wills any wrong for (His) servants. To completely understand God's justice, we must think of both this world and the Hereafter. This world is temporary, it will come and go. The true and eternal life is in the Hereafter. This world is only a field for the Hereafter. Illnesses and calamities will count as worship for those who are believers and are patient. And for those believers who fall under these and are deprived of the transient worldly goodness in this short lifetime, if they remain patient, they will be rewarded with limitless rewards that others will be unable to see forever. God will take one He had given and give back endlessly, as long as humans wholeheartedly believe in this and are patient, respectful and thankful.

Fifth: God sends humans to this world for worship. True peace and happiness is being a friend of God and attaining His favor. Compared to those who live in ease and abundance, those who were faced with illnesses, troubles, tribulations, and calamities understand their helplessness easier, and feel the need to submit to God. Their worship will be more involved and, whenever possible, they will struggle to do good and earn good deeds. And isn't this the true reason for our existence in this world? If so, and if these conditions don't result from our mistakes, they shouldn't be thought of as punishment. Maybe they should be seen as God's favor. Of course, when a perfect believer is faced with illness, disability, tribulation, and calamity, he will be patient and say, *"Surely we belong to God (as His creatures and servants) and surely to Him we are bound to return"* (al-Baqarah 2:156).[134]

QUESTIONS

1- In the sentence, "Wealth and children are trials from humans," what does "trial" mean?
   a. Weakness
   b. Test
   c. Delusion
   d. Case

2- Which of the following are false?
   a. God only tests humans with hunger and fear.
   b. Tribulations and calamities along with goodness are means of being tested.
   c. When, where, and with what we will be tested is unknown.
   d. The true reason for the existence of humans in this world is worship.

3- Al-Baqarah's 155th verse decrees that people will be tested with various things. Which of the following is not one of them?
   a. Hunger
   b. Defects in wealth, life, and earnings
   c. Fear
   d. Long life

4- According to a noble saying of our Prophet, who are the ones that face the most severe tribulations?
   a. The Prophets
   b. The people of the other Prophets
   c. The saints
   d. The righteous servants

---

[134]   Küçük, Muhittin, *Sorularla Açılan Pencereler-1*, İstanbul: Muştu, 2009, pp. 92–95

9.

TOLERANCE AND EASE

Let not those among you who are favored with resources swear that they will no longer give to the kindred, the needy, and those who have emigrated in God's cause (even though those wealthy ones suffer harm at the hands of the latter). Rather, let them pardon and forbear. Do you not wish that God should forgive you? God is All-Forgiving, All-Compassionate. (an-Nur 24:22)

Tolerance Is the Attribute of a Believer

Tolerance and simplicity plays a major role in the Islamic faith. Displaying gentleness and tolerance while conveying the truth, is a great value. Many insensitive souls have melted amidst the warmth of gentleness and tolerance in the past, and embraced the Islamic circle of light. Indeed, God demands this from us, He commands us to be tolerant and approach people with gentleness.[135]

In the words of the eminent scholar Fethullah Gülen, a person of tolerance constantly gains in every aspect of life and never loses. While living the present, living for the future at the same time is the dimension of Divine favor and wisdom reserved for people of tolerance. Those favored with this are the sole inheritors of the world beyond.[136]

A believer granted the morals of the Qur'an should eliminate evil with kindness, and never heed to impolite behavior. He must always opt for tolerance and gentleness and be forgiving towards those who act unfavorably.

---

[135] Ta-Ha 20:44
[136] Gülen, M. Fethullah, *Asrın Getirdiği Tereddütler-4*, İstanbul, Nil, 2011, p.

The Islamic culture is a culture of forbearance. Our Lord, Who describes Himself in the beginning of the verses of the Qur'an as Merciful and Compassionate in the words *Bismillahirahmanirahim* (In the Name of God, the All-Merciful, the All-Compassionate), and the noble Prophet who said "Have mercy on those on the earth so God and angels will have mercy on you"[137] are calling upon us to live without offending others and to be a civilization of tolerance.

Millions of decent people who have been educated and disciplined according to the Islamic faith, and in particular the companions of God have always represented the culture of tolerance and forbearance in the most excellent manner. The noble Prophet's warning to those who became angry at a man who entered the mosque after drinking alcohol, and Julaybib the Companion who the Messenger of God saved from the whims of his youth with his words of advice as a young man, and later the beloved Prophet finding him martyred on the battle field, taking him into his arms and praying for him, are just two of the scenes of mercy of the Most Excellent Human.

Iron melted and coal turned into diamonds in the compassionate hands of Islam's guides who bore souls of enlightenment. Every command of Islam is the means of compassion. Both the prohibitions and punishments of the Islamic faith are aimed at saving and protecting its societies. Even in terms of the clear punishments in the Qur'an and Traditions of the Prophet, it is recommended that forgiveness should be favored. So in these terms, Islam is a religion bearing compassion in its every command, and gives major importance to forgiveness, mercy, tolerance and ease.

Members of the Islamic faith should make this emotion and conception their guide in every aspect of life. Indeed, Fethullah Gülen described the manner required of a believer in this poem:

Our Mode and Fashion

Our mode is based on love, our lives devoted to passion,
Our hearts keep beating unconditionally.

---

[137]   *Sunan Abu Dawud*, Adab, 58

Our stir is to access all people by compassion;
Especially as Muhammadian Spirit embraces our souls.
No matter we might remain as the last soldier of this front,
Determined we are, to wait till the day of resurrection,
Loving all within the hope to attain Haqq,
As passionate as Majnun's quest for Layla in deserts…
Headed to the depth of our hearts,
Adding an ethereal ferment to the existence;
We shall run to the freshness of the holy mercy,
Ridding of hate and malice in our souls…
Another light shines on the arbor we shall walk on,
We shall pass over cliffs that are caved by hate;
All people are in peace in the Hereafter,
We feel the spring blossoming just a little ahead…

So How Does God Mention Ease in the Qur'an?

In the Qur'an, the word *"yusr*/ease" is mentioned 41 times. God does not grant a human burdens or difficulties beyond their capability of endurance; He only burdens them with responsibilities they are capable of sustaining.[138] *"God does not charge a soul with a duty except in what He has (already) granted it (of capacity to discharge that duty). God will bring about, after hardship, ease"* (at-Talaq 65:7) God does not want hardships for humans, He wants ease.[139] Because humans were created weak and do not want hardship, God wants to ease their heavy burden.[140]

Religion was deemed easier by God.[141] In addition to the general rulings of worship commanded in the Islamic faith under normal conditions called *"azima"* (acting with piety), there are also aspects of ease/convenience for a valid reason referred to as concessions, and in addition, the gates to repenting for sins remain wide open.

Forcing people to do things is noncompliant with human nature. Therefore, enforcing religion on people was forbidden in the Islamic faith. Indeed, religion is an aspect of belief and choice. In the state-

---

138   Al-Baqarah 2:286
139   Al-Baqarah 2:185
140   An-Nisa 4:28
141   Hajj 22:78

ments of the Qur'an, there is no compulsion in religion.[142] Nobody can force another person to become a Muslim. Indeed, if God willed, He could have made everyone on earth Muslims.[143]

However, we must also emphasis the point: The command "There is no compulsion in religion" is regarding people being forced into becoming Muslims, not a Muslim practicing his religion. After a person voluntarily accepts the Islamic faith, he is obliged to fulfill the Islamic commands.[144] If an individual abstains from fulfilling the commands of God without a valid excuse after embracing Islam, then he will face certain results both in this world and the Hereafter. This is not compulsion in religion, but is disciplining those who voluntarily chose the Islamic faith to live on the right path in accordance with the life he chose, and ensuring that this path of righteousness concludes with success.

READING TEXT
The Weapon of Tolerance against the Gun

One day, the new muezzin came to the imam of the mosque, who had been waiting for a muezzin for a long time. Vehbi, a man from the congregation was so pleased: "Congratulations imam effendi, at last you have been appointed a muezzin!"

The imam smiled reluctantly and said: "He is not an appointed muezzin; he is a muezzin that I earned with compassion and tolerance! He pointed a gun at me, and I responded with my weapon of tolerance, he took me hostage first then I took him hostage. Now he has displayed his loyalty by becoming our muezzin."

Vehbi was confused. The imam began to explain: "One morning at dawn I locked the mosque, as I left and walked out of the gate on my way home, a voice startled me: "Imam effendi, raise your hands or I will shoot!"

I looked, but I did not recognize the man, he held a gun at me, and pointing in a certain direction said: "Walk that way!"

---

142   Al-Baqarah 2:256
143   Yunus 10:99
144   Al-Ahzab 33:36

So with my hands on my head, I walked in the direction he said. We eventually reached the graveyard. On the command of the voice coming from behind me we walked around the graveyard for a while, and without turning around I inquired, "Can I ask why we are walking around the graveyard?" His answer was very interesting: "I am the son of so and so, a member of the congregation whom you loved dearly, I am looking for my father's grave."

I was both relieved and extremely surprised: "Your father's grave is over there," so I took him to his father's grave.

Suddenly he gave another command: "Kneel down and recite the *Surah* Ya-Sin!"

Despite my increasing confusion, I recited this *surah* of the Qur'an. In the meantime, I noticed from the corner of my eye that the young man had put the gun in his pocket and was now crying. After I had recited the chapter, he said: "You have fulfilled your duty, you can go now!"

I replied: "No, I cannot go and leave you like this. I want to know why you did this."

He began to sob. When he calmed down he explained: "Unfortunately I drink alcohol. Last night I become drunk again. I saw my father in my dream. He was angry with me and said: 'What kind of son are you? I died all those years ago, but I have not received even one gift from you, is that my reward?' When I woke up, I wanted someone to recite the Qur'an at my father's graveside. I appreciate what you did, but you can go now, leave me alone. I have ruined my life." I replied: "No! You are not ruined. Even if that is the case, if you drop gold onto the ground it does not lose its value. The only thing you have to do is escaping the pit of sin and finding your true essence. Come on, I'll take you to my house."

He was hesitant at first, but I insisted, and we walked home together. He considered himself unworthy of kindness. I told him: "A man like your father cannot be the father of a bad son, there is a time and place for everything, and this is your time to change." We became friends, and this friendship developed to the point that he wanted to be the muezzin of our mosque. Briefly, he pulled a gun on me and I revealed my weapon of compassion and tolerance; he frightened me at first, but then I took him hostage.[145]

Islam is a Religion of Ease

The One who knows a human the best is God, the Creator of all things. God, who knows the human power, capacity and capability, planned the human servitude and worship accordingly, and when He demanded something from a human, He commanded this according to the human's means and capabilities. God is the One of absolute justice... He gave these commands based on the capacity of humans.

The Qur'an clearly states that God gave these commands in accordance with human power:

(O believers, if you are worried that God will take every soul to account even for what the soul keeps within it of intentions and plans, know that) God burdens no soul except within its capacity: in its favor is whatever (good) it earns, and against it whatever (evil) it merits. (So, pray thus to your Lord:) "Our Lord, take us not to task if we forget or make mistakes. Our Lord, lay not on us a burden such as You laid on those gone before us. Our Lord, impose not on us what we do not have the power to bear." (al-Baqarah 2:286)

In other words, God has not burdened responsible humans with any form of worship, either physically or spiritually, beyond his power. On the contrary, He gave His commands according to the ability of the human structure and understanding.

In the duties God made incumbent upon His servants, He considered the capacity of the individuals. For example, Hajj was not deemed obligatory on every Muslim, but for those who possess specific financial means and conditions: *"Pilgrimage to the House is a duty owed to God by all who can afford a way to it"* (Al Imran 3:97). In addition, regarding the ritual of purification, the preparation for worship as important as prayer, the option of performing *tayammum* (ablution

---

Refik, İbrahim, *Hayatın Renkleri*, İstanbul: Albatros, 2001, p. 138

with clean soil) when the conditions are not suitable, clearly indicates that the command is based upon capacity.[146]

God never burdens His servants with things that he would not be able to endure; and due to this He does not want His servants to impose anything beyond their own duties and responsibilities.[147]

Ease in servitude and worship is a very important principle in the Islamic faith. The essence of all these principles is expressed in these words: *"God wills to lighten for you (your burdens), for human has been created weak (liable to err)"* (an-Nisa 4:28). Scholars on the commentary of the Qur'an say that this verse is applicable to the commands of the Islamic religion on a whole, and that God granted this convenience in every aspect of the Islamic religion.[148]

When we look at the noble Prophet's life of servitude, we clearly see that convenience and ease as a principle. The Companions related this in the following *hadith*: "Whenever the Prophet had to choose between two options, he would choose the easier of the two."[149] And in another narration, the Prophet said: "Make things easy not difficult, give tidings and do not create repulsion."[150]

The fact that Islam is a religion of ease and convenience is emphasized twice in this verse of the Qur'an: *"Then, surely, with hardship comes ease. Surely, with hardship comes ease"* (ash-Sharh 94:5–6).

Indeed, certain forms of worship were made easier so that worship can be performed in any environment and conditions, so that Muslims can execute their servitude with ease. Observing the fast at a later date if a person is unable to observe the fast during the month of Ramadan, praying in the sitting position when unable to perform the prayer standing, performing the *tayammum* when there is no water or water is unobtainable, and shortening the prayer on a journey are a few of the common aspects of ease in Islam.

---

146   Al-Ma'idah 5:6
147   Al-Ma'idah 5:101
148   Radi, *Al-Mafatih al-Ghayb*, 10/55
149   *Sunan Abu Dawud*, Adab, 4; *Al-Muwatta*, Husnu al-Huluq, 2
150   *Sahih al-Bukhari*, Ilm, Maghazi 60; Adab, 80: *Sahih Muslim*, Jihad, 4

In view of the individual's capacity and requirements, there are many other aspects of convenience in Islam. Therefore the commands of the Islamic faith may be fulfilled at any time and place.

The Tolerance of God's Messenger

The beloved Prophet bore a heart of tolerance. His name was accompanied by "the All-Merciful, the All-Compassionate." The Prophet's dear wife, our mother Aisha reported: "He never spoke evil of anyone. He never said or did anything improper. He would not raise his voice and not respond to evil with evil, but he would forgive."

She also said: "Whenever the Messenger of God was given an option between two things he would chose the easier of the two as long as it was not a sin. But if it was a sin he would abstain from it."[151]

She continued: "The Prophet never beat anyone with his hand, neither a woman nor a servant, but only, in the case when he had been fighting in the cause of God and he never took revenge for anything unless the things made inviolable by God were made violable; he then took revenge for God, the Exalted and Glorious."[152]

Qadi Bayzawi explains this subject in these words: "It is clear that the Messenger of God was gentle, patient and just. If he had not served the rights of God and the people, then this would have been contempt. If he sought revenge for himself, then this would have been classified as impatience. The Messenger of God avoided the two extremes, and adopted tolerance and justice in the most positive, gentlest manner."

Anas ibn Malik, one of the Companions narrated: "One day when I was walking with the Messenger of God, a Bedouin came and grabbed on God's Messenger's cloak with such strength that I could see the marks of the cloak on his neck, and said 'O Muhammad! Give me some of God's wealth you have.' The Messenger of God turned to the Bedouin and laughed, and ordered that he should be given some money."[153]

---

[151]   *Tajrid* 9/276
[152]   *Sahih Muslim*, Fadail, 79
[153]   Köksal, M. Asım, *İslam Tarihi-9*, İstanbul: Şamil, 1987, p. 450

According to another narration by Anas, God's Messenger has never said anything that may upset someone to their face or reproach people for their mistakes. He explained things that were forbidden and must be avoided in general rather than mentioning specific individuals so they would not be offended. Nevertheless, the Messenger of God, who classified every sign as a command, displayed great care to avoid offending the people.

God's Messenger noticed that one man used an unpleasant scent that was disturbing everyone; it was yellow in color and clearly visible. He remained silent. But after the man left, the Messenger of God told those present: "Tell him in a gentle manner so that he will not use this unpleasant, yellow scent again."

The Companions related, "When God's Messenger disliked something, this was apparent from the look on his face." The following *hadith* bears great wisdom: "None of you should tell me anything bad about another person, for when I meet you I want my heart to be clean."[154]

The Messenger of God Always Chose Tolerance and Dialogue

When we look at the life of the noble Prophet, we clearly see that for effective communications with people, he constantly strived to establish an environment of dialogue. For example, despite the severe conditions, his approach of accepting the Treaty of Hudaybiya in order to establish an environment of peace is clear evidence of this.

Indeed, he was commanded to guard the atmosphere of peace and dialogue with the Treaty of Hudaybiya in these verses of the Qur'an: *"God does not forbid you, as regards those who do not make war against you on account of your Religion, nor drive you away from your homes, to be kindly to them, and act towards them with equity. God surely loves the scrupulously equitable"* (al-Mumtahana 60:8) and *"... so long as they remain true to you, be true to them"* (at-Tawbah 9:7). According to this, despite objections and that he had embraced Islam, in view of one of the clauses in the treaty the Messenger of God was forced to hand over Abu Jandal

---

154   *Sunan Abu Dawud*, Kitab al-Adab, 36/4842

who had taken refuge with the beloved Prophet, to his father Suhayl, thus displaying his loyalty to the treaty and desire for dialogue.

As a result, the Hudaybiya peace treaty meant that the Meccans and the tribes who were their allies would not experience any problems, including war, for ten years. The Messenger of God sent envoys to the rulers of neighboring countries in an attempt of establishing dialogue. In a short time, this proved to be successful. One of these leaders was Negus (Najashi).

So first, let's go back a little further into the history of Islam. Immediately following the Battle of Badr, Negus called Jafar ibn Abi Talib and his companions who were in Abyssinia. These Muslims were astonished to see Negus sitting on the ground wearing an old gown. Why would a king sit on the ground wearing old clothing for no reason!

Negus explained to the Muslims why he had invited them in these words: "I called you here to give you good tidings! One of my men has just returned from your country and informed me that God assisted His Messenger and perished the enemy. They came across them in Badr at a place known for its *miswak* trees. It's almost as if I can see the place, I used to tend to my camels there."

Before they departed, the Muslims who rejoiced at the news given to them by Negus asked: "O Majesty! Why do you sit on the ground and not on a throne or cushion, and why are you wearing old clothes?"

He replied: "I found in what was revealed to Jesus, that one of God's rights on His servants is that the servants should be humble before God whenever He gives them from His blessings. As God Almighty has given me the new blessing of Muhammad, I wanted to give you these tidings in the state of humbleness."

Fundamentally, this is the result of respecting others and displaying a kind attitude, having an open mind, not insisting that "You cannot think differently to me," and everybody recognizing their own status in life. None of the correspondences, the letters that were sent or the pursuit of an atmosphere of dialogue was in vain, but in the name of faith was establishing the foundation stone for a new civilization.

A short time after, the Meccans, who had still not recovered from the shock of defeat in the Battle of Badr, sent Amr ibn al-As and Abdullah ibn Abi Rabia to Abyssinia once again in an attempt of bringing the Muslims back to Mecca and getting revenge on them at least. They said:

"Let's bring those from whom we will take our revenge back from Abyssinia! We will send an envoy to the king and ask him to return Muhammad's companions and kill them in retaliation for our men they killed in Badr!"

So once again they gave the envoys valuable gifts to present to the king, and warned that they must take greater care to avoid experiencing a fiasco as they did previously. However, they were mistaken again.

In a short time, the Messenger of God heard of this and immediately sent Amr ibn Umayyah to Negus with a letter. Once again, this mutual dialogue was to give results; Negus was not to be deceived by their valuable gifts or elaborate words, but instead sent them back to Mecca empty handed.[155]

READING TEXT

Assessments regarding Tolerance and Leniency

- Even if their ideas differ from ours, we must be tolerant towards others and show them respect.
- It is not our duty to destroy souls, but rather to cleanse souls.
- We must always remember that we are the community of the Messenger of God, who even towards those who beat and wounded him prayed, "O God! Forgive and guide them to the path of truth for they do not recognize me; if they knew they would not do such a thing!" and not underestimate the problems this important man faced. (M. Fethullah Gülen)
- The demand in this period is not a new religion composed of the various world faiths, but tolerance and respect among the members of different religions.

---

[155] Mukrizi, *Imta al-Asma*, 1/22; Qurtubi, *Al-Jami*, 6/255; Hamidullah, Muhammad, *Al-Wasaiqu's-Siyasiyyah*, 99

- The golden rule of conduct is mutual toleration, seeing that we will never all think alike and we shall always see the truth in fragments and from different angles of vision. (Ghandi)
- When a person looks at a flower, how can he experience the beauty that flower spreads if he goes back to the past and observes the ugly visions in his imagination.
- Instead of complaining that the rosebush is full of thorns, be happy that the thorn bush has roses. (Goethe)

QUESTIONS

1- How should we perceive the verse *"There is no compulsion in religion"* (al-Baqarah 2:256)

   a. Everyone may practice the Islamic commands that they consider easy.

   b. Nobody can force another person to accept Islam.

   c. No one can be forced into practicing the religious commands.

   d. Anyone can perform the duties they wish and nobody can interfere.

2- What is the following verse of the Qur'an mainly emphasizing? *"Then, surely, with hardship comes ease. Surely, with hardship comes ease"* (ash-Sharh 94:5–6).

   a. That there is ease in everything in life.

   b. That there is ease in practicing religion.

   c. It is easy to obtain Paradise.

   d. A person can do anything he/she wishes.

3- Who were the Prophets to whom God gave the command *"Go, both of you, to the Pharaoh for he has exceedingly rebelled. But speak to him in gentle words, so that he might reflect and be mindful or feel some awe"* (Ta-Ha 20:43–44).

   a. Enoch and Jethro

   b. Jacob and Joseph

   c. Jesus and Muhammad

   d. Moses and Aaron

4- In this paragraph, which of the options below should fill the empty spaces? "Religion was made easy by God. In addition to the general rulings under normal conditions regarding the forms of worship prescribed in the Islamic faith called ...., there are also aspects of ease due to a valid excuse referred to as ...."

    a. concessions-commands

    b. permission-rulings

    c. commands-concessions

    d. rulings-permission

5- "A believer granted the morals of the Qur'an should eliminate evil with kindness, and never heed to impolite behavior. He must always opt for tolerance and gentleness and be forgiving towards those who act unfavorably."

What is emphasized in the paragraph above?

    a. We must be tolerant.

    b. We must be violent towards non-believers.

    c. We must retaliate for what others do to us.

    d. It is wrong to show kindness to those who do not appreciate kindness.

10.

BEING A COMMUNITY

"And hold fast all together to the rope of God, and never be divided" (Al Imran 3:103).

What is a Community?

A community is a structure comprising of people who consciously unite around a specific vision, thought and belief. God created the human as a social being, and sent him into this world dependent on his fellow creatures. Humans can only live and be content in a society. The Islamic faith gives great importance to Muslims living in communities and assisting each other both materially and spiritually.

The Qur'an states that God loves the believers who fight in His cause in ranks like solid structures.[156] In one of the Traditions, the Messenger of God said: "Believers are like the limbs of a body, when one limb hurts the entire body hurts."[157]

A community is a protecting shield and barrier against the melting and destroying waves of our age. The likelihood of a Muslim living alone making mistakes compared with those who live in communities is much greater. In addition, those who live individually are deprived of the radiant atmosphere granted to those living in communities. Communities act in a collective manner, and this is how it should be. There is a greater opportunity of direction and reaching the required targets in a community. On one hand is the solidarity of emo-

---

[156] As-Saff 61:4
[157] *Sahih al-Bukhari*, Adab, 27; *Sahih Muslim*, Birr, 17

tions and thoughts, and collective awareness of many people, while on the other, even if the person is a genius, there is the thoughts and ideas of a single individual... Indeed, there is no comparison between the two. Thus the wisdom in the words: "God is with the community."[158]

Communities are a Constant Source of Strength

In one of the *hadith*s, it is stated that a community is a source of strength and compassion while division is a source of destruction.[159] Additionally, we must never forget that any form of worship performed in congregation is twenty seven times more superior to individual worship.[160]

While 1 individually is of no particular value, if you put two 1's together this becomes 11 and when three 1's come together this becomes 111. Now following this example of simple numbers, let's consider this by comparing the light spread by 11 torches with that of 111 torches. This is the case when lifting something alone and in a group. So what if the alliance of capability and thought is then added to this. In addition, if there is collective exertion and determination together with the solidarity of effort and ideals, this begins to have an insuppressible impact on the hearts.

In the words of Fethullah Gülen, if you want to be a fruit producing tree exposed to compassion, then strive to be a tree in the forest. When you are alone, there is no compassion, you may become weak. However, compassion will certainly descend on the forest, and you will benefit from that compassion abundantly.[161]

As we explained earlier, humans were created as a social being. A person living alone may face difficulties against the winds of misguidance blowing deviously all around, and even worse, may become the target of the Satan's poisonous arrows of evil. Therefore, every human

---

158   *Sunan at-Tirmidhi*, Fitan, 7
159   *Al-Musnad* 4/145
160   *Sahih al-Bukhari*, Adhan, 30
161   Gülen, M. Fethullah, *İnancın Gölgesinde-2*, İstanbul: Nil, 2011, pp. 203–204

should avoid living alone and take refuge within the structure of the community.

READING TEXT

I Consider Living Among a Community a Guarantee of Salvation!

Maybe I am not a very fortunate person in terms of my relationship with God, if only I was; however, I am fortunate in terms of being among this distinguished community of unique people. I have thousands of self-sacrificing companions and tens of thousands of heroic brothers and sisters. Thousands of people, whose names and characters are unknown to me, continue to investigate various things around the world for the sake of our mutual ideals. Most of them are not acquainted with one another, they have never sat and spoke with me, but then what do I possibly have to give to these people?

However, these infatuated individuals journeyed out into the universe with sublime emotions; teaching humanity. In this aspect, at first they acquired certain disciplines from those they considered a source of reference; but then developed a system of thought, a conception of life and world philosophy; and are striving to revive this throughout the entire world. In view of this, I consider myself extremely fortunate. In fact, there are two aspects in which I consider myself fortunate:

Firstly; the movement of these volunteers, the heroes of no expectation, represents a great collective spiritual personality, and when this combines with their sincere efforts, this adds up to a significant number contributing to a huge system individuals could not achieve alone. They classify me as a member of this collective spiritual personality. I consider this the greatest means in terms of global prosperity, and a guarantee of the eternal bliss in the world beyond.

Secondly; I anticipate that at least one person from among so many individuals will witness my desolation as they pass by me on the Day of Reckoning, and will surely not abandon me to a life of such misery, but will assist me and intercede for me. Indeed, I bear hope that I will reach salvation by virtue of the intercession of my companions.

In all sincerity, I harbor this belief of all my companions and remember them all with great admiration. In particular, those I first mentioned, each of whom is a king, bear a special place in my heart. I consider all of these loyal companions in this manner; I am offended when they are offended, I am saddened when they are not taken seriously, and grieved when they are not appreciated.

Indeed, those who offend these devoted flag bearers offend me; those who underestimate these individuals, underestimate the service on the path of God, done in the difficult periods.[162]

There is a Demand of Communal Spirit

The solidarity of the hearts and actions is not only one of the key principles, but is also one of the main targets in the Islamic faith. In the name of expressing this reality, God revealed in the Qur'an:

> And hold fast all together to the rope of God, and never be divided. Remember God's favor upon you: you were once enemies, and He reconciled your hearts so that through His favor, you became like brothers. You stood on the brink of a pit of fire, and He delivered you from it. Thus, God makes His signs of truth clear to you that you may be guided (to the Straight Path in all matters, and be steadfast on it.) (Al Imran 3:103)

In view of this and similar verses of the Qur'an, Islamic scholars said: After recognition and bearing witness to the truth "There is no deity but God and Muhammad is the Messenger of God", there is a third fact that must be recognized, that believers are the brothers and sisters of one another, in other words, that they must live as a community and act accordingly.

The principles prescribed as a condition of the Islamic faith such as performing the prayers in congregation, the wealthy giving charity to the poor, performing the Hajj, and the Friday prayers and Eid Prayers being a weekly and yearly event for celebration are clear evidence of the importance Islam gives to guarding the community and communal spirit, and the necessity of reviving and maintaining this

---

162   Şimsek, Osman, *İbretlik Hatıralar*, İstanbul: Işık, 2012, pp. 281–282

spirit. The Messenger of God established brotherhood with the Ansar as soon as the Meccan migrants (the Muhajirin) reached Medina, but what was this emphasizing? Is this not signifying the necessity of communal spirit and the importance of establishing this spirit?

Particularly during a period surrounded by sin, the sentiment and opinion, "I can live both my religion and my faith alone" is by no means a sound conception. Almost everywhere is full of scenes enticing sin, whether this is in the streets, on the television, on the Internet, in newspapers, magazines and shop windows. Indeed, resisting such a terrible attack, guarding faith and morality in such a situation can only be achieved if the Muslims bond together and carry out the duty which represents the collective spiritual personality of Islam.

What are the Signs of Guarding the Communal Spirit?

1. We must never insult others, and avoid speech and actions that will harm the feelings and dignity of others. A believer must be self-criticizing and supportive to others. Investigating the shortcomings of others is an immoral act, and relating these shortcomings to others is a sinful act. If we do see mistakes in others, we should warn them with kindness and in a suitable manner.

2. A person must never consider himself superior to others, and should display humbleness. A believer must avoid succumbing to conceit and pride, and even if an individual holds a position of superiority, must never consider himself superior to others. Performing in such an honorable act, not only signifies the individuals maturity, but also the spiritual excellence of the community of which he is a member.

3. A believer must avoid disorder and corruption at all times, and must favor amendment. Indeed, true believers are the constant maintainers of peace, tranquility and security.

4. There is trustfulness between individuals of communal spirit. They trust one another and encourage trustworthiness. They

never disappoint their friends, or discourage them in their faith, devotion and enthusiasm in their service towards the Qur'an.

5. Success must not be attributed to the individual or to personal excellence, but rather to the Divine favor granted to the collective spiritual personality of the community. Such awareness is not only the means of unity and friendship, but is also a form of spiritual gratitude.

READING TEXT
The Most Excellent Community

Sufyan ibn Uyaynah related: "If people gather and mention the name of God, the Satan and the world depart. The Satan says sadly to the world: "Can you see what these humans are doing?"

The world consoles the Satan saying: "Do not approach them now... When they leave I will entice them one by one, and submit them to you."

This is why God's mercy is upon the community. Decisions regarding various beneficial actions emerge from communities, and the first seeds of the fruits of prosperity are sown in such gatherings.

If a person attends these gatherings frequently and conveys this spirituality into his home or workplace, this individual will reach salvation from the enticements of the Satan and the transient world. The atmosphere of these gatherings should be conveyed into every environment, the topics should be conveyed to others and life should be adorned with the enlightening discussions and opinions of these gatherings.

Those who say "If I am not there, I am with you spiritually" are the ones deprived of the atmosphere and light showering down upon such gatherings. As their deprivation is apparent from their actions in this world, it will also be apparent when those who attend these gatherings are rewarded in the Hereafter.

The words "I am with you spiritually" are as invalid as saying "I wish I was there" to those at a table-spread, and this is as unbeneficial as a student who demands a diploma without attending a school of Medicine but says "My heart was there."[163]

How Does Bediüzzaman Said Nursi Relate the Necessity of a Community?

In the words of Bediüzzaman Said Nursi, the sincere, loyal and devoted individuals who act with the collective principle in aspects regarding the Hereafter, each of the individuals who make solidarity and cooperation a principle between them and enforce this are not a single tongue, a single mind and a single heart, but are probably tongues, minds and hearts totaling their numbers of brothers who perform worship consciously and repent. In other words, thousands of tongues and hearts retaliate against the sins which attack from a thousand angles, and are therefore guarding themselves from the physical or spiritual dangers and damages.

There is a huge difference between an individual working alone and working in a community. As those who provide a service within a community not only benefit from those with whom they operate, but they also benefit from the representation in collective issues according to the honor of the community they represent and the commitment of their mutual agreements. Operating in a disorganized manner is not only extremely difficult, but its production is also limited. Whereas, based on an agreement and contract, each of the individuals who combine their various skills and practices with loyalty, who embraced their duties with passion and enthusiasm and advanced with the community are not only rewarded for their own efforts, but will also gain more than their fair share of the efforts and benefits of their fellow companions of cause. As a result, those of faith and piety who strive for the revival of Islam will not only obtain the rewards of their own actions and efforts because they have established a spiritual corporation of faith and piety, but they will also be granted the abundance and favors of God's exceptional prosperity and blessings.

---

163   Akar, Mehmet, *Mesel Ufku*, İstanbul: Timaş, 2008, p. 85

There are certain conditions of being a member of the collective spiritual personality, and benefitting from the general prosperity and profits of the community in the future such as loyalty, service, piety, performing obligatory duties, praying for friends of the same cause, and acting according to the laws of brotherhood. An individual may only benefit from the compassion and abundance if these conditions are fulfilled, and according to his intention. Therefore, those who secure eternal bliss may be a part of the community.

The Mercy of God Is with the Largest Group

In terms of good deeds, living in a community is quite a profitable move. Because when deeds which are simple and relatively insignificant are performed in a group or congregation, these are transformed into communal deeds and rewards. Indeed, living in a group or community means joining a spiritual organization that was established for the eternal world alone. The benefits of an organization which continues to operate with millions of participants will undoubtedly be much greater than that of an individual.

In the words "God's mercy, blessings and protection are with the largest group of Muslims,"[164] it is clear that God's compassion, benevolence and mercy are upon communities. Therefore, a community represented by a collective spiritual personality of devoted people must have such spirituality and awareness, that they may profit abundantly from the Divine mercy granted to the community.

Any individual who claims that he can overcome difficult material or spiritual issues alone is seriously mistaken. Deliberately abandoning ease and prosperity is clearly choosing destruction and deprivation. As this individual will attempt to solve, comprehend, see, hear and overcome issues with a single mind, a single heart, one pair of eyes and one pair of ears, or in other words by individual power and decision. Whereas those who live in a community, can solve problems and operate by meeting, conferring and obtaining opinions and skills of innu-

---

164   *Sunan at-Tirmidhi*, Fitan, 7; *Sunan an-Nasa'i*, Tahrim, 6

merous minds, hearts, eyes and ears, in brief, an extensive power and immense determination.

When the Messenger of God said, *"He who deviates from the largest group of Muslims, even as much as a hand span, has himself cut off his connection with Islam"*,[165] he is clearly expressing that Islam is a religion of collectivity, that it is necessary for Muslims to contribute to the community spirit, and live their religion as a community.

READING TEXT

A youth named Safa, who worked in one of the Central Asian countries while studying university there explained: "One of our friends qualified to study on a state grant. We were studying in the same class and faculty. He previously graduated from a vocational high school. He was staying in a student hostel belonging to the state university. When he went home during the summer holidays, his father noticed a huge change in him. His father, who became worried due to these negative changes said: "Son! There has been an immense change in you; I am not allowing you to return! Despite his persistence, but young man was unable to persuade his father. When he began to plead with his father, "But what about my education…" his father conditioned him, "I will only agree to send you if you live among decent, well behaved people."

So he agreed and promised that he would do as his father said. At the beginning of the term, because we were in the same class, he came to me and explained what had happened, and it was almost as if he was pleading with me to help him. He said "If I am going to study here, I must stay with you and your friends. This was my father's condition, or he will not allow me to remain here." I told him, "Well… maybe, but I must speak to my friends first." So I spoke to them almost immediately, but they were reluctant because he did not have a very good reputation. Despite my persistence, they did not agree. He came over to me every day in the classroom and asked "What happened?" Each time I

---

165   *Sunan at-Tirmidhi*, Amsal, 3

tried to pass it off by saying, "I am going to speak to them," hoping that he may understand.

His persistence continued, and I continued in my efforts of persuading my friends. Eventually, they said: "If you really want to, go and live with him yourself!" So I agreed, and I invited him to stay with me in an apartment I rented with a few other friends. Before long, this young man began to change and abandoned his bad habits. After a while, he turned into a completely different person, he spread light to all those around him. Both the youth, and other members of the neighborhood visited us frequently, they all loved him dearly.

One day, he suddenly became ill. We rushed him to the hospital, but the doctor "It's too late!" His appendix ruptured and somehow went unnoticed for a long time, and over time the leak from the appendix spread to other internal organs destroying them completely. We were advised: "Inform his family so they can come and see him for the last time." We phoned his family immediately. Indeed, his father arrived just before his death.

A few months passed. One night I saw him in my dream. We were sitting on the floor talking and drinking tea. He was sitting on one side, and another friend was sitting on the other. I asked him: "How did they treat you?"

He replied: "They treated me as if I am one of you. Here they do not cast people like you into Hell. This is why they admitted me into Paradise."

I woke up. I had tears rolling down my face. I was under the influence of that dream for hours. I sincerely hope that this extraordinary dream comes true."

Bediüzzaman Said Nursi gives tidings that, God willing, those who serve the Qur'an and faith will be rewarded with the eternal bliss, calling them as "believers and people of salvation."

May God increase the numbers of these people. His benevolence is unlimited. His gates of compassion are open to every plea performed with sincerity. As long as His servants do not stray from His caravan of eternity, His paths of radiance, from truth and justice, they are the fortunate ones.[166]

What Should Those Living in a Community Pay Attention To?

Those living in a community must pay attention to the points below, and make these a vital part of life:

1. They must love their fellow members of service for the sake of God and remain constantly in contact with them.

2. They must adopt the principle of becoming absorbed, lost in companionship. Losing oneself in companionship means reaching maturity in mutual love and affection, bearing a morality such that individuals willingly give preference to their brother or sister rather than themselves in every kind of material or spiritual favor. In which case, individuals enter into their world of thoughts and emotions and share their joy and sorrow.

3. They must never do anything without consultation, and respect the common views and opinions of their friends.

4. They should be at peace with everyone, and not argue with anybody.

5. They must be respectful to their elders and compassionate to the young.

6. They should base their behavior upon kindness.

7. They must pray for the material and spiritual success of their companions who constitute the collective spiritual personality, in the world and the Hereafter.

Grouping Should Not Be the Means of Division

Establishing a group or community is normal; the abnormal aspect is transforming these groups into the means of dispute and division. Just as there is an intense relationship between individuals constituting any group, the same relationship between the different groups is also

---

[166]   Akar, Mehmet, *Mesel Ufku*, İstanbul: Timaş, 2008, p.138

essential. When this is not executed, grouping results in division, disintegration and eventually fading away, whereas this is a huge disadvantage in Islam. The only means of avoiding this is integrating and guarding solidarity. However, at this point it will be beneficial to reflect certain principles regarding the matter:

1. No religious group should oppose another.
2. The members of groups should act respectfully towards the leaders of other groups and speak of them in a polite, respectable manner.
3. All of the religious groups should show concern with one another's problems, and share their joy.

Even if certain aspects may be difficult, it is our duty to force and convince ourselves regarding the matter.[167]

How Should We Perceive the *Hadith* "The Differences among My Community Are a Mercy"?

The word "differences" in the *hadith*, "The differences among my community are a mercy"[168] should be perceived as being the "differences in serving justice, in declaring different views and presenting different interpretations." Although Muslims believe in the same truths and principles, every person bears an individual character and structure of thought. This is why it is quite natural to have different approaches and views while analyzing events.

If Muslims are to solve their problems by consulting others, then everyone expresses their opinions in an open, sincere manner and states their knowledge and views in their own particular fields of expertise. In these terms, this will be a source of physical and spiritual development.

When Bediüzzaman Said Nursi interprets this *hadith* in his work called *The Letters*, he discusses it in the context of three question and answers, and also gives examples.

The question and answers are as follows:

---

[167]   Gülen, M. Fethullah, *Fasıldan Fasıla-1*, İzmir: Nil, 1997, p. 170
[168]   Nawawi, *Shar as-Sahih Muslim*, 11/91-92; Al-Qurtubi, *Al-Jami li Ahkam al-Qur'an*, 4/159; As-Suyuti, *At-Tadribu'r-Rawi*, 2/175

"**Question:** A Tradition says: "Difference among my community is a mercy." Difference requires partisanship that, although a social disease, does relieve the oppressed masses from an oppressive elite that, if united, tends toward tyranny. If there are [political] parties, the oppressed may protect themselves by joining one. Also, do you agree that different opinions and ideas allow the truth to shine forth?

Answer: In such a context, difference is positive, meaning that it allows each side to promote and propagate its own argument, to improve and reform a competing view instead of destroying it. The Prophet rejects a negative difference, for it seeks to destroy another side because of partisan bias and hostility. Those who are at each other's throats cannot act positively (toward each other). Partisanship in the name of truth can be a refuge for those seeking their rights. But the current biased and self-centered partisanship is only a refuge and a focus of support for the unjust. If devilish people support those engaged in biased partisanship, such partisans will call God's blessings upon them. Moreover, if angelic people join another side, the same partisans will call God's curses upon them.

If people differ in the name of truth, this is only a difference of means. In reality, it is an agreement and a unity with respect to aim and basic purpose. Such a difference can reveal all aspects of truth, and so serves justice and truth. But a confrontation between biased, partisan opinions driven by egotism and fame-seeking, one engendered by a tyrannical, carnal self, only can bring forth the flames of dissension. Opposing views based upon such a source can never converge, for only differences based upon seeking the truth in the name of a united purpose can do so. Since they do not differ in the name of truth, they split into extremes and give rise to irreconcilable divisions."[169]

Following these explanations we gave in brief, Bediüzzaman Said Nursi warns the believers in these words:

> O people of belief! If you wish to avoid such a fate, come to your senses. Take refuge in the citadel of your fellow believers and fight

---

169   Nursi, Said, *The Letters*, New Jersey: The Light, 2007, pp. 286–287

those oppressors who exploit your differences. If you do not, you cannot preserve your lives or defend your rights. While two champions fight each other, even a child can beat them. If two mountains are balanced in the scales, even a small stone can cause one to rise and the other to fall.

So, my fellow believers, control your passions and hostile partisanship, otherwise your strength will weaken so much that even a small force can beat you. If you have any commitment to a collective life of social harmony and solidarity, make the principle of "the believers are together like a firm building, one part of which supports the other" your guiding principle in life! This will deliver you from humiliation in this world and wretchedness in the next.[170]

READING TEXT

The Islamic Faith Is One Religion, So Why Do We Need Groups or Communities?

Let's attempt to answer this question by giving an example. Every organ in the human body performs different duties, and each bear different roles in sustaining life. So if the eye was to suggest "Come! All of you do my duty." This would be both damaging and impossible. Therefore, it is more appropriate for each of the organs to say "We should all have one objective, let each of us use its own power to maintain the body and life."

So we can also consider the differences in religious groups, schools of thought and spiritual orders in the same way. Each is like the different organs of the body. But each must bear a single objective, "serving humanity for the sake of God." When the objective is one, then it bears no significance if each bears a different name.

Another important aspect is that these groups fulfill their own duties without criticizing the other. If people are asked "Who is the world's greatest mother?" in general, each person will say "My mother is the greatest." Undoubtedly, every individual is right in his own way

---

[170]   Nursi, Said, *The Letters*, New Jersey: The Light, 2007, pp. 288–289

in responding like this. But this does not mean that other mothers are not great.

If we are asked what is the best occupation, the best temperament or school of thought? Obviously everyone will say "Mine is the best." And the others may also think the same, and nobody will consider this strange. In which case, the discrimination and hostility fades away.

Religious groups and communities are like limbs which strive to maintain the spiritual life of the society. In other words, these groups are, so to speak, the faculties of the university of Islam. And for as long as they bear a single objective in sharing this duty then—God willing—they would have attained God's pleasure.

In the same way that our existence is a blessing of God, our course of life is a role defined by God. In other words, God has provides us with everything necessary for being human. He does not need any other power to achieve this. Thus, certainly the foundation of Prophethood which systemized the regulations stipulated by God was established, and is managed by God. Therefore, primarily the Qur'an, then the Traditions of the Messenger of God are our means of guidance. The schools of legal thought which benefit from these two sources are religious organs which bring us closer to God. The principles and regulations that these schools convey are based entirely on the Qur'an and the Traditions of the noble Prophet. In view of this, they are the indispensable constituents of faith and Islam.

If these groups are based entirely on piety and the pleasure of God, then they are considered to be guides in the Islamic faith. Indeed, scholars who lead these groups have good comprehension of self-interrogation: "How can I earn God's pleasure, how can I unite these people with God?" Due to this, we must consider every order they give in accordance with the principles prescribed by God, as a part of the Islamic faith, because whatever they convey originates from the Qur'an and the Traditions of the Prophet.[171]

---

171   www.hikmet.net

QUESTIONS

1- Which of the words below should fill the empty space in this verse? "*And hold fast all together to the .... of God, and never be divided*" (Al Imran 3:103).

   a. hand

   b. rope

   c. power

   d. throne

2- Which of the following is not a necessity in bearing the communal spirit?

   a. A person must avoid words and actions which may hurt the feelings and honor of others.

   b. A believer must avoid provocation and always be in favor of reform.

   c. An individual must have a career.

   d. A person should not consider him/herself superior to others, and must display humbleness at all times.

3- Which of the following options should fill the empty space in this tradition of the Prophet? "God's .....and ......are with the largest group of Muslims."

   a. kindness and assistance

   b. mercy and power

   c. mercy, blessings and protection

   d. kindness and power

4- Establishing a group or community is normal; the abnormal is transforming these groups into the means of dispute and division. In order to practice this, which of the following should not be taken into consideration?

   a. No religious group or order should oppose another.

   b. Every religious group or order should impose their own ideas and opinions on the other groups, and create an atmosphere of dispute by doing so.

c. The individuals of these groups should act respectfully towards the leaders of these groups and speak of them in a polite, respectable manner.

d. All of the religious groups should be concerned with one another's problems, and share their joy.

5- What will be the result of having no commitment to a collective life of social harmony and solidarity?

a. Humiliation in this world and wretchedness in the next

b. Success

c. Fame

d. Power

11.

SENSITIVITY REGARDING THE PROHIBITED AND THE LAWFUL

Numan ibn Bashir said: "I heard the Messenger of God say, 'What is lawful is clear and what is unlawful is (also) clear. But between the two are doubtful matters of which many people do not know. He who protects himself from doubtful matters clears himself in regard to his faith and honor. But he who falls into doubtful matters is like a shepherd who grazes (his sheep) around a sanctuary, and (liable) to graze therein. Surely, every king has a sanctuary. Surely, the sanctuary of God is His prohibitions. Surely, in the body is a piece of flesh, and if it is sound, the whole body is sound; and if it is damaged, the body is diseased. Surely, it is the heart.'"[172]

What Do Lawful and Prohibited (*Halal* and *Haram*) Mean?

Lawful defines that which is not prohibited in the Islamic faith, whereas prohibited defines that which is not lawful.

That which has not been defined as prohibited is permissible. God revealed: *"It is He Who created all that is in the world for you"* (al-Baqarah 2:29) *"Do you not see that God has made all that is in the heavens and all that is on the earth of service to you"* (Luqman 31:20). These verses of the Qur'an state that God created many blessings for mankind. That which was not prohibited to eat, drink or use in the Qur'an and Traditions of the noble Prophet are permissible, and that prohibited is unlawful.

Sahih al-Bukhari, Iman, 39

In this chapter, we will be discussing and analyzing the prohibitions and lawful aspects of food, drink, clothing, household goods, the fields of work and income, occupation and transactions which exist in both the family and social lives, and generally aspects which mainly concern the younger members of the Islamic faith.[173]

1. The Prohibited and Lawful Aspects Regarding Food and Drink

Complying with certain conditions, all foods and drinks, with the exception of those stipulated in the Qur'an, are stated as being permissible,[174] in addition, it also states that nobody has the right to render what God has deemed prohibited as permissible, or what God has deemed permissible as prohibited.[175] One of the points emphasized in the Qur'an is that sustenance should be "lawful and pure."[176] Even if these foods are lawful, the Qur'an still forbids excessiveness and waste in terms of eating and drinking.[177]

One of the main aims in forbidding certain foods and drinks is to maintain the physical and spiritual health of humans. The substances which are proved to be damaging to the human body both physically and spiritually are classified forbidden in the Islamic faith. Substances which have an intoxicating effect are also among the things prohibited in Islam.

Animals Whose Meat is Permissible and Prohibited

1. ANIMALS THAT LIVE ON LAND

The religious ruling regarding eating the meat of land animals can be categorized according to their characteristics as follows:

---

173   Information in this section regarding the Islamic principles was obtained from the *Ilmihal* published by the Turkish Religious Foundation.

174   Al-An'am 6:140; al-A'raf 7:32

175   Al-Ma'idah 5:87; al-An'am 6:140; at-Tahrim 66:1; at-Taubah 9:37

176   Al-Baqarah 2:168; al-Ma'idah 5:88; al-Anfal 8:69; an-Nahl 16:114

177   Al-An'am 6:141; al-A'raf 7:31

a) Scholars are in agreement that there are four groups of animals whose meat is permissible:

1. Domesticated animals such as cattle, sheep, goat, camel, rabbit, chicken, goose, duck and turkey.

2. Wild animals such as deer, antelope, mountain goats, wild cattle and zebras.

3. Islamic scholars are in agreement that the meat of birds such as pigeons, sparrows, quail, starlings and herons is permissible.

4. Locust is also included in the grouping of animals permissible to eat due to the special ruling in the Tradition of the Prophet stating that it may be eaten.[178]

b) There are three groups of animals whose meat is classified as prohibited by the consensus of the scholars:

1. The clear ruling in the Qur'an states that swine meat (pork) is prohibited.[179] The pig is the only animal to be prohibited by species in the Qur'an.

2. The prohibition of eating meat slaughtered in a name other than that of God is also based on the clear ruling in the Qur'an.[180]

3. The prohibition of eating meat which was not slaughtered in accordance with the Islamic ruling and the meat of dead animals (animals that died due to material causes) is also based on Qur'anic jurisprudence.[181]

c) Eating the meat of animals not listed in the groups above is a topic of dispute among scholars.

While certain animals are classified as either permissible or prohibited by the consensus of a majority of scholars, we see that opinions regarding some animals are distributed equally.

---

178 *Sahih al-Bukhari*, Zabaih, 13: *Sahih Muslim*, Zabaih, 52
179 Al-Baqarah 2:173
180 Al-An'am 6:121
181 Al-Baqarah 2:173

Animals categorized as beasts of prey, in other words animals that hunt and catch their prey using the four fangs found in their upper and lower jaws, and protect themselves with these fangs—whether domesticated or not—such as wolves, lions, tigers, leopards, monkeys, hyenas, dogs and cats, and birds of prey namely falcons, hawks, eagles and vultures that catch their prey with their claws, and although they do not bear these features, birds which generally feed on filth such as ravens and crows, and creatures which are filthy by nature such as rats and snakes and insects like scorpions, flies and spiders, are all classified as prohibited by a majority of Islamic scholars.

2. SEA CREATURES

It is revealed in the Qur'an that foods obtained from the sea are lawful.[182] The noble Prophet replied to a question regarding the sea in these words, "Its water is pure and its dead are lawful."[183] Both these statements and the principle of the permissibility of subjects that have no special ruling, constitutes the basis for the ruling of creatures living in the sea.

1. All kinds of fish are permissible according to all schools, and slaughtering fish is not necessary. However, according to the Hanafi school, it is not permissible to eat fish that died due to material causes and floats on the water surface. The Hanafi opinion on this matter is based on health aspects. But fish that die due to the extreme heat or cold, being trapped in ice or water and washed up onto the shore are not classified as dying due to material causes, and can be eaten. Again, if fish die after throwing fish poison into the water while trying to catch the fish, but die before being caught and it is absolutely clear that they died due to this reason, or if larger sea creatures such as the sword fish is killed by a blow to the head with a heavy object before it is taken out of the water, it can be eaten.

---

182   Al-Ma'idah 5:96; Fatir 35:12

183   *Sunan Abu Dawud*, Tahara, 41; *Sunan at-Tirmidhi*, Tahara, 52

2. According to the Hanafi school, eating sea creatures other than fish (mussels, frogs and crabs) is not permissible, whereas according to the other three legal schools, any creature which lives in water—even if it dies due to material causes—is permissible and can be eaten. There is an opinion in the Shafi school, in parallel with the Hanafi view, that water creatures resembling land animals whose meat is permissible is allowed, and those which resemble land animals whose meat is prohibited are classified as unlawful.

Drinks

In the Islamic faith, every kind of drink which causes intoxication, affects the mental and spiritual balance, and numbs the nervous system was prohibited.[184] The noble Prophet related these words on the subject: "Everything that intoxicates is alcohol and alcohol is forbidden"[185] "Whatever intoxicates in large quantities is forbidden in small quantities."[186]

In view of the Qur'anic verses and Traditions of the Prophet regarding this topic, any kind of drink which intoxicates was deemed prohibited by all legal schools. Over a period of time, drinks which cause intoxication become addictive. A person who drinks these in small quantities will eventually begin to drink more, because as the addiction develops the need to increase this amount will also increase as it will not have the same effect.

In one of the *hadith*s, those who produce wine (alcoholic drinks), those who have it produced, who drink it, transport it, to whom it was delivered, who serves and sells it, those who benefit from its income, those who purchase it and the ones for whom it was purchased are seriously condemned.[187] In view of this *hadith*, a majority of scholars

---

184   Al-Baqarah 2:219; An-Nisa 4:43

185   *Sahih al-Bukhari*, Abad, 80; *Sahih Muslim*, Ashriba, 73

186   Tirmidhi Drinks 3; *Sunan Abu Dawud*, Ashriba, 5

187   *Sunan Abu Dawud*, Ashriba, 2; *Sunan at-Tirmidhi*, Buyu', 58; *Sunan ibn Majah*, Ashriba, 6

are in agreement that, to avoid assisting others to commit sin,[188] it is prohibited even to sell grapes to wine producers.

Is Smoking Prohibited?

One of the most widespread and probably the most disputed addiction is the addiction of smoking.

As it is impossible to claim in this day that smoking is not harmful, it is quite evident that the topic should be within the boundaries of the religious prohibitions. Scientists emphasize that in addition to cancer and defects in the nervous system, the nicotine found in cigarettes and the smoke from cigarettes causes huge damage and many other diseases. God Almighty states in the Qur'an: "*...do not ruin yourselves by your own hand*" (al-Baqarah 2:195). The Messenger of God emphasized that not harming oneself or others is an Islamic principle: "There should be neither harming nor reciprocating harm."[189] Taking into consideration that smoking harms the individual and those around him, then we can say that the rights of God and the rights of others are violated.

There is also the aspect of waste. Waste is spending money without necessity. The Qur'an tells us "*...eat and drink, but do not be wasteful...*" (al-A'raf 7:31), and the noble Prophet commanded the people to behave with moderation at all times, and forbade them to spend extravagantly. If we consider the addiction of the individual addicted to smoking, the conception that the expenditure on cigarettes, or indeed what can be considered as a significant provision of constitutional needs, is not wasteful expenditure—in addition to wasteful expenditure, the aspect of smoking being harmful—is totally inconsistent. The fact that a person may be wealthy does not eliminate the factor that this expenditure is a waste.

This point should not be ignored: The head of the family is the man; he cares for his wife, children, members of the family and relatives in need, and bears the responsibility of providing for them. Those under

---

[188]   Al-Ma'idah 5:2
[189]   *Sunan ibn Majah*, Ahkam, 17; *Muwatta*, Aqdiya, 31

such a huge financial commitment spending money on cigarettes to the extent that they fail to fulfill this duty is not only unacceptable religiously, but also humanely and morally unacceptable.

The religious ruling regarding smoking may be considered from many different angles, in particular aspects such as the damage to health, waste and the responsibility of maintaining a family. In view of all these facts, we can say that smoking is unlawful. Addictions such as the water pipe (*narghila*) and snuff can also be evaluated on the same basis. In addition, due to the fact that the effects of drugs such as marijuana, heroin, cocaine and morphine exceed that of alcohol, these substances are also prohibited.

READING TEXT
There is One Account that I Cannot Answer for!

Fethullah Gülen narrates: "On his deathbed, my uncle continuously lost consciousness just like my father did, and when he opened his eyes, told those at his bedside, "There is one right that I cannot overcome!" At the time, Seyfettin effendi, the imam's son was beside him.

Whenever he had the strength to speak, he repeatedly said "Seyfettin effendi, they brought a cart full of accounts before me!" There was no need for you to walk down so and so street, why did you go there? When you went to so and so place, you should have lowered your gaze, why did you lift your head and gaze at what was forbidden? Why did you not guard your ears at so and so place and you heard bad things? There were so many accounts to be given… He groaned "I am trying to answer all these questions; I am struggling to overcome these sensitive questions with honor. But there is one question that I just cannot answer for!" Yes, my mother's elder brother, my blessed uncle…

If only I knew what that question was, I would give anything to settle this account; and I would suffer the consequences to relieve him of this burden. But I have no idea what it was."[190]

* * *

---

[190]   Şimsek, Osman, *İbretlik Hatıralar*, İstanbul: Işık, 2012, pp. 43–44

Osman Şimsek explains: In the opinion of our honorable teacher, even if a person—because he has no other income—eats and drinks things which are not forbidden but are doubtful, it is wrong for him to restrict his family's livelihood accordingly. A person must provide for his family with legitimate means. Our respected teacher, Fethullah Gülen, has always recognized his duty of guidance—and personally—his duty of servitude; he considered the state income earned in return for his services questionable, and only used a necessary portion of this salary.

He spent a major part of his life in extreme poverty; and remained hungry for days in fear of "unlawful earnings." During the years when he worked for the state on a low income, his salary, which he spent mainly on his travels and efforts on the path of serving the faith and virtues, was limited. It would have been difficult for this honorable scholar, who lived such a humble life that he was content with eating boiled potatoes due to financial hardship, to provide for somebody else under such difficult conditions; even if this was for the livelihood of a family, it would have been almost impossible for him to undertake such a responsibility.

In the earlier stages of his life when he considered marriage, he asked himself frequently, "Will I be forced to resort to an illegitimate livelihood? Will I abandon my main duty and aspire the worldly pleasures?"[191]

2. The Permissible and Prohibited Aspects of Clothing and Adornment

In general, among the whole of existence covering the body is a virtue unique to humans. In every era, nudity has been considered an act of shame and immodesty by societies of conscience and reason.

The command of covering the body in the Islamic faith is aimed at various objectives including guarding the spiritual health and honor of individuals, the general morality of the society, to maintain the balance between denominations and people in relationships, and establish a family life befitting to the human honor. The different rulings in the

---

[191]   *Ibid.*, p. 89

covering of males and females are a distinction made to guard the characteristics in the creation of man and woman.

In Islamic literature, the parts and organs of the body prohibited to reveal, display and look at are defined as *"awrat"* (private parts). In addition to the obligation of males and females covering the necessary parts of the body in general, the term *satr al-awrat* is mainly used to define covering the specific parts of the body during the Prayers. Just as covering the private parts of the body during the Prayers is a religious obligation, covering these parts of the body in general is also classified as a religious duty. However, the limits of covering the body vary according to sexes and whether those present are permissible to marry or not in the Islamic faith. Therefore, in the Islamic jurisprudence, covering the body can be divided in three categories; covering during the Prayer, covering before close family, and covering before strangers.

The parts of the body that males must cover during the Prayers and generally before other men, and women other than their wives, is the area from the navel to the knees. This is the general opinion of a majority of Islamic scholars, but there are certain differences in opinion regarding the boundaries of covering the private parts.

According to the Hanafi and Shafi schools, the private parts a woman must cover before other women and their *mahram* (males never permissible to them for marriage) is the same as males (from the navel to the knees). The majority opinion in the Maliki and Hanbali schools is that before *mahram* males, all parts of the body with the exception of the hands, face, head, neck, arms, feet and calves are classified as private parts and must be covered.

A woman's *awrat* in front of non-*mahram* males (males permissible for marriage) is the whole body with the exception of the face, hands and feet.

ARE MEN PROHIBITED FROM WEARING GOLD AND SILK CLOTHING?

In the Islamic faith, men are prohibited from wearing gold and silk clothing. The Messenger of God said gold and silk are forbidden for men, but are permissible for women,[192] and that whoever wears silk in this world will not wear it in the Hereafter.[193]

The Prophet, who prohibited believers from eating and drinking from gold utensils,[194] warned the believers in another *hadith* that whoever wears silk, on the Day of Judgment, God will dress him in a garment of fire.[195]

Scholars of Islamic law say the reasons for the prohibition of men wearing gold and silk is extravagance and conceit, that this will incite envy among the poor and changing the nature of men, will make them appear feminine.

3. The Permissible and Forbidden Regarding Art and Entertainment

IS PAINTING AND SCULPTURING PROHIBITED?

Islam, the religion of unification eliminated polytheism, a widespread form of belief and worship during that period. Polytheism was based on glorifying and worshipping paintings and sculptures. In view of the noble Prophet's words, Islamic scholars objected to pictures and sculptures. The Arabs of that period worshipped the paintings and sculptures they drew and created with their own hands. Due to the fear that the people would revert to their old customs, the Messenger of God chose to forbid the paintings and figures that would remind them of these customs.

These are a few of the Prophet's Traditions on the subject: According to a report by the Prophet's dear wife Aisha, the Prophet broke everything in his house that was made in the shape of a cross.[196]

---

[192]   *Sunan ibn Majah*, Libas, 19; *Sunan Abu Dawud*, Libas, 1; *Sunan at-Tirmidhi*, Libas, 1

[193]   *Sahih al-Bukhari*, Libas, 25; *Sahih Muslim*, Libas, 6,7,21; *Sunan Abu Dawud*, Libas, 7

[194]   *Sahih al-Bukhari*, At'ima, 28; *Sahih Muslim*, Libas, 5

[195]   Haysami, *Majma al-Zawaid wa Manba al-Fawaid*, 5/141

[196]   *Sahih al-Bukhari*, Libas, 90

"On the Day of Judgment, artists will experience the severest of punishments. On the Day of Judgment, those who create figures will be commanded, "Give life to your creation" and when they fail they will be punished."[197]

Once, the noble Prophet's dear wife Aisha brought a cushion with pictures (of animals) on it. When Aisha noticed the sign of displeasure on the Prophet's face, she said, "O Messenger of God! I ask forgiveness from God and His Messenger. Have I committed sin?" Indicating the cushion, the noble Prophet asked "What is this?" His dear wife said, "I brought it for you to sit and recline on." The Messenger of God replied: "Those who create these pictures will be punished on the Day of Judgment. They will be commanded, "Give life to your creation." And he added: "The angels do not enter houses where there are pictures."[198]

Our mother Aisha hung a curtain at the door of her house. When the Messenger of God returned from a journey and saw the curtain, he said "Those who will receive the severest punishment on the Day of Judgment are the ones who try to create a resemblance of God's creation."[199]

As we mentioned earlier, Islam emerged during a period in which polytheism was a widespread practice. Therefore, the Messenger of God acted with great caution towards anything that may distance the people from belief in unification and encourage polytheism. So we must analyze the noble Prophet's words above accordingly, and fully understand the wisdom in these statements.

Incidentally, Islamic scholars emphasize that painting and hanging pictures of scenery such as mountains, trees and rocks, and pictures of figures which do not completely reflect the human body is permissible.

READING TEXT

There were many God fearing people who worshiped Him day and night. They had great affection for Him, and He loved them and never

---

197   *Ibid.*, 89
198   *Ibid.*, 95
199   *Ibid.*, 91

rejected their supplications. The people had great love and respect for these servants loved by God. So the Satan decided to take advantage of the situation.

When these companions of God died, the Satan mingled among the people, and with every opportunity began to remind them of these companions of God they loved so dearly.

"What were they like?"

"Good gracious! What kind of a question is that? They were totally devoted to God, and He never rejected their prayers."

"How much do you miss them?"

"We miss them immensely, our grief is indescribable."

"So you long to see them, is this true?"

"Yes, we want to see them so much!"

"Then why do you not look at them every day?"

"What do you mean? Is this possible? They are dead, they have departed from this world."

"In that case, you can look at their paintings and statues!"

So the people are convinced by the Satan's words, they do paintings and drawings of these righteous individuals, and begin to look at these paintings every day in an attempt of relieving their sorrow. Over a period of time, they turn to statues. They place these statues in their homes and their temples.

Those who first created these paintings and statues were worshipping God, and not associating any partners with God. They realized that these statues were made of stone, and were of no benefit or harm however, they persisted in glorifying these objects of stone. Day by day, these statues increased in number, and as the statues increased, the people's respect for them became even greater. Displaying respect and devotion to these statues became a way of life, and to such an extent that when a righteous person died, making a statue of that person immediately after his death was considered an important duty.

As generations passed, children and grandchildren witnessed their fathers and grandfathers respecting, bowing before and worshipping these statues. The children overshadowed their fathers in respect for the statues, in time they began to prostrate and pray to them for their requirements, and had also began sacrificing animals for the statues.

Eventually, these statues became an object of idolization, and each had become an interceder of polytheism. So, once again the Satan had defeated his eternal enemy.

IS LISTENING TO MUSIC PERMISSIBLE?

Music is probably one of the most controversial, most disputed topics among Islamic scholars of the present day. In view of the basis for reasons, both in favor and against music, we reach the conclusion that music was not completely forbidden.

However, singing songs and listening to music containing words of blasphemy and encouraging disobedience, words considered unfavorable in Islam or which entice forbidden things such as sexual provocation and obscenity is strictly forbidden.

IS GAMBLING PROHIBITED?

Gambling is the means of unjustified income which encourages human idleness, eliminates earning by effort, sows the seeds of grudge and hostility among people, destroys families and entices people from their duties of servitude. All kinds of gambling was deemed unlawful in the Qur'an: *"And do not consume your wealth among yourselves in false ways (in vanities, sins and crimes such as theft, usurpation, bribery, usury, and gambling)"* (al-Baqarah 2:188) and *"O you who believe! Intoxicants, games of chance, sacrifices to (anything serving the function of) idols (and at places consecrated for offerings to any other than God), and (the pagan practice of) divination by arrows (and similar practices) are a loathsome evil of Satan's doing; so turn wholly away from it, so that you may prosper (in both worlds)"* (al-Maedah 5:90).

As revealed in the Qur'anic verses, gambling is unjustly obtaining the wealth of others. In addition, this is a deceiving disease which induces sins such as lying, drinking alcohol, greed, revenge and murder. This is why the Messenger of God told the people to abstain when such a sin is even mentioned by saying: "When any of you says to his friend 'come let us gamble' he should give alms in expiation."[200]

IS PLAYING CHESS AND BACKGAMMON PROHIBITED?

In order for the game of chess to be classified as permissible, there are for conditions:

1. The players should not become so engrossed in the game that they forget the Prayers.
2. Chess should not be played with the expectation of winning money or the like, in other words, the winner or loser must not stipulate conditions of gain.
3. Those who are playing must avoid speaking unfavorably, lying, gossip and abuse during the game.
4. Whoever plays chess should not become addicted to the game to the extent that he cannot give up.

In which case, chess is permissible on the condition that the player does not overindulge, that the game does not prevent the duties of servitude or encourage sin.

The Islamic scholars, who approach the permissibility of chess because of the nature of the game, abstain from backgammon and describe the difference between chess and backgammon in these words: "Backgammon is a game is based on the dice, whereas chess is based on thought and mental skill."

As a result, it is only possible to build the structure of jurisprudence after understanding the principle. The principle here is: If these kinds of games are based on thought and calculation, then they are permissible. This is the case with chess. However, if a game is based on the dice and prediction, then it is prohibited, which is the case with backgammon.

4. The Prohibitions and Lawful Aspects of Sexual Relations

The Islamic faith, which adopts the principle of fulfilling not only the psychological and spiritual requirements, but also the physical require-

---

200   *Sahih Muslim*, Ayman, 5

ments in a reasonable and balanced manner, deals with human sexuality as a fact of life, however, by placing certain restrictions in an attempt of guarding and maintaining sexual life, it also aims at preventing behavior contradictory to human honor and values.

Marrying and guarding chastity, fulfilling the bodily desires within the lawful boundaries, and maintaining a regular and healthy sexual life is an act which Islam commands and encourages, and is therefore included in the concept of "worship." The Qur'an reveals, *"And among His signs is that He has created for you, from your selves, mates, that you may incline towards them and find rest in them, and He has engendered love and tenderness between you. Surely in this are signs for people who reflect"* (ar-Rum 30:21) and refers to believers who guard their chastity and are content with the lawful sexual relations within marriage with praise.[201] The Messenger of God encouraging marriage, advising the believers to guard the union of marriage whenever possible, ascribing certain roles regarding the subject on parents and the state, disapproving of celibacy and criticizing those who practiced monasticism are aimed at the same objective, as the other religious duties can be performed better within a balanced, peaceful family life.

In the same way that guarding chastity and honor constitutes the general religious and moral law of sexual life in the Islamic faith, the forbiddance of fornication and prohibition of actions which may lead to unlawful relations and violating honor were measures in guarding the same law. Because guarding a value is only possible if it is protected, either directly or indirectly from aspects of threat which may cause violation.

ALL ACTS OF FORNICATION ARE PROHIBITED

Since the early times, fornication (*zina*), which means sexual relations between two individuals who are not married, was deemed an act that corrupted the mind, morality and legal order, and considered wrong, shameful and evil among the other Divine religions, and totally forbid-

---

[201]   Al-Mu'minun 23:5-6

den by the Islamic faith, is considered one of the major sins and certain measures were taken to prevent this evil act.

However, forbidding fornication alone would not be sufficient in guarding the individuals within the society and family life, and ensuring a healthy sexual life. In addition, it is necessary to fight against all aspects of immodesty, prostitution and obscenity considered evil and shameless both in religion and by human nature, and amending environments which support and generalize these acts of evil. This is why the Islamic faith not only prohibited fornication, but in an attempt of guarding and improving family life also made a point of preventing aspects which lead to fornication and obscenity, to excessiveness in male and female relations and extreme permissiveness, and in addition imposed moral maturity on individuals and personal responsibility, and gave certain rights and duties to partners regarding sexuality.

In the Qur'an, fornication and prostitution are classified as major sins, and it also mentions the punishment of fornication in this world and the Hereafter,[202] and also commands men and women to guard their eyes from looking at anything unlawful and to cover their private parts, thus signifying that one of the paths leading to fornication will be obstructed.[203] In one of the Traditions, by mentioning the fornication of organs such as the tongue, mouth, hands, feet and eyes,[204] the Messenger of God defines that any kind of unlawful relationship, flirtation and intimacy which are the basis of fornication, are acts of immorality and commanded the people to avoid such acts. As chastity and modesty are an entirety, the only means of protecting this is by avoiding all kinds of evil and sin which are a threat.

Males and females are a sexual stimulant to one another. Therefore it is necessary for the men and women (those permitted to marry) to maintain a "distance." Again, in view of the problems that may arise, a man and woman are not permitted to be alone together. In Islamic law, a man and woman who are permitted to marry being alone together is referred to as "*khalwat*" (seclusion, isolation). In one of the Traditions,

---

202   Al-Imran 3:135; an-Nisa 4:15-16; al-Isra 17:32
203   An-Nur 24:30–31
204   *Sahih Muslim*, Qadar, 5

the Messenger of God said: "Whoever believes in God and the Last Day should never be in privacy with a woman without her *mahram* (close family member), because the third one present is the Satan."[205] Such a situation could provoke temptation, lead to fornication or gossip, and cause damage to the honor of the individuals in question.

In relationships between the sexes, it is a collective responsibility of both the men and women to guard their moral principles. Based on the characteristic of sexual stimulation, women are ordered to act with greater care. When speaking to a man, women must make a point of speaking in a serious manner that will not arouse doubt or lead the other person to any misunderstanding,[206] they must not display their beauty and adornments to men,[207] thus covering themselves in an appropriate manner when they leave the home[208] is a command aimed at this point.

The Messenger of God considered it unfit for women to wear perfume outside the home to the extent that others can smell the scent.[209]

IS WATCHING OBSCENE FILMS AND LOOKING AT OBSCENE PICTURES PROHIBITED?

In general, moral corruption begins by looking at obscenity, and this develops with the persistence of these glances and eventually turns to sin. Furthermore, the eyes record the images they see, and store this in the records of the imagination. Wherever the person goes, these images continuously appear in his mind. If this individual is a student, it prevents him from studying, if the person works, he cannot focus on his job, or if the individual is a man of thought, he cannot concentrate; so there is a probable decline, deterioration in every aspect. In order to avoid such a situation, the Islamic faith imposes prohibitions regarding looking at obscene images, thus saving Muslims from succumbing to such detriment.

---

205   *Sahih Muslim*, Hajj 74; *Sunan at-Tirmidhi*, Rada, 16; *Al-Mustadrak* 1/114
206   Al-Ahzab 33:32
207   An-Nur 24:31
208   An-Nur 24:31; al-Ahzab 33:59
209   *Sunan at-Tirmidhi*, Adab, 35; Rada, 13; *Al-Musnad* 4/414, 418

Whether these are aimed at sexual provocation or not, producing and making films and pictures classified within the Islamic boundaries of nudity is prohibited. Watching and selling these films and pictures is also prohibited. It is prohibited because fundamentally, direct nudity, or observing nudity by watching films and looking at pictures is aimed at the same unlawful objective.

We must not restrict nudity or obscene films and pictures to women alone. There is no discrimination between the sexes, as the sin for the nudity of women and men is equal. Whoever it may be, exposing and looking at what is classified as the private parts is prohibited.

READING TEXT
Why the Young Man Held His Finger over a Flame

Harikzadeler Street... This is the name of one of the streets I encountered while walking down from Şehzade Mosque towards Laleli Mosque. Harikzadeler... That is, "those escaping the fire"...

Who knows which number this fire constituted in İstanbul's wooden buildings? It was a night where the chill of winter burnt like fire. The formidable fire that was to later become the eponym of that street had also broken out in the latter half of such a night, in a wooden house. Those who were able to escape the flames that engulfed the area within a short time managed to save themselves. The young woman who tore herself away onto to the street, in the light of the flames, was one of these. Confused as to what to do and where to go, a light coming from the windows of one of the *madrasa*s adjoining the Şehzade Mosque had given her hope. She could no longer have withstood this cold, which caused her teeth to chatter. She opened the door of the *madrasa*, which is currently a dormitory for female students, and entered.

When the engrossed student, studying a Qur'anic commentary under the light emitted onto the walnut reading desk by the oil lamp, raised his head, he could not make any sense of this: "Who are you? Human or ghost? What are you doing here at this time of night?"

"I am not a ghost, but one of your sisters in faith. The fire which erupted in our neighborhood engulfed us also. I was barely able to escape and took refuge here."

"No way! I am a student who is currently studying the commentary of the Qur'an. I have to steer clear of behavior that raises suspicion. If they see you here, it will be impossible to stop the rumors. You must leave right away!"

"If I leave at this time of night, I'll freeze!"

Murmuring something under his breath, the student of the Qur'an began to think...

"I hope this isn't a bad sign. Perhaps we are being tested?"

A few minutes' silence...

"Then wrap yourself up in the rug below this wall over here and take a rest in the corner."

Continuing his perusal and study of Baydawi's exegesis, the student began to struggle with his devil as the minutes went by.

At one point exclaiming, "No!" he held his finger over the flame and insisted on keeping it there until his skin contracted.

The struggle continued until morning. The finger held several times to the flame was a good deal burned, with a wound even emerging on its tip. It was almost daybreak. The student who was later to graduate from Law and become a judge left the *madrasa* with the recital of the morning call to Prayer and went to the mosque. When he returned to see that no one was left in his room, he breathed a sigh of relief.

The young woman, who rushed to the scene of the blaze with the daylight, screamed when she saw her father and mother frantically searching for her.

"Father, mother, I am here, I am here!"

"Where were you last night?"

"Right here, in a room in the *madrasa*, near one of the students."

And the young woman explained what had happened.

Her father, an Ottoman Pasha, then took his daughter with him to the presence of the teacher of Qur'anic exegesis at Şehzade Mosque, requesting him to gather his students. The teacher was downcast and his students bewildered. They were concerned that one student exhibited behavior towards the young woman that was deemed improper...

Surveying the gathered students one by one, the young woman eventually indicated to one in particular and said: "That's him, father! The student whose fingertip is bandaged."

The teacher of Qur'anic exegesis asked with great astonishment: "Salahaddin, I would never have expected this from you! How could you give rise to such a complaint?"

Just as Salahaddin lowered his head and was unable to utter a single word due to his shame before his teacher, the young woman's father intervened:

"Respected teacher, do not worry your esteemed student. We sought him not for complaint but as a result of our admiration and so as to congratulate him. Ask him why he has bandaged his finger thus!"

In the face of their insistence, the embarrassed student explained: "As Satan directed his evil promptings at me, I held my finger to the flame of the lamp and asked myself, 'Can you run the risk of enduring this?' It was then that I burnt my finger and was forced to bandage it."

The father, a Pasha of the Ottoman Empire, explained: "Respected teacher, not only do I wish to cover all the expenses of this student until he completes his study, but I also seek to give my daughter to him in marriage and, as such, be honored with having him as a son-in-law."

The only words falling from our lips before this historical incident is none other than the well-known adage: Even the reverie of certain years long past are worth the entire world!

5. The Lawful and Prohibited with Respect to Daily Life

Certain matters encountered frequently in daily life will be touched upon here.

IT IS NOT PERMISSIBLE TO NEGLECT
THE PRESCRIBED PRAYER

The prescribed Prayer is a believer's most vital duty of servanthood. When we examine the Qur'an, we see that our Lord has enjoined the

Prayer seventy times, commensurate with its importance. There is no other worship that is as emphasized as persistently as the Daily Prayers.

The prescribed Prayer is a form of worship which promises us felicity in two worlds. God Almighty declares in the Qur'an that abandoning the Prayer is a characteristic of the denizens of Hellfire.[210]

Moreover, stating, "What lies between a person and disbelief is the abandonment of the Prayers," God's Messenger[211] expresses the fact that observing the prescribed Prayer is a mark of a believer.

Indeed, the Daily Prayers are a mark of belief, the light of the heart, and the ascension of the believer. That is to say, a believer advances by means of the Prayer and ascends to the sphere of the Almighty's approval and good pleasure. Neglecting the prescribed Prayer is disobedience to God, rebelling against Him, and is a grave sin. God Almighty explains the predicament and fateful end of such people in the Qur'an as follows: *"Then, there succeeded them generations who neglected and wasted the Prayer and followed (their) lusts (abandoning the service of God's cause). They will meet perdition (as their just deserts)"* (Maryam 19:59).

Stating, "One who breaches a trust has no belief and one who is not careful about cleanliness and who neglects the Prayer has no religion. The position of the Prayer in religion is like that of the head to the body,"[212] God's Messenger indicates in another Tradition also that the first matter upon which a person will be called to account in the Hereafter is the prescribed Prayer and that a person with perfect Prayers will experience ease in their subsequent examination.

Scholars taking into account the Traditions[213] of God's Messenger which state that children must be instructed to perform the Prayer at age seven and must be compelled to observe the Daily Prayers at ten years of age, have considered the omission of the Prayer of a child who has reached the age of puberty within the same category.

---

[210]   Al-Muddathir 74:42–43

[211]   *Sahih Muslim*, Iman 134; Ahmad ibn Hanbal, *Al-Musnad*, 3:389

[212]   Haythami, *Majma' al-Zawa'id*, 1:292

[213]   *Sunan Abu Dawud*, Salat, 26; *Sunan at-Tirmidhi*, Salat, 299

Moreover, those who fail to place the required importance on the positions of bowing and prostration in the Prayer have been cautioned with the Prophetic Traditions[214] which state that the greatest thief is one who steals from the Prayer. That the punishment of those who abandon the congregation, despite being able to do so, is also mentioned in books pertaining to the sins, is also of a cautionary nature.[215]

Alongside neglecting the prescribed Daily Prayers, performing them before or after their set times, deliberately and without a valid excuse, have also been considered among the major sins.

Some scholars have also asserted that failure to perform the prescribed prayers in congregation without justifiable reason can also be evaluated within this same category, based on the important admonishments that God's Messenger makes in relation to performing the Prayers in congregation.

Furthermore, the compulsory nature of the Friday Prayer is also established in the Qur'an. Stating that the heart of one who abandons three Friday prayers without valid reason will be sealed[216] by God, the Messenger of God also affirms the gravity of the matter in another Tradition: "Either some people stop neglecting the Friday Prayers, or God will seal their hearts and they will be among the heedless."[217]

SPEAKING UNTRUTH AND LYING UNDER OATH ARE OF THE MAJOR SINS

Lying is a moral degeneration. It is a major sin which sets communities against one another and severs the bonds between them. A believer must not deviate from truthfulness and must not speak untruth, even if a situation against their own interests is in question. Children must be raised free from lie and untruth from an early age. In addition, it is also important to note that those words commonly described in society as "little white lies" are also composed of untruth. Lies do not have a color. A lie is a lie and is a sin leading the human being to deep abysses.

---

214 Ahmad ibn Hanbal, *Al-Musnad*, 5:310; Zahabi, *Al-Kaba'ir*, 50
215 Zahabi, *Al-Kaba'ir*, 53
216 *Sunan ibn Majah*, Salat, 93
217 *Sahih Muslim*, Jumu'ah, 12

God Almighty declares in the Qur'an[218] that He will not allow liars to prosper and He curses those who have made a habit of lying.[219]

God's Messenger, who states, "Lying leads to wrongdoing and wrongdoing leads to the Fire. A person keeps telling lies till they are recorded before God, a liar,"[220] has in another Tradition deemed lying as one of the signs of hypocrisy.[221]

What befits a Muslim is holding their tongue; however, they must speak propitious words where it will be of benefit. There is salvation in silence. The Messenger of God points to this, stating: "Whosoever believes in God and the Last Day should either speak good or remain silent."

A person who lies under oath deceives the people by means of holding God as witness to their oath. This is essentially exploitation of the exalted Name of God and is slander leveled against Him. Slander against God is most certainly forbidden and is of the major sins. This is a very severe predicament. A believer must steer clear of such a grave sin, even be it in jest.

God's Messenger has expressed in many of his Traditions that lying under oath is a great sin[222]. Stating in one of his *hadith*s that God Almighty will not look upon three groups of people with mercy on the Day of Judgment, God's Messenger enumerates these people in the following manner:

1. One who reminds (others of their charity or favors);
2. One who sells their goods by swearing a false oath;
3. The person who drags their garment (behind them) out of conceit.[223]

In another *hadith* stating, "Whosoever makes an oath to God and adds a lie even equivalent to a gnat's wing, that oath will constitute a

---

218 Mu'min 40:28–29
219 Adh-Dhariyat 51:10–11; Al Imran 3:61
220 *Sahih al-Bukhari*, Adab, 69; *Sahih Muslim*, Birr, 103, 104
221 *Sahih al-Bukhari*, Iman, 25; *Sahih Muslim*, Iman, 25
222 *Sahih al-Bukhari*, Ayman, 15; *Sahih Muslim*, Iman, 220
223 *Sahih Muslim*, Iman, 171

(black) stain on their heart until the Day of Judgment,"[224] God's Messenger also affirms that, "Anyone who swears a false oath to get hold of some property belonging to a Muslim to which they have no right should prepare for their place in Hellfire. Let those present here convey this to all those who are not present."[225]

There have also been scholars who have included in this sin, making false oaths and making frequent oaths, though they may be true.

ALL KINDS OF FORTUNE-TELLING AND SOOTHSAYING ARE PROHIBITED

Humankind, throughout history, has attempted to understand and discover the mysteries concerning both themselves and their environment, to acquire knowledge about their future, and to possess command over their own fate. Playing an important role in this also, is most certainly the curiosity and interest in the unknown and enigmatic. Consequently, from time immemorial, human beings have not been able to remain indifferent to the assertions and hints put forth in relation to their hidden dimensions and future; this characteristic has prepared the grounds for such pursuits as black magic, sorcery, fortune-telling, and soothsaying to become established in society and much sought after.

The Qur'an reveals that absolute dominance over both the senses and the realm beyond them belongs to God[226] and the pagan practice of divination by arrows widespread during the Age of Ignorance is fiercely prohibited.[227] Soothsaying has also been prohibited in the Prophetic Traditions. Being viewed within this same context, taking ominous meanings from certain names and objects or the behavior of animals, as well as fortune-telling using items such as pebbles, chickpeas or broad beans have also been forbidden.[228] Severe reproof is also given in another Prophetic Tradition, where those relying on and believing in the results of such pursuits as fortune-telling are considered to have

---

224   Hakim, *Al-Mustadrak*, 4:327
225   Tabarani, *Al-Mu'jam al-Kabir*, 1:275; Hakim, *Al-Mustadrak*, 4:327
226   Az-Zumar 39:46; at-Talaq 65:12
227   Al-Ma'idah 5:3
228   *Sunan Abu Dawud*, Tib, 23

denied that which was revealed to God's Messenger and it is stated that their Prayers would not be accepted for forty days.[229] For this reason, in Islam, all kinds of undertakings threatening belief in God's absolute sovereignty and oneness, carrying traces of pagan customs such as consulting with idols and appealing to them for help, and preventing the human being from appealing to real sources of knowledge and causes have been deemed falsehood; considered within this scope, fortune-telling and soothsaying have thus been prohibited.

In the Qur'anic verses and the Prophetic Traditions, all forms of superstitious belief, falsehood, and practice which carry claims of knowing the unseen, changing a person's fate and seeing the future, which purport to receive help from beings other than God, and which prevent people from applying to reliable sources of knowledge and true causes, have been prohibited. Consequently, every kind of fortune-telling and soothsaying gaining wide currency in diverse cultures in various ways, such as divination by salt, coffee reading, pouring molten lead into water, palm reading, and divination with books contravene the belief and knowledge system of Islam.

IS BLACK MAGIC AND SORCERY PROHIBITED?

Perhaps the most severe of claims to give information of the unseen, soothsaying, and paranormal activity is sorcery. Referred to in Arabic with the word *sihr*, the art of producing paranormal occurrences by mesmerizing human beings through magic and deception involves sorcery, amulet-making, and clairvoyance first and foremost, and also encompasses the misuse of physical and immaterial instruments for certain ends.

The concept of *sihr* has been frequently referred to in the Qur'an in various contexts. These verses, in brief, affirm the verity of the revelation given by God to the Prophets and to Prophet Muhammad, peace and blessings be upon him, as well as the Messengership of each of them, and declare that this is not sorcery or wizardry. The opposition and slander campaigns mounted against previous Prophets by magicians are touched upon, and the magicians' being liars and imposters

---

[229]   *Sahih Muslim*, Salam, 125; *Sunan ibn Majah*, Tahara, 122

who will never prosper is also mentioned.[230] Sorcery has been included among the seven cardinal sins in the Prophetic Traditions.[231]

Sorcery has a long past, with origins that can be traced back to primeval communities. As sorcery or black magic is an undertaking that has at its base self-interest, it does not recognize religion or the sacred. In sorcery is the pretension of accomplishing affairs above Divine will and power. The religion of Islam deems conjuring and having spells made as being among the major sins and has opposed it with a vengeance. The debate concerning the reality and influence of witchcraft to one side, Muslim scholars have affirmed that no harm from magic can come to a person independent of the Divine will and that a Muslim's involvement in black magic and sorcery is utterly prohibited.

For those who have been spellbound to appeal to the assistance of those who have made a profession out of sorcery and casting spells is objectionable. The first thing that must be done is to seek refuge in God, observe one's worship and entreaty to Him, and to give in charity to the impoverished. In the event of a God-fearing and reliable scholar's providing assistance to those afflicted by sorcery, it is also possible to benefit from them.

READING TEXT

If Only You Could Have Guarded Your Gaze!

A teacher explains: I once had a student who was exceptionally bright and successful and with a talent rare among students. He excelled in both (worldly and spiritual) aspects in equal harness. I guessed from the events that he explained that he spent some of his nights in great spiritual fervor. The beauty within him had projected onto his countenance. His face used to glow and all those who saw him would be left in admiration.

From time to time, he would bring his classmates and include them in the discussions of a spiritual nature. He wished for everyone

---

[230]   Al-A'raf 7:116; Yunus 10:76-77; Ta-Ha 20:69; az-Zukhruf 43:30; adh-Dhariyat 51:52

[231]   *Sahih al-Bukhari*, Wasaya, 23; *Sahih Muslim*, Iman, 144

to taste of these blessings. All those who knew him, myself first and foremost, used to look at him as the future of Turkey, but God's Messenger had beseeched God, "Do not leave us alone with our carnal souls, for even an instant." When returning from the fierce battle that was Uhud, he had stated: "The greatest battle is that waged against the carnal soul; the strongest wrestler is one who can overcome their carnal soul." These words had to have profound wisdom behind them. They were not spoken in vain; this is self-evident.

He was a third-year student of senior high school and was preparing for the university examinations. His goal was to get into university and serve his nation. And everyone expected a great deal from him.

Yalova is a small place. It is always possible to run into people and meet with them. When I once saw him walking with his girlfriend in an alleyway, I became quite uneasy, as the thought that he might become distracted with petty things and be detained or diverted halfway occurred to me. I am not in the habit of prying into the affairs of others. However, his spiritual world was going to become overcast, his momentum would suffer, and consequently, he would be unable to reach his aim. I considered counseling him at an opportune time. How close can fire and gunpowder be, after all?

When I told him that he needed to be guarded and prudent in his behavior, he innocently responded that he was simply conveying the message to his friend. His friend, God willing, was to soon begin observing the prescribed Prayer. Appearing convinced, I then left.

What I feared happened. The communication of the message eventuated in the reverse and his pristine world had turned upside down. His nights were in disarray and his days wretched. Dear brother! If only you could have guarded your gaze!

6. Key Offences Committed Against Individuals and Property

The religion of Islam has rendered the human being the most precious and noble of all creation and has deemed the preservation of human life as one of the chief objectives of religion. The Qur'an maintains that one who kills an innocent person unjustly has committed as grave a crime as killing all humanity, and that saving the life of a single human being is as sublime and meritorious an act as giving life to all human beings.[232] For this reason, murder constitutes one of the major sins in Islam. It proclaims that one who unjustly and willfully kills a believer is—subject to the demand of family and relatives—to be killed in retaliation,[233] that they will be subjected to an eternal punishment in the Fire, and that they will face the wrath and condemnation of God.[234]

Addressing all Muslims during the Farewell Pilgrimage, God's Messenger declared, "Just as you regard this month, this day, this city as sacred, so regard the life and property of every Muslim as a sacred trust (under the responsibility of society and guaranteed by the law),"[235] and thus indicated the inviolability of the human right to life. In another Prophetic Tradition, he states: "Avoid the seven noxious things. (These include the) killing of one whom God has declared inviolate without a just cause."[236]

If it has become established that a person has committed a crime despite the precautionary measures taken by Islam whether in the religious or moral sphere, or in the judicial sense, a criminal justice system based on truth and justice is adopted; this system foresees the punishment of the offender and the protection of the rights of the victim, as well as allaying the conscience of society and preventing the recommitting of that offense. As an extension of this approach, in cases of deliberate killing and provided that this is demanded by the victim's family, the killing of the murderer in retaliation is elemental.[237] If retaliation is not demanded or is not possible, blood money is paid. As a rule in cases of accidental killing, payment of blood money is made to the ben-

---

232   Al-Ma'idah 5:32
233   Al-Baqarah 2:178; Al-Isra 17:33
234   An-Nisa 4:93
235   *Sahih al-Bukhari*, Ilm, 37, Hajj, 132; *Sahih Muslim*, Hajj, 147
236   *Sahih al-Bukhari*, Wasaya, 23; Tib, 48; Hudud, 44; *Sahih Muslim*, Iman, 144; *Sunan Abu Dawud*, Wasaya, 10
237   Al-Baqarah 2:178-179; al-Ma'idah 5:45

eficiaries of the deceased.[238] As for the offender's being held liable for paying blood money, this is in one sense aimed at the broader benefit of society, and in another, enables the training of the carnal soul. As an additional penal sanction for those who kill a family member, they are deprived of that person's inheritance, thus aimed at preventing from the outset the committing of murder with a view to coming into an inheritance.

A person who willfully kills another is considered rebellious and a transgressor. Stating that the acceptance of a murderer's repentance is contingent upon God's will, scholars have noted more so than the weight of the crime, their being given the chance to reform themselves and be a good person, in the event of their not being killed in retaliation. As can be understood from the general expression in the verses concerning the forgiveness of sins,[239] the situation of the murderer before God and their end is a matter left entirely to the will and forgiveness of God.

IS SUICIDE PERMISSIBLE?

The right to life of the human being, who assumes the most honorable position among creation, is the most fundamental right conferred upon them by God. Sent to the world to know their Creator and live their lives in accordance with His will, human beings do not possess command over coming to the world and leaving it; this matter constitutes an element of the Divine will and order. That which is in the hands of the human being is to know the One Who created them, be a servant to Him and, as such, increase their esteem in His eyes.

The Qur'an indicates that saving the life of human being is as grand a gesture as saving the lives of all human beings and that taking a single life is as grave a crime and sin as killing all humanity.[240] Those aiming to commit suicide, whatever the reason, are also deemed to be among those included within the ambit of this verse. Asserting in rela-

---

238   An-Nisa 4:92
239   An-Nisa 4:48, 116; az-Zumar 39:53
240   Al-Ma'idah 5:32

tion to this matter that those who commit suicide by jumping off a cliff, consuming poison or with a lethal device will enter Hellfire and reside therein eternally,[241] the noble Prophet draws attention to suicide's being a major sin as well as its dire repercussions. This is due to the fact that persevering during hardship and bearing patiently every kind of anguish and sorrow, notwithstanding the degree of difficulty, and not losing one's faith and trust in God, must be the chief character and maxim of a Muslim. Furthermore, the patience and struggle shown on this path has great merit and value in the eyes of God. The Qur'an frequently reminds human beings that the trials and tribulations encountered in one's life are each a means of testing, and that when these are endured with patience and fortitude, one can become a good Muslim.[242] On the other hand, a person has no right to intervene in the right of life that God has granted to the human being for a certain purpose, or to see themselves as possessing authority in this regard; such a stance is deemed a great ingratitude.

Even if Muslim scholars have maintained that a Muslim who commits suicide will be subjected to tremendous punishment in the Hereafter as a result of their suicide and will even remain therein indefinitely, they have not said that one who commits suicide renounces their belief and becomes an unbeliever. This is because belief and unbelief are not connected with behavioral disorders but have to do with faith. The status of one who commits suicide is a matter between themselves and God. A Muslim who commits suicide is washed and shrouded and their funeral prayer is performed, as with other Muslim funerals, and they are buried in the Muslim cemetery. The view of the greater majority of Muslim jurists is thus.

THEFT IS PROHIBITED

Denoting, "taking secretly the property of another, from the place of its safekeeping, without their knowledge," stealing is one of the key crimes violating the right of property and ownership. The protection

---

241   *Sahih al-Bukhari*, Tib, 56
242   Al-Baqarah 2:155, 177; al-Hajj 22:35

of wealth acquired through honest work and lawful earnings is among the fundamental principles of Islam. Islam holds labor and ownership as sacred and has penalized wrongfully withholding the rights of others. For this reason, stealing has been considered a great sin and wrongdoing in Islam, as with all the Divinely revealed religions and legal systems, in the judicial sense, as well from a theological and moral perspective.

In order for the crime of theft to be firmly established and for the foreseen punishment to be dealt accordingly, certain conditions are sought. These include the absence of such reasonable grounds as hunger, need, compulsion and the like, willful and voluntary perpetration, criminal liability, the stolen property's having been under legal protection, and its being above a certain amount.

QUESTIONS

1- Which of the below are not one of the animals on which there is consensus that its meat is lawful for consumption?
   a. Deer
   b. Rabbit
   c. Monkey
   d. Pigeon

2- What are the areas of the woman that are prohibited to be seen by men who are not her close relatives, by blood, milk, or marriage?
   a. Her entire body, excluding her hair.
   b. Her entire body except her arms (elbows included).
   c. Her entire body, except her head and neck.
   d. Her entire body, excluding her face, hands, and feet.

3- What is the ruling for eating seafood other than that which falls under the category of fish (such as mussel, frog, crab) in the Hanafi legal school?
   a. It is *haram*.
   b. It is *halal*.
   c. It is *mubah*.
   d. It is allowed.

4- The prohibition of which of the following animals is expressly established in the Qur'an?

   a. Dog

   b. Cat

   c. Pig

   d. Hyena

5- Which of the following is false?

   a. *Halal* describes that which is religiously prohibited, while *haram* describes that which is allowed.

   b. God Almighty has created many bounties for humankind.

   c. Things about which there is no religious ruling are *halal*.

   d. Everything whose consumption or use has not been forbidden in the Qur'anic verses and the *hadith* is *halal*.

6- What is the ruling for wearing garments made of silk for men and women?

For Men	For Women
a. *makruh*	*halal*
b. *haram*	*halal*
c. *halal*	*haram*
d. *halal*	*makruh*

7- What is the ruling concerning drawing picture of landscapes such as trees, mountains, and rocks?

   a. All kinds of pictures are *haram*.

   b. It is permissible.

   c. It is not permissible.

   d. It is strongly reprehensible.

APPENDICES

Appendix 1: Satanic Intrigues

WHAT ARE THE SIX HUMAN AND SATANIC INTRIGUES?

The human being has been sent to the world for examination. Life continues from beginning to end as a series of trials of differing dimensions and depths. The human being is confronted with these trials starting from their childhood, and lasting until the moment when their soul is resigned to its Lord. In the Sixth Section of "The Twenty-Ninth Letter" in *The Letters*, named "The Six Attacks", Said Nursi states, "God willing, this Sixth Section will confound six stratagems of satans among jinn and men, and block up six of their ways of attack," and as such identifies the most dangerous of these trials as the desire for rank and position, the sense of fear, greed, racialism, egotism, and love of comfort.

Now, let us try to briefly elucidate these diseases that Said Nursi has identified, again from his perspective. The desire for rank and position denotes the desire to hold a particular post or position and to be famed among the people. He summarizes this feeling within the human being as follows: "Present in most people is a hypocritical desire to be seen by people and hold a position in the public view, which is ambition for fame and acclaim, and self-advertisement; it is present to a lesser or greater extent in all those who seek this world. The desire to accomplish this ambition will drive a person to sacrifice his life even."

The desire for rank and position is an evil trait that darkens the heart and paralyzes the spirit. It is always within the realm of possibility for those unfortunate souls who have yielded their hearts to such a sickness, to have their vision blurred and deviate to dead ends. In fact, the desire for rank and position may be found more or less in every individual. It is for this reason that if the endeavor is not made to satisfy this emotion within a legitimate sphere, it is inevitable that those unable to free themselves from the clutches of such an attitude will inflict harm on both themselves and the society in which they live. Such damage is virtually irreparable.

The second is the sense of fear. A person can bridle their willpower with the bridle of fear. Especially in our day, the people of heedlessness attempt to suppress human beings with the sense of fear. Said Nursi states: "One of the strongest and most basic emotions in man is the sense of fear. Scheming oppressors profit greatly from the emotion of fear. They restrain the pusillanimous with it. The agents of the worldly and propagandists of the people of misguidance take advantage of this weak point of the common people and of the religious scholars in particular. They frighten them and excite their groundless fears." In so doing, he presents the matter with consideration of its modern elements. A heart that has believed in the truth can only be freed of this sickness by means of a spiritual attentiveness and through the conviction, "May my honor, integrity, and pride be sacrificed in this cause! Death is only in the hands of God." The sole remedy for not feeling fear of anyone is to fear the One who really deserves to be feared.

The third intrigue is greed. Greed is the excessive desire to acquire or possess something, avarice, and insatiability. With the words, "If the children of Adam possessed two valleys of gold, they would surely desire a third (valley of gold); only the soil (of the grave) can satisfy their avarice. God forgives those who turn to Him in repentance," God's Messenger depicts the psychological state of those people who are enslaved to greed. The human being can only escape the clutches of greed through taking the verse, *"eat and drink, but do not be wasteful,"* (al-A'raf 7:31) as a standard for themselves and conducting their expenditure without tending to waste. Moreover, some evil spirits can enter through the vein of avarice and make believers instruments for their own loathsome ends. Nursi states: "Yes, 'the worldly' and especially the people of misguidance do not give away their money cheaply; they sell it at a high price. Sometimes something which may help a little towards a year of worldly life is the means of destroying infinite eternal life. And with that vile greed, the person draws Divine wrath on himself and tries to attract the pleasure of the people of misguidance." In so doing, he draws attention to such a danger.

The fourth matter is racialism. The notion of racialism first started in Europe and later became one of the agents paving the way for the end of the Ottoman State. They set the people of this nation, favored with the manifestation of "Divine coloring," against one another with the idea of racialism, Turks against Kurds, Kurds against Bosnians, Bosnians against Albanians. Islam opposes such an understanding of nationalism, which places racialism before religion.

Indeed, tribalism and racialism was completely abolished by virtue of the bond of belief in Islam. When the Companions of the Prophet are considered, it immediately becomes evident that the majority of them were from different races. For instance, Abu Bakr was an Arab, Bilal Ethiopian, Suhayb Byzantine, and Salman Persian. Despite all of them being people of differing climates and nations, they united in the melting pot of Islam and became brothers. The verse, "*Surely the noblest, most honorable of you in God's sight is the one best in piety, righteousness, and reverence for God,*" (al-Hujurat 49:13) documents this truth. As mentioned above, while Islam rejects a negative nationalism, which holds race above religion on the one hand, it on the other hand has established a positive nationalism, based on the fact family and lineage, nationhood, and people are also a reality.

This is, moreover, a social fact which is indicated in the verse, "*O humankind! Surely We have created you from a single (pair of) male and female, and made you into tribes and families so that you may know one another*" (al-Hujurat 49:13). Said Nursi has diagnosed this reality in a striking manner and has articulated it thus: "The idea of positive nationalism should serve Islam and be its citadel and armor; it should not take its place. For within the brotherhood of Islam is a hundredfold brotherhood that persists in the Intermediate Realm and World of Eternity. So whatever its extent, national brotherhood may be an element of it. But to plant it in place of Islamic brotherhood is a foolish crime like replacing the treasure of diamonds within the citadel with the citadel's stones, and throwing the diamonds away."

The fifth attack is egotism, the weakest and most dangerous in the human being, and is something that needs to be cast out of a person's character once and for all. For it is very difficult for those unfortunate ones swept up in the vortex of ego to see and recognize truth and reality and, as they are blindfolded, to walk towards their aim without going astray. Again, Said Nursi affirms: "My brothers! Beware, do not let them strike you with egotism, do not let them hunt you with it! You should know that this century the people of misguidance have mounted the ego and are galloping through the valleys of misguidance. The people of truth have to give it up if they are to serve the truth. Even if a person is justified in making use of the ego, since he will resemble the others and they too will suppose he is self-seeking like them, it will be an injustice to the service of the truth. In any event, the service of the Qur'an around which we are gathered does not accept the 'I', it requires the 'we.' It says: "Don't say 'I', say 'we.'" Thus, he invites us to be on guard towards this satanic characteristic.

The sixth attack is that which encumbers as a serious sickness in a great many heroes who have devoted themselves to the truth in our day, the sickness of laziness and the desire for physical comfort. Indeed, these enlightened souls who awaken the social spirit, guide the people and elevate them to true humanity, and who are devotees of the truth, must be prepared to sacrifice everything, material or spiritual, for the sake of this ideal without ever stooping to laziness. There is a story told of legend, regarding Prophet Abraham's wealth. Whilst its authenticity may be dubious, the lesson to be taken from it is significant. Prophet Abraham owned so many sheep that had so many shepherds that he is considered to be among the wealthiest in regard to his day. Some of the angels, who could not reconcile such great wealth with the office of Prophethood—notwithstanding the particular notion that it sprang from—directed the following question: "How can all this wealth be compatible with the position of Prophethood?" God Almighty then declared: "Has this wealth entered his heart or not? Go and test him!" Upon this, the angels, under the command of the angel of Revelation Archangel Gabriel, appeared in human form and went to the presence of Prophet Abraham. Here, the angels uttered the words, "Transcendent and Holy You Are, the Lord of the angels and the Spirit," loud enough for him to hear, as an expression of their knowledge of God. These words are carefully selected, in way of exaltation and glorification of God Almighty. With a heart receptive to breezes from the Divine Realm, Prophet Abraham was immensely pleased when he heard such glorification and articulated his astonishment with the words, "For God's sake, what a beautiful thing this is! May one third of my wealth be yours, repeat your words once more!" When the angels repeated the statement, Prophet Abraham said: "Let half of it be yours!" When they repeated it a third time, however, he responded saying, "I am bound in servitude to you, along with my shepherds!" Upon this, Archangel Gabriel introduced himself and said: "I am one of God's angels. I do not need any of these; however, my Lord desired to display your faithfulness and tested you with us." The angels then left. The travelers upon the path of truth must perpetually continue along their way and be wary of being swept up in the vortex of ease and comfort, despite having the approval of God as their sole intention.

In short, gazes must constantly be directed towards God in return for His infinite mercy, without losing hope in and regard for Him for even an instant, and one must act satiated with a sense of self-control and supervision. In this way, the spirit of action will not be atrophied and, by not being swept up by the intrigues known as the "Six Attacks" and through becoming freed of the shame and disheartenment of sins and drinking to repletion the celestial waters of forgiveness, it will be possible to reach the infinite mercy which gives relief to spirits.[243]

Appendix 2: Protecting Values and Prudence

KEEPING SECRETS

Guarding a secret is the same as guarding one's chastity. Those who keep a secret, whether personal or a friend's, keep themselves chaste. Conversely, those who spread secrets damage their honor and reputation by leaving them unguarded.

* * *

---

[243]   Gülen, M. Fethullah, *Prizma-3*, İstanbul: Nil, 2011, p. 36

If you want to tell someone a secret, be sure that you could trust him or her with your honor. He or she must be as meticulous about keeping your secret as he or she would be about his or her own honor. An unreliable person, one who is ignorant of the value of chastity, should not be entrusted with keeping a secret.

* * *

Keeping a secret and respecting the secrets of others, as opposed to prying into them, is a virtue related to self-discipline and sensitivity. Those who lack understanding cannot guard a secret, and those who do not care about the consequences of words and actions cannot be considered discreet.

* * *

It is usually wiser not to tell your private concerns to others, especially if they are unattractive, offensive, or lacking in merit. To do so can embarrass loved ones and delight enemies, and have other unpleasant consequences as well.

* * *

Hearts are created as safes for keeping secrets. Intelligence is their lock; willpower is their key. No one can break into the safe and steal its valuables if the lock or key are not faulty.

* * *

Bear in mind that those who carry others' secrets to you might bear yours to others. Do not give such tactless people any chance to learn even the smallest details of your private concerns.

* * *

If you entrust another secret to someone who previously disclosed one, your lack of perception and poor judgment in choosing a confidant is plain for all to see. One whose own heart is firm on this matter and who is vigilant cannot be deceived and seduced repeatedly in this way.

* * *

There are secrets related to the person, the family, and the nation. By disclosing a personal secret, you are interfering with a person's honor; by disclosing a family secret, you are interfering with the family's honor; and by disclosing a national secret, you are interfering with the nation's honor. A secret is a power only as long as it stays with its owner, but is a weapon that may be used against its owner if it passes into the hands of others. This is the meaning of one of our traditional sayings: "The secret is your slave, but you become its slave if you disclose it."

* * *

The details of many important affairs can be protected only if they are kept secret. Often enough, when the involved parties do not keep certain matters secret, no progress is achieved. In addition, serious risks might confront those who are involved, particularly if the matter concerns delicate issues of national life and its continuation.

* * *

If a state cannot protect its secrets from its enemies, it cannot develop. If an army reveals its strategy to its antagonists, it cannot attain victory. If key workers are won over by the competitors, their employers cannot succeed.

* * *

Explain what you must, but never give away all of your secrets. Those who freely publicize the secrets of their hearts drag themselves and their nation toward an inevitable downfall.[244]

GOD'S MESSENGER KEPT PREPARATIONS FOR MILITARY CAMPAIGNS CONFIDENTIAL

God's Messenger was in preparation for battle. As per usual, he kept his intention and objective extremely confidential. On this particular occasion, he kept the affair quite secret and no one, including his wives

---

[244]   Gülen, M. Fethullah, *Pearls of Wisdom,* New Jersey: Tughra Books, 2012, pp. 81–83

and closest friends, knew where this campaign would be, so much so that, upon Abu Bakr's once visiting his daughter Aisha to find her making travel preparations and asking her where God's Messenger intended to march, he received from her the response: "By God, father, I do not know either!"[245]

This is precisely how confidential the expedition was kept. Abu Bakr was the closest person to God's Messenger and the person he loved most. The Messenger of God had even chosen him as his Companion during the Emigration. In spite of this, God's Messenger kept the destination of the preparations for the military campaign hidden from even him. This is yet another dimension of just how unparalleled God's Messenger is as a commander. Taking this lesson from the Messenger of God, Mehmed the Conqueror was to one day state: "If even my beard were to know my secret, I would cut it off!" Such is the blessed commander among the spiritual heirs of God's Messenger.

The noble Prophet always employed ambiguity in his military campaigns for the sake of secrecy. He always concealed his actual aim and drew attention to allusions that would enable it to be understood in another way. It seems to me that modern military commanders do not think differently. For if they are to mount an operation in a particular place, they generate ten times the amount of noise that the assault would cause, somewhere else. They always act with many alternatives and conceal the real target. Where will they land their forces? From point 'A', point 'B', or point 'C'? It is not known. However, these are matters relating to military techniques developed fourteen centuries later. The true discoverer of these is Prophet Muhammad, peace and blessings be upon him. He did not receive an education in a school or a *madrasa*, but acquired all his knowledge from God Almighty entirely and was an unlettered Prophet who was, however, the scholar of scholars. And thus, we are compelled to proclaim once again, "*Muhammad'ur-Rasullulah* (Muhammad is the Messenger of Allah)."

Indeed, he again kept his target hidden and was on the constant alert, being aware of who was taking and bringing what—every detail

---

[245]   Ibn Hisham, *As-Sirat an-Nabawiyya*, 5:52

one by one—by means of the intelligence network he established. Irrespective of whether these were through revelation, or the sagacity and Prophetic wisdom of that great insight and discernment, he was able to keep track of the desert like the palm of his hand.

One such example: "When a Companion who fought at Badr, in an error of judgment, realized towards the end of the operation that the forces were heading towards Mecca, he sent a letter to the Quraysh informing them of this situation. This letter was couriered by a woman carrying water. Immediately summoning Ali and Zubayr ibn Awwam, God's Messenger informed them of the situation and they sped forth upon the errand of retrieving the letter from her."

This secrecy was maintained until there was only a stop left for Mecca and no one became aware of the army's arrival.

When Abbas brought Abu Sufyan to the presence of God's Messenger, there was nothing left to be done for the Meccans.[246] Even if they attempted to flee with the fastest horses and camels, they were not going to get away, for Mecca was seized.[247]

DO YOU KNOW HOW TO KEEP A SECRET?

Sultan Yavuz Selim, like many Ottoman Sultans, used to keep his military campaign preparations secret, for the security of the state. On one occasion, when one of his viziers insistently inquired as to the nation where the expedition would be directed, Sultan Yavuz Selim asked him: "Do you know how to keep a secret?"

When, with hope that he would receive a response from the Sultan, the Vizier said: "Yes, my Lord, I do." The Sultan retorted: "So do I."

Appendix 3: The Blows Dealt by Divine Compassion

Question: What are the blows dealt by Divine compassion, can you explain the concept?

Answer: A blow dealt by Divine compassion is a gentle reminder to return His servants to the right path. Bediüzzaman has put great

---

[246] *Ibid.*, 5:58-60
[247] Gülen, M. Fethullah, *Sonsuz Nur-2*, İstanbul: Nil, 2007, p. 338

emphasis on this concept and discussed it in "The Tenth Gleam" based on the verse, *"The Day when every soul will find whatever good it has done brought forward, and whatever evil it has done, it will wish that there were a far space between it and that evil. God warns you that you beware of Himself; and God is All-Pitying for the servants"* (Al Imran 3:30).

The magnitude of the blow depends on how dear the beloved is to the lover. For example, a believer who has not established a relationship with his Lord and neglects his duties of faith without an excuse might experience this blow in the form of financial damage or some calamity relating to his children. This blow is a reminder to the believer to evaluate his behavior and return to the right path. In this regard, even though this concept is described as a "blow" it is more so a blessing and a gift.

A pious believer's thoughts might stray by envying others, even though he or she usually uses intellectual capacity fully in a proper manner. This person might immediately receive one of those blows, because once a certain spiritual level is attained not even the thought of anything improper is allowed. A person who usually gets up in the middle of the night to contemplate God by praying and leaving tears on the prayer rug, might miss that opportunity one night, but then will then spend the next day in great discomfort. For a believer at that level, this is a blow dealt by Divine compassion. God raises individuals with this aptitude to a level where they, metaphorically spoken, steer the wheel of the ship. But if a person who has been at the wheel of such a Divine ship decides to shovel coal and tend to the sails like a common seaman it will be a degradation that God cannot allow. Therefore when God sends such a warning to that individual to pull him or herself together it can only be considered as a blessing. We call this blessing a blow dealt by Divine compassion.

There are many examples relating to this concept in the time of the noble Prophet or as it also called the Age of Happiness. In the night before the Battle of Uhud the Messenger of God sat and consulted with his Companions. He strongly advised to stay in Medina and fight with a defensive strategy. However the majority of his Companions, consisting of young men, wanted an offensive streak. Their passion was very sincere which is documented with the revelation of the verse, *"Among the believers are men (of highest valor) who have been true to their covenant with God: among them are those who have fulfilled their vow (by remaining steadfast until death), and those who are awaiting (its fulfillment). They have never altered in any way"* (al-Ahzab 33:23). Nevertheless the excitement these young Companions experienced actually stood in their way to grasp the intricacies of obedience to the command. More so, the soldiers entrusted with the duty to cover the back of the army equipped with bows and arrows were told to remain in their posts no matter what they saw. Whether they saw their army splitting the spoils or they saw their dead bodies being eaten by birds, they were under no circumstances to leave their posts. But when they disobeyed and left their assigned spots the enemy recuperated and pushed their army back. The repulse they experienced in that moment was their blow dealt by Divine compassion. When the Companions comprehended this warning they gathered around the beloved Prophet and went after the enemy, hence they were able to turn their mistake into a deed and their repulse into victory.

These blows are also relevant for contemporary followers of the Messenger of God. This path is an honorable conduit. God places the biggest importance on this issue in this world. If there was anything more important God would have bestowed that as duty on His Prophets. We can even say that what signifies the Angel Gabriel, what sets him apart and elevates him is being part of this grand duty. Therefore, even if it is a small mistake, any potentially harmful behavior will be responded to by God with a blow. The magnitude of that blow is determined by the individual's closeness to God and his or her sense of responsibility. Yes, nobody has the right to sacrifice even the smallest piece of this glorious ideal. The Messenger of God fulfilled all his duties which are indicated in the verse, *"O Messenger (you who convey and embody the Message in the best way)! Convey and make known in the clearest way all that has been sent down to you from your Lord. For, if you do not, you have not conveyed His Message and fulfilled the task of His Messengership"* (al-Ma'idah 5:67). After him great individuals such as Umar ibn Abdulaziz, Al-Ghazali, Abdu'l-Qadir al-Jilani, Imam Rabbani, Mawlana Halid al-Baghdadi, Bediüzzaman Said Nursi have taken this responsibility and tried to represent this message in their time to the best of their ability. Contemporaries who aspire to be part of this glorious ideal should be aware of this blessing and never neglect, get tired of or complain about serving their own people. Otherwise blows dealt by Divine compassion will be inevitable. Also, valuing existing blessings is a strong means to further ones. This is only possible through thanking God for the blessings in their own unique ways and exploring new ways to increase those blessing.[248]

Appendix 4: Prayer under All Conditions

THE PRESCRIBED PRAYER MUST BE OBSERVED UNDER ALL CONDITIONS

Nothing—work, trade, task, preoccupation, or any other excuse—can keep a believer back from performing the prescribed Prayer.[249] Our religion has provided every kind of ease in order for this duty to be performed: Those unable to find water can observe the Prayer by taking a dry ablution with clean soil;[250] those in threat of a certain danger, can perform the Prayer, standing in a place, afoot or mounted;[251] travelers, by performing four cycles of the *fard* Prayer as two cycles;[252] joining the Noon and Afternoon Prayers, and the Evening and Night Prayers in times of necessity or exigency;[253] those in battle performing the Prayer as they are able to;[254] the ill or the excused unable to stand, by performing the Prayer while sitting, and those unable to sit, performing the Prayer while lying down.[255] There is no valid excuse for not performing the Prayer, other than during menstruation or postna-

---

248   Gülen, M. Fethullah, *Prizma-3*, İstanbul: Nil, 2008, pp. 91–94

249   An-Nur 24:38

250   Al-Ma'idah 5:6

251   Al-Baqarah 2:239

252   *Sahih Muslim*, Salat al-Musafirin, 4; *Sunan Abu Dawud*, Salat, 27

253   *Sahih Muslim*, Salat al-Musafirin, 52; *Sahih al-Bukhari*, Taqsir as-Salat, 13

254   An-Nisa 4:102

255   Al Imran 3:191

tal bleeding for women, insanity, being unconscious and forgetfulness.[256]

The Daily Prayers pose no difficulty or burden for a Muslim in whose heart belief is firmly established and who has acquired the character of a true believer.[257] A believer does not delay their Daily Prayers and observes them readily and with pleasure.[258] God Almighty describes the state of those who rise to do the prescribed Prayer with reluctance[259] as the state of the hypocrites.[260]

WHAT IS THE RULING FOR NOT OBSERVING THE PRESCRIBED PRAYER?

Failure to perform the prescribed Prayer is a grave sin. One who does not observe the Prayer does so either because they do not believe in its being obligatory, because they make little of it, or due to their laziness, neglect, or forgetfulness.

One who does not observe the prescribed Prayer due to their not believing it to be obligatory or because of their disregard cannot be a believer, as this person does not believe in God's certain decree. A person who does not establish the Daily Prayers due to their laziness, carelessness, and engrossment in other activities and without valid reason, despite their believing in its being enjoined as compulsory, has committed a major sin. This is the real meaning in the Prophetic Traditions, some of which are mentioned below:

"Whosoever misses the Afternoon Prayer (deliberately), their deeds will be rendered null and void."[261]

"Do not deliberately neglect to observe a prescribed Prayer for he who neglects the prescribed Prayer deliberately will be removed from the protection of God and His Messenger."[262]

---

256   Al-Baqarah 2:239
257   Al-Baqarah 2:45
258   Al-Ma'arij 70:22–23
259   An-Nisa 4:142
260   At-Tawbah 9:54
261   *Sahih al-Bukhari*, Mawaqit as-Salat, 15
262   *Al-Musnad*, 6:421

On one particular mention of the Prescribed Prayer, God's Messenger said: "If one secures his Prayer, this Prayer will be light (in the face of darkness), evidence (of his faithfulness) and salvation (from punishment) on the Day of Judgment and for one who does not protect it, there will be no light, evidence or salvation on the Day of Judgment. Such a person will be with the Pharaoh, Qarun, Haman, and Ubayy ibn Khalaf on the Day of Judgment."[263]

Muslim scholars have asserted that only neglecting the Prescribed Prayer through denial of its obligatory nature can lead a person to unbelief and that these and similar Prophetic Traditions are directed at deterring believers from willful omission.[264]

WHY MUST WE OBSERVE THE PRESCRIBED PRAYER?

We must observe the prescribed Prayer because it is the greatest pillar of Islam after the Declaration of Faith. It is among the most important elements of religion after God's unity. It is the last will and advice of God's Messenger to the believers. The first thing for which a believer will be called to account on the Day of Judgment is the Daily Prayers.

The prescribed Prayer is the best of deeds ordained by God. It brings a person closer to God. With the Prayer, a believer gives thanks for the bounties bestowed to them by God. The Daily Prayers protect the believer from sin and wrongdoing. Moreover, they are the means to the forgiveness of sins and shield a person from punishment in the grave.

In short, the prescribed Prayer is the basis of succor, triumph, self-assurance and prosperity in both the world and the Hereafter. Hence, the believer must not neglect his Prayer whatever the circumstances in which he may find himself.

THE CONNECTION BETWEEN PRAYER, BELIEF, AND ISLAM

It is not possible to separate belief from the prescribed Prayer. Belief and the prescribed Prayer are twins that have come into existence from

---

263   *Ibid.*, 2:169
264   Jalal ad-Din as-Suyuti, *Sharh Sunan an-Nasa'i*, 1:231–233

the same womb. Belief constitutes the theoretical aspect of religion and religious life; the consolidation of that theoretical aspect and its being rendered an inner depth of one's nature is only possible through worship and with the prescribed Prayer first and foremost. For this reason, it can be said that the prescribed Prayer is a concrete belief and belief is an abstract Prayer. Those who see religion as being comprised merely of a recognition with the conscience and remove worship and devotion from the picture, despite considering their profession as being within the category of religion, have not been able to free themselves from associating partners with God, without even realizing it.

Indeed, the prescribed Prayer is the pillar of religion. The Daily Prayers are a river of penitence flowing towards eternity and a fountain of purification in which the believers cleanse themselves at least five times each day. The Daily Prayer is a very important duty which needs to be fulfilled even during the fiercest hours of struggle on the battlefield, is a secure stronghold, a vital means to gaining nearness to God.

Stating, "What lies between a person and disbelief is the abandonment of prayer," God's Messenger touches upon the very close connection between belief and the prescribed Prayer. Between belief and the prescribed Prayer is a virtuous cycle. As a servant observes the Daily Prayers, their belief strengthens, and as their belief strengthens, they embrace the Daily Prayers with an even greater fervor and devotion.

Certain people in our day who lower the dignity of the matter make the assertion that, "My heart is pure and I believe in God." It is self-evident that the notion of purity of heart exclusively will not avail them in the slightest. Expressed differently, belief is consolidated with the road leading to worship and is cemented through the establishment of the prescribed Prayer. Belief is fortified through fasting. Belief is reinforced through utilizing the means leading to the removal of miserliness from the heart. Belief is reinforced through undertaking the pilgrimage and patiently enduring a great amount of hardship. Belief is reinforced through enjoining the good and forbidding the evil. However many there are pillars in Islam, they serve as supports reinforcing belief from all directions—from its right and left, from in front and from behind, and from underneath it.

HOW IMPORTANT IS THE PRESCRIBED PRAYER?

"The prescribed Prayers (*Salah*) are Islam's pillars. To fully understand their importance, consider this parable: A ruler gives each of his two servants 24 gold coins and sends them to a beautiful farm that is 2 months' travel away. He tells them: "Use this money to buy your ticket, your supplies, and what you will need after you arrive. After traveling for a day, you will reach a transit station. Choose a method of transportation that you can afford."

The servants leave. One spends only a little money before reaching the station. He uses his money so wisely that his master increases it a thousandfold. The other servant gambles away 23 of the 24 coins before reaching the station. The first servant advises the second one: "Use this coin to buy your ticket, or else you'll have to walk and suffer hunger. Our master is generous. Maybe he'll forgive you. Maybe you can take a plane, so we can reach the farm in a day. If not, you'll have to go on foot and endure 2 months of hunger while crossing the desert." If he ignores his friend's advice, anyone can see what will happen.

Now listen to the explanation, those of you who do not pray, as well as you, my soul that is not inclined toward prayer. The ruler is our God. One servant represents religious people who pray with fervor; the other represents people who do not like to pray. The 24 coins are the 24 hours of a day. The farm is Paradise, the transit station is the grave, and the journey is from the grave to eternal life. People cover that journey at different times according to their deeds and conduct. Some of the truly devout pass in a day 1,000 years like lightning, while others pass 50,000 years with the speed of imagination. The Qur'an alludes to this truth in 22:47 and 70:4.

The ticket is the prescribed prayers, all of which can be prayed in an hour. If you spend 23 hours a day in worldly affairs and do not reserve the remaining hour for the prescribed prayers, you are a foolish loser. You may be tempted to use half of your money for a lottery being played by 1,000 people. Your possibility of winning is 1:1,000, while those who pray have a 99 percent chance of winning. If you do not use at least one coin to gain an inexhaustible treasure, something is obviously wrong with you.

Prayer comforts the soul and the mind and is easy for the body. Furthermore, correct intention transforms our deeds and conduct into worship. Thus our short lifetime is spent for the sake of eternal life in the other world, and our transient life gains a kind of permanence.[265]

PRAYER UNDER DIFFICULT CONDITIONS

The value of acts of worship is measured with the difficulty they pose for human beings. Worship carried out in times of difficulty and hardship is without a doubt more meritorious. It must not be forgotten that however much hardship there is in an auspicious undertaking and however difficult it is to obtain it, it contains merit and reward to this same degree.

However trying are the affairs in which we are engaged, however insurmountable and steep are the hills that we climb, our rewards will be just as great. Consequently, the rewards for a Prayer observed with an ablution taken perfectly—so as to overflow with positive feelings and experience worship completely and through enduring every difficulty—are going to be as great.

For, after asking the Companions, "Shall I inform you of the means by which God effaces your sins and elevates your ranks?" God's Messenger, upon him be the most perfect of blessings and salutations, enumerated the following: "Performing the ablution properly in spite of difficult circumstances, walking with more paces towards the mosque, and waiting for the next Prayer after offering a prescribed Prayer."

Subsequently, he added: "And that is *ribat* (mindfulness in establishing an intimacy with God to the level of guarding the Muslim frontiers), that is *ribat*."[266]

In one particular Tradition, God's Messenger has employed the Arabic word *isbagh* in reference to taking the ablution. This word denotes fulfilling the requirements of the ablution perfectly, washing the nose and mouth thoroughly, and washing hands and feet completely. Another term used in the Traditon is *ala al-makarih*, which entails making

---

[265]   Nursi, Said, *The Words*, New Jersey: The Light, 2005, pp. 25–26
[266]   *Sahih Muslim*, Tahara, 41

haste to the water source to perform ablution properly, notwithstanding the difficulty.

When we examine the life of God's Messenger, we see that he did not abandon the Prayer even during war, and observed the prescribed Prayer in congregation even in such extreme circumstances. The Companions observed the Daily Prayers in congregation even at the fiercest point of the Battle of Badr. The Meccan forces outnumbered the Muslims, being threefold the size of the Muslim army. A complete struggle for life and death was being waged but God's Messenger and his Companions had preferred establishing the prescribed Prayer in congregation, shoulder to shoulder, over saving their own lives.

While half of them observed the Prayer, the other half fought, and when those who had performed the Prayer were fighting, the others stood for Prayer in congregation. This matter is explained in the Qur'an, in the Chapter Nisa, verse 102.[267]

Our carnal soul as well as Satan conjures up myriad excuses to deter us from observing the prescribed Prayer: "I am so busy and can't find the time." "They don't allow me to pray at work."

So, is not the prescribed Prayer the most important task? Can we not set aside five to ten minutes during our lunch breaks and perform the Prayer? What is more, performing the Daily Prayer will be a means to our prosperity.

Some people do not observe the Daily Prayers at any time with the excuse that they cannot pray at work when, in fact, the number of the Prayer times that coincide with our time at work is one or two. During the summer, in particular, there is no serious difficulty as there is greater time between the Prayer times. During the winter, however, the Afternoon and Evening Prayer can present a challenge. Nonetheless, it is possible to observe the Prayers during one's breaks provided that one arranges their time appropriately.

---

[267]   For further information in relation to this topic, refer to M. Fethullah Gülen's sermon: "Dinin Özündeki Kolaylık ve Zor Şartlarda Namaz", http://tr.fgulen.com/content/view/16448/26/

Sometimes, the times given for rest breaks are very short and are not enough for taking ablution and performing the Prayer. But a person who has a love for the Prayer takes his ablution during one break and performs his Prayer in another. Again, if there are problems regarding time and place, one can suffice with performing only the *fard* Prayers.

There is no place to perform the Prayer in some workplaces. In such cases, one must try to at least perform the *fard* Prayers in an empty place, a storeroom, or elsewhere while at work.

There are plenty of formulas for a person who wants to observe the prescribed Prayer. So long as we experience concern for the Prayer, God will prepare both the place and the time.

Do not say, "What will come of a few Prayers being left until later?" One Daily Prayer is worth the entire world! Every moment spent in coming up with various solutions and formulas for observing the prescribed Prayer on time is considered as worship.

Indeed, the prescribed Prayer is such a form of worship that it cannot be abandoned whatever the circumstances.

Appendix 5: Love of Nation

LOVE OF ONE'S NATION COMES FROM BELIEF

The parcel of land on which peoples have settled and have waged many a struggle to live freely therein has been referred to as the nation. This is what is implied in the expression, "Soil, for whose sake there are those who sacrifice their lives, is a nation." Its protection has been encouraged with Prophetic Tradition: "Whoever is killed while defending his life, religion, honor, and property then he is a martyr."[268]

The nation is not a goal or objective, but a means of serving the goal and objective. The aim and purpose is the human being and the practice of their beliefs. This being the case, the nation in which they can freely practice their religion is preferred to that in which they cannot. However, this is only the case when one is compelled to make

---

[268]   *Sunan at-Tirmidhi*, Diyat, 22

such a choice; otherwise, changing one's nation without such a preference being necessary would be mistaken and erroneous. God's Messenger was forced to migrate to Medina when it became impossible for him to practice his religion in Mecca.

His love and longing for the city of Mecca cannot be explained only with religious sentiment; within that yearning and attachment is also the longing and love for the nation. Love of nation can only be relegated to the background when religion cannot be practiced freely. There is no harm, from the religious standpoint, in people's loving and honoring their nation. In point of fact, there are many Prophetic Traditions which praise the nation and exhort one's remaining therein.

The Tradition which states, "Love for one's nation is part of faith," is mentioned in the 155th Letter of the *Maktubat* of Imam Rabbani, one of the greatest Muslim scholars and the reviver of the second millennium, and in the Mathnawi of Mawlana Jalal ad-Din ar-Rumi.

God's Messenger has stated: "Standing guard for one day in the way of God is better than this world and all that it contains."[269]

Where is one to stand guard? Of course on the nation's frontiers... Many of the religious commandments are realized with nation and land. It is inconceivable for there to be an army but no military headquarters, a congregation but no mosque, *zakah* but no marketplace and bazaar where the *zakah* money is to be earned, knowledge and learning but no school and educational institution, laws of inheritance but no land and fields to be bequeathed.

A person can only practice their religion and live a dignified life in a free and independent nation. Statelessness is very bitter and wretched. Religion and nation are two inseparable, indivisible elements. The fact that God's Messenger settled in Medina and adopted it as his nation, immediately after leaving Mecca, indicates the importance of the concept of nation.

Fethullah Gülen expresses the nature of love of one's nation as follows:

---

269   *Sahih al-Bukhari*, Jihad, 71

Those who do not know God have never been able to love Him; indeed, they cannot. Those who are not informed of the Prophet cannot show him due respect; indeed, they cannot. And those who consider our lands to be mere geographical territory cannot be aware of the love for one's homeland; this is not possible. Any territory is valuable according to the amount of riches found on the surface and underground. Likewise, a country rises upon its unique essence and values that have been inherited from the past; it is only in relation to these values that a country can be enthroned in the heart of the people.[270]

WHY MUST WE LOVE OUR NATION?

Fethullah Gülen explains the reason why we must love our nation in the following way:

"Let me state, first of all, that I love my nation with respect to its collective spiritual personality. Otherwise, there can of course be individuals, among our nation as with every other, who can be considered deplorable from the perspective of truth, justice, and humanity. However, when taking into consideration our nation, which is generally firmly connected to their spiritual roots, it is evident that such individuals have remained a minority."

In a saying often related as a Prophetic Tradition, it is said: "Love of the homeland comes from belief."[271] This can also be expressed as, "Love of nation is a part of faith." For our exalted nation who has been the standard-bearer of our religion of Islam for centuries has frequently changed the course of the history of humanity, and has served humanity in a great many ways. It is by virtue of this that we love our nation with a sense of pride.

Without question, our nation has accomplished great feats. These "accomplishments," generally call to mind, in our day, positive and technological advancements. However, knowledge and technology itself are not everything when it comes to solving the problems of humanity and securing its happiness and peace. Moreover, that scientific discov-

---

270   Gülen, M. Fethullah, *Örnekleri Kendinden Bir Hareket*, İstanbul: Nil, 2011, p. 94

271   As-Saghani, *al-Mawdhuat*, 53; As-Sakhawi, *Al-Maqasid al-Hasana*, 297

eries and technological progress bereft of morality, virtue, and a consciousness of social responsibility each become a scourge and disaster in the hands of the selfish and self-interested, is an incontrovertible reality. Consequently, implied in our statement, "Our nation has accomplished great feats," is the human and moral values our predecessors brought to all humanity and its dispersing justice to its surrounds by virtue of that exceptional capacity of administration and politics. We take an interest in these aspects of our nation and even have an attachment to it to the degree of love.

However, I cannot know whether all these affections will avail those people who are now in the past. Perhaps recalling these favors will be a means to remembering them in kindness. We can say, "May God have mercy on our forefathers! They left for us a promising country; however, we have polluted its countenance and what falls upon us now is to re-illuminate its horizon once again," and perhaps then this would mean something. Ultimately, if we claim to take a keen interest in, have an attachment and even a great love for our nation, which has developed upon firm spiritual roots, then we must fulfill those duties towards that beloved that are incumbent upon us. The issue of real importance for us is precisely this.

For instance, our nation's fulfilling anew the historical mission that it carried out during one period in the balance of power among nations, if at the very least within its own region, and its becoming an important element of balance, holds great importance for us. It has within its spirit a notion of justice inherited from its ancestors, an understanding of integrity, and a sense of mercy. That there is a need for this, for the peace of both the people of that region as well as for our own nation, is self-evident. Consequently, we desire most fervently for our nation to arise once again with its values and reconstruct the stature of its own soul anew. In my opinion, the love we hold within us should be manifested along these lines. This expression also holds an important meaning. When describing the reality of love, Rabia al-Adawiya states: "You speak of loving God while you disobey Him; I swear by my life that there is nothing as strange as this. If you were true in your love, you would obey Him; for a lover obeys the one they love."[272]

We see a similar understanding in the approach of Said Nursi with reference to obedience to God's Messenger and attachment to him. He states, for instance, that if it were possible, we would exert great endeavor to resemble him who we hold so dearly with our manner of speaking and even our tone of voice, we would dress like him, walk and talk like him.

Indeed, love of God reveals itself through obedience and love of God's Messenger reveals itself by following, to the letter, his Sunnah. If one who claims to love God and His Messenger displays laxity in taking the message of God and His Messenger to all corners of the globe, promulgating and making it heard by everyone, this means that their words are a lie. Similarly, if one who claims to love their nation exerts no effort or endeavor in the way of its standing on its own feet, its revival, and its raising once again the statue of its soul, this means that they speak untruth with these words.

Another important aspect of the matter is this: A person who claims to love their nation must be in the concerted effort toward making the values of their nation known universally and convincing others of the true need that humanity has for these. Otherwise, if this nation is accepted as one that is not trusted and one that is discredited, it will be thrown aside and humanity will be unable to benefit from the values it has inherited from history. That being the case, when raising our nation with its own values on the one hand, it is necessary to represent it worldwide with those values which established it throughout history, on the other.

If an ant were to know intuitively that there was honey in marble, it would incessantly circle that marble in determination and resolve and find one way of reaching that honey. It would not say, like a human being who had fallen into a well and exerted no effort to get out: "Let someone come and throw down a rope and pull me out." If it possessed them, it would use its claws, feet, and nails. If its hands were chained, it

---

Ibn Asakir, *Tarikh al-Dimashq*, 69:118; Ali al-Qari, *Mirqat al-Mafatih*, 9:214

would gnaw a place for its feet to step. In short, it would most certainly strive to escape via countless ways and alternatives.

What befalls us—if we indeed believe that we have been placed upon a true path with Divine grace—is to continue along that path with God's grace and favor even more swiftly, and to overcome all obstacles and impediments, even if they number in the tens of thousands. This, it seems to be, is the true love of nation.

A person who has reached this point can lose sleep and sometimes forget the way home, as however much devotion a person shows towards a matter, to the degree of madness that is the extent to which they will remain indifferent to all other affairs. A person focused on one particular matter can sometimes experience forgetfulness in even those things in which they are well versed. They are absentminded, but not in their own matter. In that they are not woolgatherer, but diver.

The real issue, after all, is being a diver of a lofty thought and an exalted ideal. And even if you are left empty-handed despite diving countless times, diving again and again with the hope that you can find a jewel and reach that coral island... Diving, of course, has such risks as drowning, being unable to resurface, and encountering danger, but when it comes to being the diver of an ideal, it inevitably brings with it goodness as an outcome. As for absolute goodness, it cannot be abandoned due to potential danger. Accordingly, servanthood to God has such potential trials as emigration, longing, separation, and homesickness, but has an assured Paradise in return for it. They are probable, while Paradise is certain. Hence, in connection with this principle, God Almighty declares: *"God has bought from the believers their selves and wealth because Paradise is for them"* (at-Tawbah 9:111). Just as Paradise belongs to Him, your wealth, life, selfhood, and family are also His. All of these have been given to the human being in trust. In this verse God Almighty declares, in mild form of bargaining so to speak: "Return to Me the trusts that I have given to you and I will grant you an eternal Paradise and eternal felicity in return."

There is here, at the same time, a condescendingness of tone and manner whereby God holds the human being as a direct addressee and speaks to them. Declaring, "You give Me that, and I will grant you this,"

He proposes a covenant with them. These are the manifestations of the "wavelengths of condescension" with regards to Divine Speech.

Similarly to my mind, the statement, "I love my nation," can only be verified through devoting everything, one's life included, in its path. One who loves his nation must consider it in every square inch of life. For instance, if a person feels the pangs of the matter to the extent of waking up in the middle of the night and stirring others to action for the sake of their nation with an idea that has occurred to them, this means that they possess love of their nation and country. The other amounts to nothing more than an empty claim.

I am of the opinion that we need to trust in this nation, when considered from the perspective of the missions it fulfilled throughout history. This is naturally not a trust in the sense of trusting in God and relying upon Him. So then, why must we trust in our nation? Because this noble nation has never remained under subjugation for an extended period of time, and has not yielded to such abasement. This means to say that it cannot, from this time forth, tolerate and submit to degeneration indefinitely. For instance, it was broken at Gallipoli, threw itself in front of the enemy with its dead, and prevented that infernal force with its own death, but never surrendered. As acknowledged by a Western observer, "This nation is able to launch an assault at the point where all other nations grow utterly desperate in defense." And thus it really is. Our nation overcame the occupying powers with the National Struggle and purged the country of the enemy. Indeed, it never tolerated subjugation and acted with the philosophy that death was preferable to living under the enslavement of another. As far as I am concerned, a nation with such character ought to be relied upon.

Furthermore, it must not be forgotten that no other country in the Muslim world has faced the bombardment that Turkey has been subjected to. The shell exploded here and its most formidable "alpha" effects such as "burning, withering, and leaving disease in its wake," made themselves felt here. However much others were affected by beta or gamma rays that were the extent to which they were impacted. The real suffering was experienced by our nation, but it nonetheless was never able to be annihilated. Note that they are still trying to stifle our nation, but it finds another path to revival and rises up once more.

If we are currently experiencing, as an entire nation, such fervor of new birth after death and a flush of resurrection, I believe that we must focus painstakingly on the issue of collective consciousness. As the individuals of such a nation within this period, we must be in the sincere consciousness of being together, working together and solving our problems via formulating ideas and brainstorming, in complete mutual trust and reliance. That collective consciousness essentially should, to my mind, be the product of a willpower and rest upon intellect; the relationship between effort in this matter and the outcome should also be comprehended very well in order for the perpetuation and continuation of such a consciousness. If the matter is built upon such sturdy fundamentals, there can be no erring. If the human being were to realize a collective consciousness with their intellect and will-power, or in other words rest their call upon mind, logic and will, they would have relied upon knowledge and would thus hold the promise of permanence. However, a morality and culture steeped in mere habit and custom and ingrained in our being, can fall apart in the face of a serious stimulus. But, when the matter is considered by taking into consideration the connection between intellect, logic, and reasoning, and its origin and end, the steps taken will be lasting and long-term. This is akin to the situation of a merchant who conducts his investment in accordance with the laws and regulations of trade. It is unclear when their investment will yield return and what kind of products will be gained. It is even possible that they will gain nothing from their invest-ment; however, if they work within the sphere of apparent causes and exert effort to this end, they will—God willing—receive the reward of their exertion and endeavor. As calculations were made in this regard and investments were carried out accordingly.

For this reason, at a time in which we are walking towards a reviv-al as a nation, a collective consciousness must be based on reason, logic, sound judgment and human willpower, and a concerted course of action must be ensured. Moreover, the advancement of our nation and the raising of the religion of Islam must be made more effectual and efficient by making use of scientific discoveries and findings. Only through such a collective consciousness can the roads we travel become highways; and this is, of course, contingent upon sitting together and conversing, consultation, and brainstorming.

In short, a person who really loves their nation must be in the constant endeavor for the sake of its revival once again with its own values and must simultaneously experience the passion and enthusiasm of having these national and spiritual values heard universally.[273]

THE HERO

The hero is the most essential ingredient of history, and its meaning and value ascend with him. The history of a nation lacking heroes is not much different from a shallow and calm lake; no matter how grand and massive, it does not in any way exhilarate breezes of relief and comfort.

Ancient Greeks glorified their history by the flags raised by some kind of legendary heroes. Ancient Rome became a part of history by means of figures like Caesar. It was only the tutelage of Hannibal that made the voice of Carthage be heard by all of humanity. Persia could get up to the flamboyant peak of its epic sagas merely by means of the restless and prolific pen of Ferdowsi. And there are many others…

Fascinatingly enough, there existed some particular nations whose histories have been built around a "one and only" hero in the same way an arch is seated upon a single pillar. There were also some other nations whose history is based and rises upon thousands of pillars, just like a temple featuring hundreds of domes. As the ancient history of Macedonia mounts by the existence of Alexander, France does by Napoleon, Germany by Bismarck, or to a different extent by Goethe…

As for our history, however, neither counting nor naming those numerous heroes is possible. It would probably be much more proper to call it, in its totality, "a history of heroes". It is simply because this nation has raised so many heroes that it is rather difficult to put a second nation in the same category, to be compared with those innumerable deeds of heroism. If you utter the name of Umar, you inevitably hear the roar of Khalid behind; when you commemorate Mehmed the Conqueror, the

---

[273]   Gülen, M. Fethullah, *Kalb İbresi*, İstanbul: Nil, 2011, pp. 107–113

voice of Sultan Selim echoes; if you remember concurrences and the Battle of Mohács, all of Anatolia resounds all the way to Gallipoli.

Western intellectuals say that this nation does not own a serious history. That's true! Where is the tale of heroes flapping in the sky of Manzikert? Where on earth are the parables of those turtle doves that flew to the West? Where are, for God's sake, the graves and epigraphs of those who resisted the Crusaders each time? And where are the domes and tombs of those poeticized as "the heroes who did not let rascals trample their motherland"?

Where are, for God's sake, the legends of heroism of my past, each of which stands as an out-and-out history, while others have meticulously recorded the meanest cases and affairs of their histories? Why did not those like Molla Husrev write down the history of "the period of elevation?" Why was the military power and prodigy, or the marvelous ability of management and universal measures of those like Sultan Selim not recorded in their own eras? What happened to Ibn al-Kamal, a capable highbrow, that he did not ascertain the affairs of "the period of summit" with his ingenious pen? These questions kept weighing on our minds till the moment we could hear the verse of the "mourner of ruins" from the suffering poet[274] who penned the epigraphs of our last unknown hero:

"You surely shall outgrow history, if we attempt to bury you under it"[275]

And now, we have been taking solace in figuring out that there may exist some heroes whose histories are impossible to record.

Yes, there are some nations who write down legends as history and they attach glory upon their epigraphs and pasts. We may see them as nations writing history. And there exists also a specific nation who makes history and lets its legends and songs be written by others. I suppose that it is essentially this fact that lies behind the state of destitution that our historical literature suffers from. We made history by manifesting heroism, and left its acoustics be composed by our slaves and servants.

---

274   Mehmet Akif Ersoy, the poet of the Turkish National Anthem

275   A verse from the eulogy "To The Martyrs of Gallipoli", penned by Mehmet Akif Ersoy

A gladiator cannot see or perceive his own heroic struggle. It is observed and recorded much better by the spectators around the arena. Likewise, if a heroic legend is strongly required for us as well, I would like to prefer to listen to it through an admiring foreign pen. The drops falling upon the chest of my history from the appreciating eyes of Lamartine[276]; the beauty and attraction inspiring Pierre Loti[277] to be buried in the shadows of cypresses in my graveyards are far more vivid and effective—especially for our people of today and those of the West, much more than the myths of Peçevi[278]. Splendor is splendor only if others admire it. Virtue and heroism become what they are whenever they are appreciated by enemies.

There exists another kind of special heroism, a transcendental heroism, which is dimensioned and deepened towards the inner self. I would like to argue that both the East and West have never been able to know this kind of heroism. In this regard, it shall only be possible to observe this unique heroism—the veil of which has not been touched by a foreign hand—in my own country.

Yes, it is absolutely required to travel to that land to observe that specific kind of heroism. A head of the state who walks among his people with a sack of flour to suppress the arrogance growing in himself; a sober commander who blew away the most powerful armies of the West with one move, and would address himself across the treasure in the palace of the beaten king thus: "Yesterday you were a moor, today you are a victorious commander, and tomorrow you will be a mortal man under the soil ready for accounting"; the great soldier and man of administration who recommended his coffin be wrapped by his gown

---

[276]   Alphonse Marie Louis de Prat de Lamartine (1790–1869), a French writer, poet and politician. He published *Histoire de la Turquie* (The Ottoman History) in Paris in 1859.

[277] Pierre Loti (1850-1923) was a French novelist and naval officer. He published *Aziyade* (1879), a novel which was a romance and autobiography dealing with some curious experiences in İstanbul.

[278]   İbrahim Peçevi (1572–1650) was a Turkish historian (chronicler) of the Ottoman State. He was a provincial official in many places and became a historian after his retirement in 1641. He is famous for his two-volume book *Tarih-i Peçevi* (Peçevi's History) of the history of the Ottoman State, the main reference for the period 1520–1640.

stained by the mud splashed by the horse of a wise man of truth—even in a time when he was sovereign of both the East and West... All these figures emerged from the people of this country.

Yes, it is in any case necessary to stop by our country to get acquainted with the real hero who walks over the entire world leading armies, handles the entire world while sitting on the throne, and becomes a devotee praying in seclusion at nights. It is necessary because those fortunate ones—who are not overwhelmed with thrones or crowns, who keep their dignity all the time, whose beginnings and endings are the same, who do not change in front of life and affairs, who make angels lose themselves by their infatuation, enthusiasm and whining—do exist in our world.

Chastity is the lily that grows in our country. Altruism is the rose of our land; its tune is heard in our gardens. It is possible in our climate to manifest the willpower to hold the honey comb in hand without tasting it. And it is particular to our aura to forget living for one's own self and yearn so that others shall live. Our people do know very well to stand in front at times of service, but hide at times of pay. It has been our culture that has introduced the entire world the concept of loving without being loved...

Gallantry has flapped its wings in our skies. It has been our world of virtue where courageous dignity and resolution have become two badges of honor. It was our temples where choirs of prayers became compositions that united the world and the Hereafter. And for ages, our people have mentioned the Holy Names of God and contemplated that absolute harmony. Due to all these, it is vain to seek for individual heroes in this country; for they won't be found. Heroism in this country stands as chain of mountains, forever. This is agreed both by friends and enemies:

Also you shall "see and feel if you cherish conscience and faith;

What a marvelous heroism beats in the chest" of the homeland,

Of the children of that land, and of the Holy Book giving soul to them.[279]

---

[279]   Gülen, M. Fethullah, *Çağ ve Nesil*, İstanbul: Nil, 2011, pp. 153–156

ANSWER KEY

1. LOYALTY AND FIDELITY
   1. C 2. A 3. A 4. C 5. D

2. MODESTY AND CHASTITY
   1. A 2. C 3. D 4. B 5. C 6. A

3. SUBMISSION
   1. B 2. D 3. A 4. C 5. D

4. SUFFERING, ANGUISH, PATIENCE, PERSEVERANCE AND INCONSTANCY
   1. D 2. A 3. C 4. A 5. B

5. *DHIKR*, RECITATION, *JAWSHAN*
   1. A 2. C 3. D 4. A 5. A 6. C

6. SINCERITY
   1. B 2. C 3. B 4. A 5. B

7. *TAWAKKUL* (TRUST IN GOD)
   1. A 2. D 3. C 4. C 5. B 6. D

8. CALAMITY, TEST, DISORDER
   1. B 2. A 3. D 4. A

9. TOLERANCE AND EASE
   1. B 2. B 3. D 4. C 5. A

10. BEING A COMMUNITY
    1. B 2. C 3. D 4. B 5. A

11. SENSITIVITY REGARDING THE PROHIBITED AND THE LAWFUL
    1. C 2. D 3. A 4. C 5. A 6. B 7. B